P9-CLR-814

Nietzsche

VOLUME IV

Nihilism

Harper & Row Editions of

MARTIN HEIDEGGER

Basic Writings

Being and Time

Discourse on Thinking

Early Greek Thinking

The End of Philosophy

Hegel's Concept of Experience

Identity and Difference

Nietzsche: Volume I, The Will to Power as Art

Nietzsche: Volume IV, Nihilism

On the Way to Language

On Time and Being

Poetry, Language, Thought

The Question Concerning Technology and Other Essays

What Is Called Thinking?

MARTIN HEIDEGGER

Nietzsche

Volume IV: Nihilism

Translated from the German by

FRANK A. CAPUZZI

Edited, with Notes and an Analysis, by

DAVID FARRELL KRELL

1817

Harper & Row, Publishers, San Francisco

Cambridge, Hagerstown, New York, Philadelphia
London, Mexico City, São Paulo, Sydney

Acknowledgment is made for the permission of Macmillan Publishing Co., Inc., M. B. Yeats, Anne Yeats, and Macmillan Ltd., to reprint from "Nineteen Hundred and Nineteen," from *Collected Poems* by William Butler Yeats. Copyright 1928 by Macmillan Publishing Co., Inc., renewed 1956 by Georgie Yeats.

Martin Heidegger's text was originally published in *Nietzsche,* Zweiter Band, © Verlag Günther Neske, Pfullingen, 1961.

 For information address Harper & Row, Publishers, Inc., 10 East 53rd Street, New York, NY 10022. Published simultaneously in Canada by Fitzhenry & Whiteside Limited, Toronto.

FIRST EDITION

Designer: Jim Mennick

Library of Congress Cataloging in Publication Data

Heidegger, Martin, 1889–1976.
NIHILISM.

(Nietzsche; v. 4)
Translation of 2 essays from the German ed. of the author's Nietzsche, v. 2: Der europäische Nihilismus and Die seinsgeschichtliche Bestimmung des Nihilismus.
Includes bibliographical references.
Contents: European nihilism—Nihilism as determined by the history of being.
1. Nietzsche, Friedrich Wilhelm, 1844–1900—Addresses, essays, lectures. 2. Nihilism (Philosophy)—Addresses, essays, lectures. I. Krell, David Farrell. II. Heidegger, Martin, 1889–1976. Seinsgeschichtliche Bestimmung des Nihilismus. English. 1982. III. Title. IV. Series: Heidegger, Martin, 1889–1976. Nietzsche. English; v. 4.
B3317.H3713 1979 vol. 4 193s [149′.8] 82-11856
ISBN 0-06-063857-5

82 83 84 85 86 10 9 8 7 6 5 4 3 2 1

Contents

Editor's Preface

The final volume of Martin Heidegger's *Nietzsche* comprises two parts: first, a lecture course taught at the University of Freiburg during the first trimester[1] of 1940, entitled "Nietzsche: The Will to Power (II. European Nihilism)";[2] second, a treatise composed during the years 1944–46 but not published until 1961 under the title "Nihilism as Determined by the History of Being." Both texts originally appeared in Martin Heidegger, *Nietzsche,* 2 vols. (Pfullingen: Günther Neske Verlag, 1961), II, 31–256 and 335–98. (Throughout these English volumes, the Neske edition is cited as NI or NII, with page number.)

Dr. Capuzzi and I have translated the passages from Nietzsche's works in Heidegger's text afresh. But we are grateful to have had the late Walter Kaufmann's exemplary renderings for comparison. With the sole exception of the footnote on the first page of the lecture course, all footnotes are my own. The glossary, which should be used solely in order to check back to the German text, is also my own work.

Heidegger's references to *Der Wille zur Macht,* the text on which he based the lecture course, are designated by the abbreviation WM, followed by the aphorism number, not page number; e.g., (WM, 12). His references to all other Nietzschean texts are to the *Grossoktavausgabe* (Leipzig, 1905 ff.), cited in the text by volume and page—e.g., (XIV, 413–67)—and in the footnotes as GOA. I have checked most of the more important—but by no means all—of the references to the

[1] The change from the semester to the trimester system was a wartime measure of brief duration.

[2] The Roman numeral II presumably refers to the second chapter of Book One of *Der Wille zur Macht,* "Toward the History of European Nihilism," although the course is by no means restricted to that part. Current plans for the lecture in the Heidegger "Complete Edition" drop the numeral.

Grossoktavausgabe against the *Kritische Gesamtausgabe* of Nietzsche's works, edited by the late Giorgio Colli and Mazzino Montinari (Berlin: Walter de Gruyter, 1967 ff.), cited in the notes as CM, with volume and page number, except where the *Nachlass* fragments are concerned. For the latter, I adopt the full designation in CM of manuscript and fragment number; e.g., W II 5 [14]. Perhaps it is not out of place to mention the recent release of a fifteen-volume paperback edition of the *Kritische Gesamtausgabe* (Deutsche Taschenbuch Verlag, 1980). Readers would do well to check Heidegger's references to the *Nachlass* against this edition, even though the exclusion of the hardcover edition's concordances to *Der Wille zur Macht* makes that task formidable indeed.

I owe debts of gratitude, above all, to Frank A. Capuzzi for his skillful translation and cheerful collaboration; to Helm Breinig and Ulrich Halfmann for rescue operations in matters touching "the awful German language"; to Joachim W. Storck in matters pertaining to the original manuscript; to Sherry Gray, who checked the manuscript of the translation painstakingly; to Walter and Elaine Brogan; and to John B. Shopp, my editor at Harper & Row, who has supported the project from the outset and seen it bravely through.

Finally, the publication of the fourth volume of Heidegger's *Nietzsche* gives me occasion to remember with pleasure and thankfulness the first general editor of the Harper & Row Heidegger series, J. Glenn Gray, who in his own unobtrusive way countered nihilism with an unclouded gaze toward the *nihil.*

D.F.K.

die Säge
St. Ulrich

Plan of the English Edition

Volume I: The Will to Power as Art

1. Author's Foreword to All Volumes [NI, 9–10].
2. "Will to Power as Art," a lecture course delivered at the University of Freiburg during the winter semester of 1936–37 [NI, 11–254].

Volume II: The Eternal Recurrence of the Same

1. "The Eternal Recurrence of the Same," a lecture course delivered at the University of Freiburg during the summer semester of 1937 [NI, 255–472].
2. "Who Is Nietzsche's Zarathustra?" a lecture to the Bremen Club on May 8, 1953, printed in *Vorträge und Aufsätze* (Pfullingen: G. Neske, 1954), pp. 101–26, added here as a supplement to the *Nietzsche* material.

Volume III: Will to Power as Knowledge and as Metaphysics

1. "Will to Power as Knowledge," a lecture course delivered at the University of Freiburg during the summer semester of 1939 [NI, 473–658].
2. "The Eternal Recurrence of the Same and Will to Power," the concluding lecture to all three lecture courses cited above, written in 1939 but not delivered [NII, 7–29].
3. "Nietzsche's Metaphysics," a typescript dated August–December 1940, apparently deriving from an unscheduled and heretofore unlisted course on Nietzsche's philosophy [NII, 257–333].*

* "Nietzsche's Metaphysics" appears as the title of a lecture course for the winter semester of 1941–42 in all published lists of Heidegger's courses. The earliest prospectuses of the Klostermann firm cited such a lecture course as volume 52 of the Heidegger "Complete Edition" (*Gesamtausgabe*). But the Heidegger Archive of the Schiller-Na-

Volume IV: Nihilism

1. "European Nihilism," a lecture course delivered at the University of Freiburg during the first trimester of 1940 [NII, 31–256].
2. "Nihilism as Determined by the History of Being," an essay composed during the years 1944–46 but not published until 1961 [NII, 335–398].

The three remaining essays in volume two of the Neske edition, "Metaphysics as History of Being" [NII, 399–457], "Sketches for a History of Being as Metaphysics" [NII, 458–80], and "Recollection of Metaphysics" [NII, 481–90], all from the year 1941, appear in English translation in Martin Heidegger, *The End of Philosophy,* tr. Joan Stambaugh (New York: Harper & Row, 1973). *The End of Philosophy* also contains the essay "Overcoming Metaphysics" (1936–46), related thematically and chronologically to the *Nietzsche* material, an essay originally published in *Vorträge und Aufsätze,* pp. 71–99. The lecture in which Heidegger summarizes much of the material in volume two of *Nietzsche,* "The Word of Nietzsche: 'God is Dead' " (1943), appears in English translation in Martin Heidegger, *The Question Concerning Technology and Other Essays,* tr. William Lovitt (New York: Harper & Row, 1977). Other references to Nietzsche in Heidegger's works are listed in the second, revised edition of Hildegard Feick, *Index zu Heideggers "Sein und Zeit"* (Tübingen: M. Niemeyer, 1968), p. 120.

---

tionalmuseum in Marbach contains no manuscript for such a course. It does contain the sixty-four-page typescript in question, with many handwritten alterations, composed in August 1940 and revised during the months of September, October, and December of that year. One of the typescript's several title pages refers to the winter semester of 1938–39, in all probability not to any lecture or seminar in the published lists but to an unlisted *Übung* [exercise] entitled "Toward an Interpretation of Nietzsche's Second 'Untimely Meditation,' *On the Use and Disadvantage of History for Life.*" On September 29, 1975, I asked Heidegger about the discrepancy of the dates for "Nietzsche's Metaphysics" in the Neske edition (1940) and in the published lists and catalogues of his courses (winter semester 1941–42). (At the time of our conversation on this matter the above information, supplied by the archive, was unknown to me.) Heidegger reaffirmed the date 1940 as the time of composition. He explained that the material had been prepared during a seminar, title and date not specified, and conceded that he might have employed the same material for the WS 1941–42 lecture course.

The problem awaits the more patient scrutiny of the archive's curators. But this may suffice to explain why Heidegger cites 1940 (and not 1942, as the catalogues would lead us to expect) as the closing date for his early lectures on Nietzsche.

Part One

EUROPEAN NIHILISM

1. The Five Major Rubrics of Nietzsche's Thought

The first philosophical use of the world *nihilism* presumably stems from Friedrich H. Jacobi. The word *nothing* appears quite frequently in Jacobi's letter to Fichte. There he says, "Truly, my dear Fichte, it would not annoy me if you or anyone else wished to say that what I set against Idealism—which I deplore as *Nihilism*— is *Chimerism*."*

Later the word *nihilism* came into vogue through Turgeniev as a name for the notion that only what is perceptible to our senses, that is, only beings that one experiences oneself, only these and nothing else are real and have being. Therefore, anything grounded on tradition, authority, or any other definitive value is negated. Usually, however, the name *positivism* is used to designate this point of view. Jean Paul, in his *Elementary Course in Aesthetics* (sections 1 and 2) employs the word in describing romantic poetry as poetic nihilism. We might compare this usage to Dostoievsky's *Foreword* to his Pushkin Lectures (1880). The passage in question runs thus:

> As far as my lecture itself is concerned, I simply want to make the following four points regarding Pushkin's importance for Russia:
>
> 1. That Pushkin, with his profound, penetrating, and highly compassionate mind, and through his truly Russian heart, was the first to see and recognize for what it is a significant, morbid manifestation among our intelligentsia, our rootless society which seems to hover high above the common people. He recognized it, and enabled us to place graphically before our

* Friedrich H. Jacobi, *Werke* (Leipzig, 1816), III, 44; from the section "Jacobi to Fichte," which first appeared in the fall of 1799. I am grateful to Dr. Otto Pöggeler, who provided the reference to Jacobi while working on the proofs of the present book. — M. H.

> eyes the typical, negative Russian character: the character who finds no rest and cannot be satisfied with anything permanent, who does not believe in his native soil nor in the strength of his native soil, who fundamentally denies Russia and himself (or rather, his social class, the entire stratum of the intelligentsia, to which he too belongs, and which has detached itself from our folk heritage), who will have nothing to do with his own people, and who sincerely suffers from all this. Pushkin's Aleko and Onegin have evoked a great many characters like themselves in our literature. . . . (Dostoievsky, *Werke,* edited by Moeller v. d. Bruck, Division Two, XII, 95f.)

For Nietzsche, though, the word *nihilism* means something substantially "more." Nietzsche speaks about "European nihilism." He does not mean the positivism that arose in the mid-nineteenth century and spread throughout Europe. "European" has a historical significance here, and means as much as "Western" in the sense of Western history. Nietzsche uses *nihilism* as the name for the historical movement that he was the first to recognize and that already governed the previous century while defining the century to come, the movement whose essential interpretation he concentrates in the terse sentence: "God is dead." That is to say, the "Christian God" has lost His power over beings and over the determination of man. "Christian God" also stands for the "transcendent" in general in its various meanings—for "ideals" and "norms," "principles" and "rules," "ends" and "values," which are set *"above"* the being, in order to give being as a whole a purpose, an order, and—as it is succinctly expressed—"meaning." Nihilism is that historical process whereby the dominance of the "transcendent" becomes null and void, so that all being loses its worth and meaning. Nihilism is the history of the being itself, through which the death of the Christian God comes slowly but inexorably to light. It may be that this God will continue to be believed in, and that His world will be taken as "real," "effectual," and "determinative." This history resembles the process in which the light of a star that has been extinguished for millennia still gleams, but in its gleaming nonetheless remains a mere "appearance." For Nietzsche, therefore, nihilism is in no way some kind of viewpoint "put forward" by somebody, nor is it an arbitrary historical "given," among many others, that can be historically documented. Nihilism is, rather, that event of long duration in which the truth of being as a whole is essentially transformed and driven toward an end that such truth has determined.

The truth of being as a whole has long been called *metaphysics.* Every era, every human epoch, is sustained by some metaphysics and is placed thereby in a definite relation to being as a whole and also to itself. The end of metaphysics discloses itself as the collapse of the reign of the transcendent and the "ideal" that sprang from it. But the end of metaphysics does not mean the cessation of history. It is the *beginning* of a serious concern with that "event": "God is dead."* That beginning is already under way. Nietzsche himself understood his philosophy as an introduction to the beginning of a new age. He envisioned the coming century—that is, the current, twentieth century—as the start of an era whose upheavals could not be compared to anything previously known. Although the scenery of the world theater might remain the same for a time, the play in performance would already be a different one. The fact that earlier aims now disappear and former values are devalued is no longer experienced as sheer annihilation and deplored as wasteful and wrong, but is rather greeted as a liberation, touted as an irrevocable gain, and perceived as a *fulfillment.*

"Nihilism" is the increasingly dominant truth that all prior aims of being have become superfluous. But with this transformation of the erstwhile relation to ruling values, nihilism has also perfected itself for the free and genuine task of a *new* valuation. Such nihilism, which is in itself perfected and is decisive for the future, may be characterized as "classical nihilism." Nietzsche describes his own "metaphysics" with this name and conceives it to be *the* counterstroke to all preceding metaphysics. The name *nihilism* thus loses the purely nihilistic sense in which it means a destruction and annihilation of previous values, the mere negation of beings and the futility of human history.

"Nihilism," thought now in its classic sense, calls for freedom *from* values as freedom *for* a *revaluation* of all (such) values. Nietzsche uses the expression "revaluation of all values hitherto" alongside the key

* On the *Ereignis* of nihilism, see Heidegger's remarks during the first lecture course on Nietzsche (winter semester, 1936–37), in Martin Heidegger, *Nietzsche.* Vol. I: *The Will to Power as Art* (New York: Harper & Row, 1979), p. 156 n.

word *nihilism* as another *major rubric* by which he assigns his own fundamental metaphysical position its definite place within the history of Western metaphysics.

From the rubric "revaluation of values," we expect that altered values will be posited in place of earlier ones. But for Nietzsche "revaluation" means that the very "place" for previous values disappears, not merely that the values themselves fall away. This implies that the nature and direction of valuation, and the definition of the essence of value are transformed. The revaluation thinks Being for the first time as value. With it, metaphysics begins to be value thinking. In accordance with this transformation, prior values do not merely succumb to devaluation but, above all, the *need* for values in their former shape and in their previous place—that is to say, their place in the transcendent—is uprooted. The uprooting of past needs most assuredly takes place by cultivating the growing ignorance of past values and by obliterating history through a revision of its basic traits. "Revaluation of prior values" is primarily the metamorphosis of all valuation heretofore and the "breeding" of a new need for values.

If such revaluation of all prior values is not only to be carried out but is also to be grounded, then it has need of a "new principle"; that is, the establishment of a basis for defining beings as a whole in a new, authoritative way. But if the interpretation of beings as a whole cannot issue from a transcendent that is posited "over" them from the outset, then the new values and their standard of measure can only be drawn from the realm of beings themselves. Thus beings themselves require a new interpretation through which their basic character may be defined in a way that will make it fit to serve as a "principle" for the inscription of a new table of values and as a standard of measure for suitably ranking such values.

If the essence of metaphysics consists in grounding the truth of being as a whole, then the revaluation of all values, as a grounding of the principle for a new valuation, is itself metaphysics. What Nietzsche perceives and posits as the basic character of being as a whole is what he calls the "will to power." That concept does not merely delimit *what* a being in its Being *is:* Nietzsche's phrase, "will to power," which has in many ways become familiar, contains his interpretation of the *essence of power.* Every power is a power only as long as it is more power; that is to say, an increase in power. Power can maintain itself in itself, that is, in its essence, only if it overtakes and overcomes the power level it has already attained—*overpowering* is the expression we use. As soon as power stalls at a certain power level, it immediately becomes powerless. "Will to power" does not mean simply the "romantic" yearning and quest for power by those who have no power; rather, "will to power" means the accruing of power by power for its own overpowering.

"Will to power" is a single name for the basic character of beings and for the essence of power. Nietzsche often substitutes "force" for "will to power" in a way that is easily misunderstood. His conception of the basic character of beings as will to power is not the contrivance or whim of a fantast who has strayed off to chase chimeras. It is the fundamental experience of a *thinker;* that is, of one of those individuals who have no choice but to find words for what a being *is* in the history of its Being. Every being, insofar as it *is,* and is *as* it is, is "will to power." The phrase names that from which all valuation proceeds and to which it returns. However, as we have said, the new valuation is not a "revaluation of all prior values" merely in that it supplants all earlier values with power, the uppermost value, but first and foremost because power and *only power* posits values, validates them, and makes decisions about the possible justifications of a valuation. If all being is will to power, then only what is fulfilled in its essence by power "has" value or "is" a value. But power is power only as enhancement of power. To the extent that it is truly power, alone determining all beings, power does not recognize the worth or value of anything outside of itself. That is why will to power as a principle for the new valuation tolerates no end outside of being as a whole. Now, because all being as will to power—that is, as incessant self-overpowering—must be *a continual "becoming,"* and because such "becoming" cannot move "toward an end" *outside* its own "farther and farther," but is ceaselessly caught up in the cyclical increase of power to which it reverts, then being as a whole too, as this power-conforming becoming, must itself always recur again and bring back the same.

Hence, the basic character of beings as will to power is also defined as "the eternal recurrence of the same." The latter constitutes yet another major rubric in Nietzsche's metaphysics and, moreover, implies something essential: *only* through the adequately conceived essence of will to power can it become clear why the Being of beings as a whole must be eternal recurrence of the same. The reverse holds as well: only through the essence of the eternal recurrence of the same can the innermost core of will to power and its necessity be grasped. The phrase "will to power" tells *what* beings are in their "essence" (in their constitution). The phrase "eternal recurrence of the same" tells *how* beings of such an essence must as a whole be.

It remains for us to observe what is decisive here; namely, that Nietzsche had to think the eternal recurrence of the same *before* the will to power. The most essential thought is thought first.

When Nietzsche himself insists that Being, as "life," is in essence "*becoming*," he does not intend the roughly defined concept of "becoming" to mean either an endless, continual progression to some unknown goal, nor is he thinking about the confused turmoil and tumult of unrestrained drives. The vague and hackneyed term *becoming* signifies the overpowering of power, as the essence of power, which powerfully and continually returns to itself in its own way.

At the same time, the eternal recurrence of the same offers the keenest interpretation of "classical nihilism," which absolutely obliterates any end above and beyond beings. For such nihilism, the words "God is dead" suggest the impotence not only of the Christian God but of every transcendent element under which men might want to shelter themselves. And that impotence signifies the collapse of the old order.

With the revaluation of all past values, an unrestricted challenge has been issued to men: that unconditionally from, through, and over themselves, they raise "new standards" under which the accommodation of being as a whole to a new order must be effected. Because the "transcendent," the "beyond," and "heaven" have been abolished, only the "earth" remains. The new order must therefore be the absolute dominance of pure power over the earth through man—not through any arbitrary kind of man, and certainly not through the humanity that has heretofore lived under the old values. Through what kind of man, then?

With nihilism—that is to say, with the revaluation of all prior values among beings as will to power and in light of the eternal recurrence of the same—it becomes necessary to posit a new essence for man. But, because "God is dead," only man himself can grant man his measure and center, the *"type,"* the "model" of a certain kind of man who has assigned the task of a revaluation of all values to the individual power of his will to power and who is prepared to embark on the absolute domination of the globe. Classical nihilism, which as the revaluation of all values hitherto understands beings as will to power and can admit eternal recurrence of the same as the sole "end," must take man himself—that is, man as he has been until now—out of and "over" himself and must fashion as his measure the figure of the "Overman." Hence, in *Thus Spoke Zarathustra* Nietzsche says, "Now then, you higher men! Only now is the mountain of man's future in labor. God died: now *we* will that Overman live." (See Part Four, "On the Higher Man," second paragraph; VI, 418.)

The Overman is the supreme configuration of purest will to power; that is to say, of the one and only value. The Overman, the absolute rule of pure power, is the "meaning" (the aim) of what alone has being; namely, "the earth." "Not 'mankind' but *Overman* is the *goal*" (WM, 1001, 1002). From Nietzsche's point of view, the Overman is not meant to be a mere amplification of prior man, but the most unequivocally singular form of human existence that, as absolute will to power, is brought to power in every man to some degree and that thereby grants him his membership in being as a whole—that is, in will to power—and that shows him to be a true "being," close to reality and "life." The Overman simply leaves the man of traditional values behind, *overtakes* him, and transfers the justification for all laws and the positing of all values to the empowering of power. An act or accomplishment is valid as such only to the extent that it serves to equip, nurture, and enhance will to power.

The five main rubrics we have mentioned—"nihilism," "revaluation of all values hitherto," "will to power," "eternal recurrence of the same," and "Overman"—each portrays Nietzsche's metaphysics from just *one* perspective, although in each case it is a perspective that defines the whole. Thus Nietzsche's metaphysics is grasped only when what is named in these five headings can be thought—that is, essentially experienced—in its primordial and heretofore merely intimated conjunction. We can learn what "nihilism" in Nietzsche's sense is only if we also comprehend, in their contexts, "revaluation of all values hitherto," "will to power," "eternal recurrence of the same," and "Overman." By starting from an adequate comprehension of nihilism and working in the opposite direction, we can also acquire knowledge about the essence of revaluation, the essence of will to power, the essence of the eternal recurrence of the same, and the essence of the Overman. But to have such knowledge is to stand within the moment that the history of Being has opened up for our age.

When we speak here about "concepts" and "grasping" and "thinking," it is certainly not a question of a propositional delimitation of what is represented when we name these major rubrics. To grasp here means consciously to experience what has been named in its essence and so to recognize in what moment of the hidden history of the West we "stand"; to recognize whether we do *stand* in it, or are falling, or already lie prostrate in it, or whether we neither surmise the one nor are touched by the other two, but merely indulge in the illusions of common opinion and the daily round, floundering in utter dissatisfaction with ourselves. Thoughtful knowing, as a supposedly "abstract doctrine," does not simply have some practical behavior as its consequence. Thoughtful knowing is in itself *comportment,* which is sustained in being not by some particular being but by Being. To think "nihilism" thus does not mean to produce "mere thoughts" about it in one's head, and as a mere spectator to retreat from reality. Rather, to think "nihilism" means to stand in that wherein every act and every reality of this era in Western history receives its time and space, its ground and its background, its means and ends, its order and its justification, its certainty and its insecurity—in a word, its "truth."

The necessity of having to think the essence of "nihilism" in the context of the "revaluation of all values," "will to power," "eternal recurrence of the same," and the "Overman" lets us readily surmise that the essence of nihilism is in itself manifold, multileveled, and multifarious. The word *nihilism* therefore permits many applications. It can be misused as an empty slogan or epithet that both repels and discredits and that conceals the user's own thoughtlessness from him. But we can also experience the full burden of what the name says when uttered in *Nietzsche's* sense. Here it means to think the history of Western metaphysics as the ground of our own history; that is, of future decisions. Finally, we can ponder more essentially what Nietzsche was thinking in using this word if we grasp his "classical nihilism" as *that* nihilism *whose "classicism" consists in the fact that it must unwittingly put itself on extreme guard against knowledge of its innermost essence.* Classical nihilism, then, discloses itself as the fulfillment of nihilism, whereby it considers itself exempt from the necessity of thinking about the very thing that constitutes its essence: the *nihil,* the nothing—as the veil that conceals the truth of the Being of beings.

Nietzsche did not present his knowledge of European nihilism in that exhaustive context he surely glimpsed by means of his inner vision, a context whose pure form we neither know nor can ever "open up" with the fragments of his work that have been preserved.

Nevertheless, in the realm of his thinking, Nietzsche thought through what he meant by the word *nihilism* in all its essential tendencies, levels, and configurations, and he put his thoughts down in notes of varying scope and intensity. A portion of these, but only a scattered, *arbitrarily* and *randomly* selected portion, were later collected into the book that after Nietzsche's death was pasted together from his posthumous writings and that is known by the title *The Will to Power.* The fragments chosen vary widely in character: reflections, meditations, definitions, maxims, exhortations, predictions, sketches for longer trains of thought, and brief reminders. *These selected pieces* were divided into four "books" under different titles. However, this way of dividing the book, which was first published in 1906, did not arrange the fragments in the order determined by the time of their writing or revision, but assembled them according to the editors' murky and in any case irrelevant personal plan. In this fabricated "book," thoughts from entirely different periods of time and from wholly divergent levels and aspects of a question are capriciously and mindlessly juxtaposed and intermingled. True, everything published in this "book" is Nietzsche's, but he never thought it *like that.*

The selections are numbered consecutively from 1 to 1067, and, thanks to this numeration, are easy to locate in the various editions. The first book, "European Nihilism," comprises numbers 1 through 134. We needn't raise the question here as to what extent other notes —whether they have been placed in subsequent chapters of this posthumous book or are not included in it at all—might with equal or greater right belong under the title "European Nihilism." For we wish to contemplate *Nietzsche's* thoughts about nihilism, as the knowledge of a thinker who thinks in the direction of world history. Such thoughts are never the mere viewpoint of that one person; still less are they the celebrated "expression of one's time." The thoughts of a thinker of Nietzsche's stature are reverberations of the still-unrecognized history of Being in the word which that historical man utters as his "language."

We today do not know the reason why the inmost core of Nietzsche's metaphysics could not be made public by him, but lies concealed in posthumous notes—*still* lies concealed, although his literary remains have for the most part become available to us, albeit in a very misleading form.

2. Nihilism as the "Devaluation of the Uppermost Values"

From what has been said about the character of the posthumous work *The Will to Power,* we can easily deduce that it will be impossible for us to deal with the individual notes in their exact order. By proceeding in such a way, we would merely be surrendering ourselves to the pointless confusion of the editors' textual arrangement. We would continue haphazardly to jumble together thoughts from different periods, that is, from different levels and thrusts of a question or discourse. Let us instead choose individual fragments. There are three criteria governing the choice:

1. The fragment must stem from a time of utter lucidity and keen insight. These are the two final years 1887 and 1888.
2. The fragment must so far as possible contain the essential core of nihilism, analyze it with sufficient scope, and show it to us from all relevant points of view.
3. The fragment must be suitable for bringing our confrontation with Nietzsche's thought on nihilism to its proper place.

These three conditions are not arbitrarily proposed: they arise from the *essence* of Nietzsche's fundamental metaphysical position, as determined by his meditation on the beginning, the career, and the completion of Western metaphysics as a whole.

In our own meditation on European nihilism we are not attempting an exhaustive presentation and elucidation of all the pertinent statements Nietzsche made. We would like to grasp the innermost essence of the history that is called *nihilism* so as to approach the Being of what is. If we occasionally connect parallel statements or similar notes, we must always bear in mind that for the most part they derive from distinct strata of thinking and that a statement yields its full import only when the often subtly shifting stratum is also co-defined. It does not matter whether we come to know all the "passages" on the "theme" of nihilism, but it is vital that by means of suitable fragments we establish a durable relationship with what it is they are addressing.

Note 12 satisfies the three conditions we have set. It was sketched in the period between November 1887 and March 1888 and bears the title "The Decline of Cosmological Values."* We cite in addition notes 14 and 15 (XV, 152 f.; spring–fall, 1887). We introduce this meditation with a note of Nietzsche's written about the same time and correctly placed by the editors at the beginning of the book.† It runs, "What does nihilism mean? *That the uppermost values devaluate themselves.* The aim is lacking; the 'why?' receives no answer" (WM, 2).

This brief note contains a question, an answer to the question, and an explanation of the answer. The question asks about the essence of nihilism. The answer is *"that the uppermost values devaluate themselves."* We immediately perceive that in the answer there is something decisive for any understanding of nihilism: nihilism is a *process,* the process of devaluation, whereby the uppermost values become valueless. Whether or not that exhausts the essence of nihilism is left undecided by the description. When values become valueless, they collapse on themselves, become untenable. The character exhibited by this process of "decline" of "the uppermost values," the extent to which it is a *historical* process and in fact the basic process of our Western history, the way in which it constitutes the historicity of the history of our own era—all these can be comprehended only if we first

* CM lists the title of this aphorism (W II 3 [99]), which Nietzsche reworked during the summer of 1888, simply as "Critique of Nihilism." Otherwise GOA (XV, 148–51) reproduces the text adequately.

† "Correctly placed by the editors" is perhaps an exaggeration: WM, 2 is part of a much larger note consisting of WM, 23, 2, 22, and 13 (cf. CM, W II 1 [35]), and even its two sentences are presented in inverse order.

know what something such as "value" really "is," whether there are "uppermost" ("highest") values, and *which ones* these are.

To be sure, the explanation of the answer offers a clue. The devaluation of values, hence nihilism too, consists in the fact that "an aim" is lacking. However, the question remains: Why an "aim"? An "aim" for what purpose? What is the inner connection between value and aim? The explanation says that the " 'Why?' receives no answer." The question "why?" asks why something is this or that way. The answer provides what we call the "grounds." The question repeats itself: Why must there be grounds? How and why is the ground a ground? In what way does this exist—a ground? What is the inner connection between ground and value?

We have already seen, thanks to our introductory remarks about the essential connection between "nihilism" and the "revaluation" of all prior and indeed uppermost values, that the concept of value plays a major role in Nietzsche's thought. As a result of the impact of his writings, valuative thought is familiar to us. One speaks of the "vital values" of a people, or the "cultural values" of a nation. It is said that the supreme values of mankind are worth protecting and preserving. We hear that things of "great value" are carried to safety, meaning that works of art, for example, are guarded from air attacks. In this case, "value" means the same as "goods." A "good" is a being that "has" a particular "value"; a good is a good on grounds of value, is that in which a value becomes an object and thus a "valuable."

What is a value? We know, for example, that the freedom of a people is a "value," but here again we basically take freedom to be a good that we possess or do not possess. Freedom would not be a good if it were not as such first a value, the sort of thing we esteem as something worthwhile, something valid, something that "matters." Value is what validates. Only what is valid is a value. But what does "validate" mean? What is valid plays the role of a standard of measure. The question is whether a value is valid because it is a standard of measure, or whether it can be a standard of measure because it is valid. If the latter, then we ask anew: What does it mean to say that a value is valid? Is something valid because it is a value, or is it a value because it is valid? What is value itself, that it should be valid? "To be valid" is of course not nothing, but the mode and manner in which value, indeed *as* value, "is." To be valid is a mode of *Being.* There can be value only in being-a-value.

The question about value and its essence is grounded in the question of Being. "Values" are *accessible* and capable of being a standard of measure only where things such as values are esteemed and where one value is ranked above or below another. Such esteeming and valuing occurs only where something "matters" for our behavior. Here alone is the kind of thing educed to which any comportment first, last, and always returns. To esteem something, to hold it worthwhile, also means to be *directed* toward it. Such direction *toward* has already assumed an "aim." Thus the essence of value has an *inner* relation to the essence of aim. Once again we encounter the vexing question: Is something an aim because it is a value, or does something only become a value insofar as it has been posited as an aim? Perhaps this either-or formulation betrays a question that is still insufficient and does not yet reach out into the truly questionable.

The same reflections might result from a consideration of the relation between value and ground. If value is what always matters in everything, then it also shows itself to be that in which everything that matters is grounded and derives its sustenance and permanence. Here the same questions present themselves: Does something become a ground because it has validity as a value, or does it succeed in validating values because it is a ground? The either-or fails here too, perhaps because the essential limits of "value" and "ground" cannot be determined on the same plane.

No matter how these questions are resolved, they at least sketch in outline form an inner bond connecting value, aim, and ground. However, the most pressing issue that still remains unclarified is why Nietzsche's valuative thought has far and away dominated all "world view" thinking since the end of the last century. In truth, the role that valuative thought plays is *by no means self-evident.* That is already demonstrated in the historical recollection that valuative thought was first advanced expressly in these terms during the second half of the nineteenth century and that it progressed to the status of a truism. We are all too willing to be diverted from that fact, because every historical investigation usurps a currently dominant mode of thought and makes it the guiding principle according to which the past is examined and rediscovered. Historians are very proud of these discoveries and fail to notice that they had already been made before the historians began to ply their belated trade. And so as soon as valuative thought emerged, there came—and still comes—the empty talk about the "cultural values" of the Middle Ages and the "spiritual values" of antiquity, even though there was nothing like "culture" in the Middle Ages nor anything like "spirit" and "culture" in ancient times. Only in the modern era have spirit and culture been deliberately experienced as fundamental modes of human comportment, and only in most recent times have "values" been posited as standards for such comportment. It does not follow, of course, that earlier periods were "uncultured" in the sense that they were submerged in barbarism; what follows is that with the schemata "culture" and "lack of culture," "spirit," and "value," we never touch in its essence the history, for example, of the Greeks.

3. Nihilism, *Nihil,* and Nothing

If we remain with Nietzsche's note, then we must first of all answer the one central question we posed earlier: What does nihilism have to do with values and their devaluation? In its literal sense, "nihilism" surely says that all being is *nihil,* "nothing," and presumably a thing can only be worth *nothing* because and inasmuch as it is already null and nothing in itself. The determination of value and the valuation of something as valued, as valuable or valueless, are first grounded on a determination of *whether* and *how* something *is,* or whether it is *"nothing."* Nihilism and *nihil* are not necessarily or essentially connected with valuative thought. Why is nihilism nonetheless (and with no particular justification) conceived of as "devaluation of the uppermost values" and as a "decline" of values?

Now, it is true that for us the word and concept *nothing* usually carries the concomitant tone of a value, namely, of disvaluation. We say *nothing* when some desired, anticipated, sought, demanded, expected thing is *not* at hand, *is* not. When a well is drilled somewhere for a "petroleum find," for example, and the drilling is fruitless, one says "Nothing was found"; that is, the anticipated finding, the find—the entity that one sought—was not found. "Nothing" implies a thing's not being at hand, its not being. "Nothing" and *nihil* therefore mean beings in their *Being* and are concepts of *Being* and not of *value.* (We should keep in mind what Jacob Wackernagel says in his *Lectures on Syntax,* Series II, (second edition, 1928), p. 272: "In the German *nicht[s]* . . . lies the word which in its Gothic form *waihts* . . . serves to translate the Greek *pragma.*")*

* Hermann Paul's *Deutsches Wörterbuch,* 6th ed. (Tübingen: Niemeyer, 1966), describes the word *nicht* as a contraction of the Old High German expression *ni (eo) wiht,*

The root meaning of the Latin word *nihil,* which even the Romans pondered (*ne-hilum*), has not been clarified up to the present day. At any rate, according to the concept of the word, *nihilism* is concerned with the nothing and therefore, in a special way, with beings in their nonbeing. But the nonbeing of beings is considered to be the negation of beings. We usually think the "nothing" only in terms of what is negated. In drilling for oil, "nothing" was found; that is to say, *not* the entity sought. In that case, one answers the question "Is oil present?" with "No." True, in drilling for oil "nothing" was found, but in no way did we find *"the nothing,"* because it was not drilled for, and cannot be drilled for, especially not with the help of mechanical drilling rigs or other such contrivances.

Does the nothing ever let itself be found, or even searched for? Or is it the case that it does not need to be sought and found at all, because it "is" *that* which we least—that is to say, never—lose?

The nothing here signifies, not the particular negation of an individual being, but the complete and absolute negation of all beings, of beings as a whole. But, as the "negation" of everything "objective," nothingness "is" for its part not a possible object. To talk about the nothing and to pursue it in thought are shown to be projects *"without object,"* vacuous word games that furthermore do not seem to notice that they are always flatly contradicting themselves, because no matter what they stipulate about the nothing they always have to say that the nothing *is* such and such. Even when we say simply that the nothing "is" nothing, we are apparently predicating an "is" of it and making it into a being; we attribute what ought to be withheld from it.

No one would want to deny that such "reflections" are easily followed and are "striking," especially as long as one moves in the realm of facile explanations, putters about with mere words, and lets oneself be struck by all such thoughtlessness. In fact, we cannot treat the

---

literally, "not any thing." (Compare the English word *nothing.*) The word *wiht* is a close relative of the English "wight," a thing, creature, or being, anything that has a modicum of "weight"—another related word. In its article on the archaic substantive "wight," the *Oxford English Dictionary* in fact derives the Gothic word *waihts* from *two* of the principal Greek words for being, *eidos* and *pragma.* The words *nichts* and *nothing* thus preserve their reference to being—as does the ostensibly negative English expression, "Not a whit!"

nothing as the counteressence to all beings except by saying that the nothing "is" such and such. But for the most part this has "only" a limited and precise meaning: the nothing too, even the nothing, still remains rooted in the "is" and in Being. What, then, do "Being" and the "is" mean? By correctly reciting these statements, so plausible and seemingly incisive, bearing on the impossibility of saying something about the nothing without thereby proclaiming it a being, one suggests that the essence of "Being" and the "is," which one is supposedly misattributing to the nothing by speaking about it, is the most evident, well-clarified, and indisputable matter in the world. One gives the impression that one has a clear, demonstrative, and unshakable hold on the truth of the "is" and of "Being." This opinion has long been endemic to Western metaphysics. It co-constitutes the ground on which all metaphysics rests. Most often, therefore, one dispenses with "the nothing" in a brief paragraph. It seems to be a universally convincing fact that "nothingness" is the opposite of all being.

On closer inspection, the nothing turns out also to be *the negation* of beings. Denying, nay-saying, nullifying, negation—all that is the opposite of affirmation. Both negation and affirmation are basic forms of judgment, assertion, *logos apophantikos.** The nothing, as a

* Aristotle (*On Interpretation,* 17a, 1–4) distinguishes *logos apophantikos* from *logos sēmantikos* in the following way: while the latter includes all meaningful statements, such as questions, commands, or requests, *logos apophantikos* is restricted to statements "that have truth or falsity in them," statements of predication, or, as the tradition calls them, "propositions." A recurrent problem in Heidegger's thought is the relationship between *logos apophantikos* and the "truth" (*alētheuein*) or "falsity" (*pseudesthai*) that are somehow "in" it. Heidegger suggests that truth is not located in propositions, as traditional logic insists, but that our speech in some way addresses primordial truth as disclosure, *a-lētheia.* Thus in his first logic course (winter semester, 1925–26) Heidegger defines *apo-phainesthai* literally as "letting (a being) be seen . . . on its own terms," and equates it with *a-lētheuein,* uncovering, unveiling, or removing (a being) from concealment. The word *phainesthai* thus points toward the very origins of the discipline that calls itself *phenomenology,* and it also suggests a kind of thinking that will have to devote itself to *alētheia.* The key text is Martin Heidegger, *Being and Time,* tr. John Macquarrie and Edward Robinson (New York: Harper & Row, 1962), section 7B, "The Concept of Logos"; section 33, "Assertion as a Derivative Mode of Interpretation"; and section 44b, "The Original Phenomenon of Truth and the Derivative Character of the Traditional Concept of Truth." See also the detailed analyses in Heidegger's first logic course, now published as Martin Heidegger, *Logik: Die Frage nach der Wahrheit* (Frankfurt am Main: V. Klostermann, 1976), §§ 9–12, pp. 62–161, and esp. section 11, pp. 127–35.

product of negation, has a "logical" origin. Certainly man needs "logic" in order to think correctly and methodically, although what one merely thinks does not have to be; that is, does not have to occur as something actual in reality. The nothing of negation or no-saying is a mere mental image, the most abstract of abstractions. The nothing is purely and simply "nothing," what is most null, and so unworthy of any further attention or respect. If the nothing is nothing, if it is not, then neither can beings ever founder in the nothing nor can all things dissolve in it. Hence there can be no process of becoming-nothing. Hence nihilism is an illusion.

Were that so, then we would be able to consider Western history saved and would be able to renounce all thoughts of "nihilism." But perhaps the matter is quite different with nihilism. Perhaps it is still as Nietzsche says in *The Will to Power* (WM, 1, from 1885–86): "Nihilism stands at the door: whence comes to us this uncanniest of all guests?" In note 2 of the Preface (XV, 137), Nietzsche says, "What I shall relate is the history of the next two centuries."

Certainly the prevailing opinion and the traditional convictions of philosophy are right to insist that the nothing is not a "being," no "object." But that does not satisfy the question as to whether this nonobjective matter really "is," inasmuch as it determines the essential unfolding of Being. The question remains whether what is not an object and never can be an object therefore "is" simply *nothingness,* and this in turn a "nullity." The question arises whether the innermost essence of nihilism and the power of its dominion do not consist precisely in considering the nothing merely as a nullity, considering nihilism as an apotheosis of the merely vacuous, as a negation that can be set to rights at once by an energetic affirmation.

Perhaps the essence of nihilism consists in *not* taking the question of the nothing seriously. In point of fact, if one leaves the question undeveloped, one remains obstinately fixed in the interrogative scheme of that familiar either-or. With general approbation, one says that the nothing *either* "is" something thoroughly null *or* it must be a being.

Among the references to *apophainesthai* in Heidegger's later thought, see "Logos," in Martin Heidegger, *Early Greek Thinking,* tr. D. F. Krell and F. A. Capuzzi (New York: Harper & Row, 1975), p. 64.

But because the nothing obviously can never be a being, the only other alternative is that it is the purely null. Who would wish to repudiate such compelling "logic"? All due respect to logic! But correct thinking can be called on as a court of last resort only if one has previously established that *what* is to be "correctly" thought according to the rules of "logic" also exhausts everything thinkable, everything that is to be thought and is given over to thinking.

What if in truth the nothing were indeed not a being but also were not simply null? And what if the *question* about the essence of the nothing, with the help of that either-or, had not yet been adequately formulated? Finally, what if the *default* of a developed question about the essence of the nothing were *the grounds* for the fact that Western metaphysics had to fall prey to nihilism? Then nihilism, conceived and experienced in a more original and essential way, would be that history of metaphysics which is heading toward a fundamental metaphysical position in which the essence of the nothing not only *cannot* be understood but also *will* no longer be understood. Nihilism would then be the essential nonthinking of the essence of the nothing. Here, perhaps, is the reason why Nietzsche was forced into what from his point of view was "complete" nihilism. Because Nietzsche surely recognized nihilism as a movement of modern Western history but was unable to think about the essence of the nothing, being unable to raise the question, he had to become a classical nihilist who expressed the history that is now happening. Nietzsche knew and experienced nihilism because he himself thought nihilistically. Nietzsche's concept of nihilism is itself nihilistic. Consequently, in spite of all his insights, he could not recognize the hidden essence of nihilism, because right from the outset, *solely* on the basis of valuative thought, he conceived of nihilism as a process of the devaluation of the uppermost values. Nietzsche had to conceive of nihilism that way because in remaining on the path and within the realm of Western metaphysics, he thought it to its conclusion.

In no sense did Nietzsche interpret nihilism as a process of devaluing the uppermost values merely because valuative thought played a role in the course of his education or in his "private" views and positions. Valuative thought played this part in Nietzsche's thought because Nietzsche thought *metaphysically,* on the path of the history of metaphysics. But it is no accident that valuative thought took precedence in metaphysics, at the core of Western philosophy. In the concept of value there lies concealed a concept of Being that contains an interpretation of the whole of beings as such. In valuative thought the *essence* of Being is—unwittingly—thought in a definite and necessary aspect; that is, in its nonessence. This is to be shown in the following reflections.

4. Nietzsche's Conception of Cosmology and Psychology

Nietzsche's note 2, which we mentioned earlier, gives us a preliminary glimpse into the nihilistically thought essence of nihilism, an insight into Nietzsche's orientation in thinking about nihilism. Nihilism is the process of the devaluation of the uppermost values. Nihilism is the inner lawfulness of this process, the "logic" according to which the decline of the uppermost values is played out according to its essence. In what is such lawfulness grounded?

To understand the Nietzschean concept of nihilism at all as the devaluation of the uppermost values, we must now come to know what is meant by such values, to what extent they contain an interpretation of the being, why we necessarily arrive at that valuative interpretation, and what transformation is wrought in metaphysics by means of it. We shall reply to these questions by way of an elucidation of note 12 (November 1887–March 1888). The fragment, entitled "Decline of the Cosmological Values," is divided into two sections (A and B) of unequal scope, and is rounded off by a concluding remark.

The first section (A) runs thus:

> *Nihilism* as a *psychological state* will have to enter on the scene, *first,* when we have sought a "meaning" in all events that is not in them: so that the seeker eventually becomes discouraged. Nihilism, then, is the recognition of the long *squandering* of strength, the agony of the "in vain," the insecurity, the lack of any opportunity to recuperate and to regain tranquillity—being ashamed of oneself, as if one had *deceived* oneself all too long. . . . That meaning could have been: the "fulfillment" of some supreme ethical canon in all events, the ethical world order; or the growth of love and harmony in social intercourse; or the gradual approximation to a

state of universal happiness; or even the departure toward a state of universal nothingness—any goal constitutes at least some meaning. What all these notions have in common is that something is to be *achieved* in the process —and now one grasps the fact that becoming aims at *nothing* and achieves *nothing*. . . . Thus disappointment regarding an ostensible *purpose of becoming* as the cause of nihilism: whether with regard to a specific purpose or generalized insight into the fact that all previous hypotheses about purposes that concern the whole "evolution" are inadequate (man *no longer* the collaborator, let alone the center, of becoming).

Nihilism as a psychological state arises, *secondly*, when one has posited a *totality*, a *systematization*, indeed any *organization* in all occurrences, and beneath all occurrences, so that a soul that craves to adore and revere wallows in the general notion of some supreme form of domination and governance (if the soul be that of a logician, complete consistency and a *Realdialektik* quite suffice to reconcile it to everything). Some sort of unity, any form of "monism": and in consequence of such faith, man, rapt in the profound feeling of standing in the network of, and being dependent on, a totality that is infinitely superior to him, as a mode of the deity. . . . "The well-being of the universal demands the devotion of the individual"—but behold, there *is* no such universal! At bottom, man has lost faith in his own value when no infinitely valuable totality works through him; that is to say, he conceived such a totality *in order to be able to believe in his own value*.

Nihilism as psychological state has yet a *third* and *final* form. Given these two *insights*, that becoming aims at no goal and that underneath all becoming there is no grand unity in which the individual could submerge completely as in an element of supreme value, one *escape* remains: to condemn the whole world of becoming as a deception and to invent a world that would lie beyond it, as the *true* world. But, as soon as man finds out how that world is fabricated, solely out of psychological needs, and that he has absolutely no right to it, the final form of nihilism emerges: it embraces *disbelief in any metaphysical world* and thus forbids itself any belief in a *true* world. Having reached this standpoint, one concedes the reality of becoming as the *only* reality, forbids oneself every kind of clandestine access to afterworlds and false divinities—but one *cannot endure this world, which, however, one does not want to deny*. What has happened, at bottom? The feeling of *valuelessness* was attained with the realization that the overall character of existence may not be interpreted by means of the concept of *"purpose,"* the concept of *"unity,"* or the concept of *"truth."* Existence aims at nothing and achieves nothing; a comprehensive unity in the plurality of

> occurrences is lacking; the character of existence is not "true," is *false*. . . . One simply lacks any grounds for convincing oneself that there is a *true* world. . . . In short, the categories *"purpose,"* "unity," "Being," by which we used to invest some value into the world—we *withdraw* again; and now the world seems *valueless*.

According to the inscription, the matter in question is the decline of *"cosmological"* values. It appears that a *special* class of values has been named, the decline of which constitutes nihilism. In the more orthodox articulations of metaphysical doctrine, "cosmology" embraces a particular region of beings, the "cosmos" in the sense of "nature," the earth and stars, plants and animals. "Psychology," as the study of soul and spirit, and especially of man as a rational creature, differs from "cosmology." "Theology" parallels and surpasses psychology and cosmology, not as the canonical interpretation of biblical revelation, but as the "rational" ("natural") interpretation of the biblical doctrine of God as the first cause of all beings, of nature and of man, of history and its works. But, just as the frequently quoted expression *Anima naturaliter christiana* ["The soul is naturally Christian"] is not a purely indubitable "natural" truth, but is a *Christian* truth, so too natural theology has the ground of its truth only in the biblical teaching that man was fashioned by a creator God who also endowed him with knowledge of his Creator. Because natural theology as a philosophical discipline cannot validly permit the Old Testament to be the source of its truths, the contents of that theology must be diluted to the statement that the world must have a first cause. That does not prove that the first cause is a "God," assuming that a God would ever let Himself be debased into an object of proofs. It is important to have some insight into the essence of rational theology, because Western metaphysics is theological even where it opposes church theology.

The words *cosmology, psychology,* and *theology*—or the threesome of *nature, man,* and *God*—circumscribe the realm in which all Western representation operates when it thinks beings as a whole in a metaphysical way. Consequently, when we read the inscription "Decline of Cosmological Values" we immediately suppose that from the three traditional domains of metaphysics Nietzsche has selected one in particular—cosmology. This supposition is erroneous. Here cosmos does not mean "nature" as distinct from man and God; rather, it signifies the "world," and "world" is the name for beings as a whole. "Cosmological values" are not a separate class of values ranked with or above others. They determine "where . . . [human life], 'nature,' 'world,' the whole sphere of becoming and transience, belong" (*Toward a Genealogy of Morals,* 1887, VII, 425). They designate the widest circle that encloses everything that is and becomes. Outside it and beyond it nothing exists. Nihilism, as the devaluation of the *uppermost* values, is the decline of *cosmological* values. If we understand its title correctly, the fragment concerns the essence of nihilism.

Section A is divided into four paragraphs, the fourth of which summarizes the other three with respect to their essential import; namely, the meaning of the decline of cosmological values. Section B affords us a view of the essential consequences of the decline. It shows that with the decline of cosmological values the cosmos itself does not fall away but is merely freed from the valuations of prevailing values and made available for a new valuation. Thus nihilism does not at all lead us into nothing. Decline is not simply collapse. But what must occur if nihilism is to lead to a rescue and recovery of beings as a whole is intimated by the concluding remark appended to the entire fragment.

The first three paragraphs of section A begin in a similar fashion: "*Nihilism* as a *psychological state*"—"will have to enter on the scene," "arises *secondly,*" "has yet a *third* and *final* form." For Nietzsche, nihilism is the covert, basic law of Western history. In this fragment, however, he expressly defines it as a "psychological state." So the question arises as to what he means by "psychological" and "psychology." For Nietzsche, "psychology" is not the psychology being practiced already in his day, a psychology modeled on physics and coupled with physiology as scientific-experimental research into mental processes, in which sense perceptions and their bodily conditions are posited, like chemical elements, as the basic constituents of such processes. Nor does "psychology" signify for Nietzsche research into the "higher life of intelligent mind" and its processes, in the sense of one kind of research among others. Neither is it "characterology," as the doctrine of various human types. One could sooner interpret Nietzsche's concept of psychology as "anthropology," if "anthropology" means a *philosophical* inquiry into the essence of man in the perspective of his essential ties to beings as a whole. In that case, "anthropology" is the "metaphysics" of man. But, even so, we have not hit on Nietzsche's conception of "psychology" and the "psychological." Nietzsche's "psychology" in no way restricts itself to man, but neither does it extend simply to plants and animals. "Psychology" is the question of the "psychical"; that is, of what is living, in that particular sense of life that determines becoming as "will to power." Insofar as the latter constitutes the basic character of all beings, and inasmuch as the truth of the whole of beings as such is called "metaphysics," Nietzsche's "psychology" is simply coterminous with metaphysics. That metaphysics becomes a "psychology," albeit one in which the "psychology" of *man* has definite preeminence, lies grounded in the very essence of modern metaphysics.

Western history has now begun to enter into the completion of that period we call the *modern,* and which is defined by the fact that man becomes the measure and the center of beings. Man is what lies at the bottom of all beings; that is, in modern terms, at the bottom of all objectification and representability. No matter how sharply Nietzsche pits himself time and again against Descartes, whose philosophy grounds modern metaphysics, he turns against Descartes only because the latter *still* does *not* posit man as *subiectum* in a way that is complete and decisive enough. The representation of the *subiectum* as ego, the I, thus the "egoistic" interpretation of the *subiectum,* is still not subjectivistic enough for Nietzsche. Modern metaphysics first comes to the full and final determination of its essence in the doctrine of the Overman, the doctrine of man's absolute preeminence among beings. In that doctrine, Descartes celebrates his supreme triumph.

Because the will to power unfolds its pure powerfulness without restraint in man—that is to say, in the figure of the Overman—"psychology" in Nietzsche's sense as the doctrine of will to power is therefore always *simultaneously* and *from the outset* the realm of the *fundamental questions of metaphysics.* Thus Nietzsche can say, in *Beyond Good and Evil* (VII, 35 ff.),

> All psychology to date has got stuck in moral prejudices and fears: it has not dared to descend into the depths. To conceive of psychology as the morphology and *doctrine of the development of will to power,* as I do—no one has yet come close to this in his thought.

At the end of the section, Nietzsche says it is imperative "that psychology be recognized again as the queen of the sciences; the other sciences must minister to her. For psychology is once again the path to the fundamental problems." We could also say that the path to the fundamental problems of metaphysics is the Cartesian *Meditationes* on man as *subiectum.* Psychology is the name for the metaphysics that posits man (that is, mankind as such, not simply the individual "I," as *subiectum*) as measure and center, as ground and aim of all being. If nihilism is construed as a "psychological state," this means that nihilism concerns the position of man amid beings as a whole, the way in which man puts himself in contact with the being as such, the way he forms and sustains that relationship and thereby himself. But that implies nothing less than the way in which man is historical. That way is determined by the basic character of beings as will to power. Taken as a "psychological state," nihilism is inherently viewed as a configuration of *will to power,* as the occurrence in which man is historical.

If Nietzsche speaks of nihilism as a "psychological state," he will also operate with "psychological" concepts and speak the language of "psychology" when he explains the essence of nihilism. That is not accidental and is therefore not an extrinsic form of communication. Nonetheless, we must detect a more essential content in such language, because it refers to the "cosmos," beings as a whole.

5. The Provenance of Nihilism and Nihilism's Three Forms

In the first three paragraphs of note 12(A) Nietzsche identifies three conditions under which nihilism enters on the scene. In asking about such conditions, he is seeking to illuminate the *provenance* of nihilism. Here provenance does not mean the "whence" but the "how"—the form and manner in which nihilism comes to be and is. In no way does provenance mean a historically reckoned genesis. Nietzsche's question about the provenance of nihilism, as a question about the cause of nihilism, is nothing other than the question of its essence.

Nihilism is the process of the devaluation of the uppermost values hitherto. If these uppermost values, which grant all beings their value, are devalued, then all beings grounded in them become valueless. A feeling of futility, of the nullity of everything, arises. Hence nihilism, as the decline of cosmological values, is at the same time the emergence of nihilism as a *feeling* of utter valuelessness, as a "psychological state." Under what circumstances does the state arise? Nihilism "must enter on the scene," *first,* "when we have sought a 'meaning' in all events that is not in them." Thus a precondition for nihilism is that we seek a "meaning" in "all events"; that is, in beings as a whole. What does Nietzsche intend by "meaning"? An understanding of the essence of nihilism, which Nietzsche often identifies with the rule of *"meaninglessness"* (see WM, 11), depends on the answer to this question. "Meaning" signifies the same thing as value, since in place of "meaninglessness" Nietzsche also says "valuelessness." Still, we lack an adequate determination of the essence of "meaning." "Meaning," one would like to think, is understood by everyone. And, in the milieu of everyday thought and vague opinions, it is. But as soon as we become aware that man seeks a "meaning" in all events, and as soon as Nietzsche indicates that this search for "meaning" is frustrated, we cannot circumvent questions about what meaning means, about why and to what extent man seeks meaning, why he cannot accept possible disappointment in this matter with indifference, but is troubled and endangered, even shattered by it in his very substance.

By "meaning," Nietzsche understands "purpose" (see paragraphs 1 and 4). We think of purpose as the why and wherefore of every action, comportment, and event. Nietzsche enumerates what the desired "meaning" could have been; that is, what from the historical point of view *has been* and in its remarkable transformations *still is:* the "ethical world order"; "the growth of love and harmony in social intercourse"; pacifism, eternal peace; "the gradual approximation to a state of universal happiness" as the greatest good of the greatest number; "or even the departure toward a state of universal nothingness." For even *this* departure toward *this* aim still has a "meaning": "any goal constitutes at least some meaning." Why? Because it has a purpose, because it *is* itself a purpose. Is nothingness an aim? Certainly, because the will to will nothingness still allows the will its *volition.* The will to destruction is will nonetheless. And, because volition is to will oneself, even the will to nothingness still permits willing—that *the will itself* be.

Human will "*needs an aim*—and would sooner will *nothingness* than *not* will at all." For "will" is will to power: power to power, or as we might also say, *will to will,* will to stay on top and retain command. The will shrinks, not from nothingness, but from *not willing,* from the annihilation of its ownmost possibility. This trepidation before the emptiness of not-willing—this *"horror vacui"*—is "the fundamental fact of human will." It is precisely from the *"fundamental fact"* of human will—that it prefers *to will the nothing* rather than *not to will* —that Nietzsche derives the basic proof for his statement that the will is in its essence will to power. (See *Toward a Genealogy of Morals,* 1887; VII, 399.)* "Meaning," "aim," and "purpose" are what allow and enable will to be will. Where there is will, there is not only a way, but first of all an aim *for* the way, even if this is "simply" the will itself.

* At the beginning of the third and last division of his *Genealogy of Morals,* "What Is the Significance of Ascetic Ideals?" Nietzsche writes,

But those absolute "purposes" have never yet been attained in the history of man. Every effort and pursuit, every enterprise and activity, every stride on life's way, every proceeding, all "processes"—in short, all "becoming"—achieves *nothing,* attains nothing in the sense of the *pure* realization of those *absolute* purposes. Expectations in that regard are disappointed; every attempt seems valueless. One begins to doubt whether there is any purpose at all in positing a "purpose" for beings as a whole or in seeking a "meaning." What if not only the effort to fulfill purposes and accomplish meaning but even the search for a positing of purpose and meaning are all delusions? The uppermost value would thereby be made to totter, to lose its indubitable character, and to "devalue itself." The "purpose" toward which everything is supposed to tend, which is in itself absolutely valid *prior to* and *for* everything, the uppermost value, becomes untenable. The decrepitude of the uppermost values edges toward *consciousness.* In accord with the new consciousness, the relation of man to being as a whole and to himself is changed.

Nihilism as a psychological state, as a "feeling" of the valuelessness of beings as a whole, "arises *secondly* when one has posited a *totality,* a *systematization,* indeed any *organization* in all occurrences, and beneath all occurrences," which is never realized. What is now introduced as the highest value for beings as a whole has the character of *"unity,"* understood here as an all-pervasive unification, arrangement, and organization of all things into one. Such "unity" appears to be less

---

But the fact that the ascetic ideal has meant so much to man is an expression of the fundamental fact concerning the human will, namely, its *horror vacui: it needs an aim*—and it would sooner will *nothingness* than *not* will at all.

And, at the conclusion of that division (as of the book itself):

> One simply cannot hide those things which were willed by a willing that took its orientation entirely from the ascetic ideal: such a hatred of the human, and even more of the animal, and still more of the material; such revulsion before the senses, and before reason itself; fear in the face of happiness and beauty; longing to escape from all semblance, change, becoming, death, desire, and from longing itself—it all signifies (let us dare to grasp it) a *will to nothingness,* a counterwill to life, rebellion against life's fundamental presuppositions; but it is and remains a *will!* And, to say again at the end what I said at the beginning: man would rather will *nothingness* than *not* will at all.

questionable in its essence than "meaning," the first "cosmological value" named. Nevertheless, even here we immediately ask ourselves why and to what extent man *"posits"* such a "ruling" and "dominant" "unity," how such positing is grounded, whether it can be grounded at all, and, if not, how it can be legitimately posited.

At once a further question arises as to whether and how this "positing" of a "unity" for beings as a whole is bound up with the previously mentioned "quest" for "meaning," whether these two are the same, and if they are, why this "same" is construed in different concepts. It can always be shown *that* man searches for meaning and posits a supreme, all-pervasive unity for beings. Nonetheless, the question of *what* the quest is and in what it is grounded must be kept open for now. At the end of the second paragraph, which describes the positing of "unity," for which Nietzsche also uses the similarly bland term "universality," he gives an indication of the *ground* of this positing, so that he might at the same time point out what happens when what is posited is *not* verified or fulfilled. Only if the *whole of beings* "works" through man, only if man is drawn into "unity" and is "submerged" in it "as in the element of highest value," only then does man have a "value" for himself. Thus, Nietzsche concludes, man must take into account such a totality and unity of beings *"so that he can believe in his own value."*

It is presupposed that man's capacity to believe in his own "value" is necessary. It is necessary because there is everywhere a concern for man's self-assertion. For man to remain certain of his own value, he must posit an uppermost value for beings as a whole. But if the belief in a unity that pervades reality is disappointed, this gives rise to the insight that nothing is aimed at by any given act or deed ("becoming"). What is implied in such an insight? Nothing less than the idea that all such realizing and becoming are nothing "real" and not truly in being, but are mere delusion. "Realizing" is therefore unreal. "Becoming" now appears to be not only aimless and meaningless but also of no consequence in itself, therefore *unreal.* However, to be able to rescue such unreality and secure for man his own value, one must in spite of everything posit *a true world* beyond "becoming," beyond the "mutable," the properly unreal and merely apparent, a world in which the permanent is preserved, untouched by any change, lack, or disappointment. Of course, the positing of this "true world," the transcendent beyond, proceeds at the expense of the earthly "world." The latter is condemned to a brief odyssey—brief when measured against eternity—through the transitory, a sojourn whose toil will find its recompense in eternity, insofar as it obtains its value from there.

From the positing of a "true world," as the world of permanent beings in themselves above a false world of change and appearance, there springs "yet a *third* and final form" of nihilism; namely, when man discovers that this "*true* world" (the "transcendent," the beyond) has been fabricated solely out of "psychological needs." Nietzsche does not explicitly name these "psychological needs" here. He has already identified them in explaining the dethronement of unity and totality. A value must be placed on beings as a whole in order that the self-worth of man remain secure; there must be a world beyond in order that this earthly world can be endured. But when it is recounted to man how, by counting on a "true world" beyond, he has only been accounting for himself and his "wishes" and has elevated a merely desirable thing into a being in itself, then the "true world"—the uppermost value—begins to totter.

It is no longer a mere matter of feeling the valuelessness and aimlessness of becoming or of feeling the unreality of becoming. Nihilism now becomes outright disbelief in anything like a *meta*-physical world, that is, a world set "above" what is sensuous and what becomes (the "physical"). Such disbelief prohibits any clandestine paths to an afterworld or heaven. Thus nihilism arrives at a new stage. It is no longer simply a matter of feeling the valuelessness of the world of becoming, of feeling its unreality. Rather, when the *supersensuous,* "true" world has fallen, the world of becoming shows itself to be the "*only* reality"; that is, the one authentic "true" world.

A peculiar transitional state emerges: first, *the world of becoming*—that is, life as lived here and now, along with its changing realms—can no longer be denied as *real;* but, second, this world, which *alone* is real, has at the outset no aims and values and so is not to be endured. It is not simply the feeling of the valuelessness of reality that dominates but also a feeling of *helplessness* within what alone is real. What is missing is an insight into the grounds for the predicament and the possibility of overcoming it.

It should already be clear from our elucidation of section A so far that Nietzsche has not juxtaposed just any "three forms" of nihilism. Nor does he merely want to describe three ways in which the hitherto uppermost values are posited. We can easily see that the three forms of nihilism designated sustain an inner relation to one another and together constitute a particular movement; that is to say, *history*. True, nowhere does Nietzsche identify any historically recognized and demonstrable forms of the positing of the uppermost values, nor the historically representable contexts of such positings, which we might describe as fundamental metaphysical positions. Nevertheless, he has such a thing in mind. He wants to show how nihilism not only arises on the ground of the inner relation of these positings of the uppermost values but also becomes a unique history that drifts toward an unequivocal historical state. Nietzsche sums up his portrayal of the three "forms" of nihilism thus:

> What has happened, at bottom? The feeling of *valuelessness* was attained when one grasped the fact that the overall character of existence may not be interpreted by means of the concept of *"purpose,"* the concept of *"unity,"* or the concept of *"truth."* Existence aims at nothing and achieves nothing; a comprehensive unity in the plurality of events is lacking: the character of existence is not "true," is *false*. . . . One simply lacks any grounds for convincing oneself that there is a *true* world.

It does seem, in this summary, as if the search for meaning, the positing of a unity, and the ascent to a "true" (supersensuous) world are merely three equivalent interpretations of the "overall character of existence" in which "nothing" is ever "achieved."

How little Nietzsche is thinking of merely defining various brands of nihilism and the conditions for their emergence is betrayed by the concluding sentence of this summary: "In short, the categories *'purpose,'* 'unity,' 'Being,' by which we used to invest some value into the world—we *withdraw* again; and now the world seems *valueless.*"

Before we show how the whole of section A is to be understood in accord with this concluding sentence, the wording of the sentence must be explained in two specific respects.

6. The Uppermost Values as Categories

Nietzsche abruptly calls the uppermost values *categories,* without giving the term a more precise explanation that might establish why the uppermost values are apprehended also in that way, and why "categories" can be conceived of as uppermost values. What are "categories"? The word, of Greek derivation, is familiar yet foreign to us. We say, for example, that someone belongs in the category of malcontents. We are speaking about a "particular category of people," and we understand *category* here to signify "class" or "sort," which are also foreign words, except that they are Romanic; they stem from the Latin. Depending on the matter at hand, the terms *category, class,* or *sort* are used to delineate a region, schema, or pigeonhole into which something is deposited and so classified.

This use of the word *category* corresponds neither to its original concept nor to the related meaning that it has preserved as a key philosophical word. Nonetheless, our current usage of the word derives from philosophical usage. *Katēgoria* and *katēgorein* arise from *kata* and *agoreuein. Agora* means a public gathering of people as opposed to a closed council meeting, the *openness* [*Öffentlichkeit*] of deliberations, of court proceedings, of the market, and of communication. *Agoreuein* means to speak openly, to announce something openly to the public, to make a revelation. *Kata* implies going from above to something below, a view onto something. *Katēgorein* therefore means that, in an explicit view on something, we reveal what it is and render it open. Such revelation happens through the word insofar as the word addresses a thing—any being at all—with regard to what it is, and identifies it as being in one way or another.

This kind of addressing and setting forth, of making public in words, is most emphatically present when charges are preferred against someone in open court proceedings, stating that he is guilty of something or other. Addressing and setting forth has its most striking and therefore most common form in such open charges. Thus *katēgorein* especially signifies a setting forth, an address, in the sense of a "charge," which implies the basic meaning of a claim that reveals something. The noun *katēgoria* can be used in that sense. *Katēgoria* is then the addressing of a thing to what it is, in such a way that through the address the being itself is, as it were, brought into words in what *it itself* is; that is to say, it comes into appearance and into the openness of publicity. A *katēgoria* in this sense is the word *table,* or *chest, house,* or *tree,* or any similar word; or *red, heavy, thin, bold*—in short, any word that addresses some being in its particularity and so proclaims how that being looks and is. The aspect in which a being shows itself as what it is, is called in Greek *to eidos* or *hē idea.* A category is the addressing of a being to the particularity of its aspect, and so is its *proper name* in the widest sense. The word is also used by Aristotle in this sense (*Physics,* B 1, 192b 17), although that in no way makes it an expression reserved for philosophical language (a "term").

A *katēgoria* is a word in which a thing is "indicted" as what it is. This prephilosophical meaning of *katēgoria* is far removed from that lifeless and superficial foreign word *category* that still persists in our language. The Aristotelian usage just cited corresponds much more fully to the spirit of the Greek language, which, to be sure, is implicitly philosophical and metaphysical and is therefore, along with Sanskrit and cultivated German, distinguished above every other language.

Now, philosophy as metaphysics deals with "categories" in a special sense. It speaks of a "doctrine of categories" and "table of categories"; Kant, for example, in his major work, *The Critique of Pure Reason,* teaches that the table of categories can be derived and deduced from the table of judgments. What does *category* mean here, in the language of the philosophers? How is the philosophical term *category* related to the prephilosophical word *katēgoria?*

Aristotle, who also used the word *katēgoria* in its usual meaning as the address of a thing in its aspect, for the first time and in a way that was decisive for the next two thousand years raised the prephilosophical expression *katēgoria* to the rank of a philosophical term that names what philosophy, in keeping with its essence, must ponder in its thinking. The elevation in rank of the word *katēgoria* was carried out in a genuinely philosophical sense. Presumably no merely derivative, arbitrarily conceived, and—as we love to say—"abstract" meaning was foisted onto the word. The thrust of the word itself, in the spirit both of the language and of the matter itself, points toward a potentially, perhaps necessarily, different and more essential meaning. When we address "that thing there"—that "door," for instance—as a door, there is another, prior claim in regarding it so. What claim? We already identified it when we said "that thing there" is addressed as a door. In order that we can address the named as a "door" and not as a window, what is meant must have already shown itself as *"that thing there"*—as what is present in some way or other. Before we address the thing meant as a "door," the unexpressed claim has already been made that it is a "that thing there"—a thing. We could not regard the named as a door if we did not first of all let it encounter us as a thing existing for itself. The claim (*katēgoria*) that it is a thing underlies the address "door." "Thing" is a more fundamental and original *category* than "door," a "category" or claim that states in what mode of Being a designated being shows itself: that it is a being for itself, or, as Aristotle says, a something that of itself is for itself—*tode ti.*

A second example. We ascertain that this door is brown (not white). To be able to address the thing named as brown, we must regard it in its color. But even the coloration of a thing appears to us as this color and as no other only if the thing confronts us as being constituted in a particular way. If the thing were not already addressed in its constitution, then we could never address it as "brown"; that is, as brown-colored, as constituted (qualified) in a particular way.

Underlying and sustaining (as its ground) the prephilosophical address (*katēgoria*) of something as "brown" is our addressing it as "constituted in a particular way," the category "constitution," *poiotēs, poion, qualitas.* In relation to the category "quality," the prior claim is identified as a category in that it names what must ground every quality, the *underlying ground: hypokeimenon, subiectum, substantia.* "Substance," quality, as well as quantity and relation are "categories":

distinctive ways of speaking to beings, addressing a being with regard to what it is *as a being,* whether it be a door or window, table or house, dog or cat, and whether it be brown or white, sweet or sour, big or little.

Metaphysics is defined as the truth of beings as a whole, truth that is enjoined in the words of thinking. These words express the claims of the being as such in its composition—categories. Thus the categories are the basic words of metaphysics and are *therefore* names for the fundamental philosophical concepts. That these categories are silently expressed as claims in our ordinary thoughts and everyday comportment toward beings, or that they are really never experienced, acknowledged, or even conceived of as such tacit claims by most men throughout their "lives," neither these nor other such reasons are sufficient grounds for thinking that these categories are something indifferent, something construed by a philosophy that is supposedly "far removed from life." That the ordinary understanding and general opinion neither knows nor needs to know anything of these categories, merely certifies that something incontrovertibly essential is to be explained here, provided that nearness to essence is the privilege—but also the fate—of only a few. That there exists something like a diesel engine, for example, has its decisive and wholly sufficient ground in the fact that the categories of mechanically and technically useful "nature" were once expressly and thoroughly thought out by philosophers.

There is nothing wrong if the "man in the street" believes that there is a "diesel engine" because Herr Diesel invented it. Not everyone needs to know that the whole business of invention would not have been able to advance one step if philosophy, at the historical moment in which it entered the realm of its nonessence, had not thought the categories of nature and so first opened up this realm for the research and experiments of inventors. Of course, that does not mean that one who knows the true provenance of modern power machinery is thereby in a position to build better motors. But he is perhaps uniquely situated to ask what machine technology *is* within the history of man's relationship to Being.

In contrast, the question of what machine technology means for human progress and culture is of little consequence and ought to be bypassed in any case. For technology signifies exactly what "culture," which is contemporaneous with it, also signifies.

The categories are ways of addressing the being with regard to what the being as such is in its composition. The categories are therefore expressly known as such ways in a meditation on what is already tacitly co-expressed and addressed in the usual modes of addressing and discussing beings. The basic form of our everyday response to beings is assertion—Aristotle's *logos apophantikos,* a saying that is capable of letting the being show itself from itself. Guided by such *logos,* Aristotle was the first to articulate the "categories," which are not expressed in assertions but sustain all assertion. For him it was not a question of a "system" of categories. Coming after Plato, he faced the most ennobling task of first showing *that* such categories belong to the domain of what philosophy (as *prōtē philosophia*) primarily and properly has to ponder. Assertion, *enuntiatio,* is then understood as judgment. The different modes of address—categories—lie hidden in the various modes of judgment. Therefore, Kant in his *Critique of Pure Reason* teaches that the table of categories must be acquired through the guidance of the table of judgments. What *Kant* expresses here—although of course its form had changed in the meantime—is the same as what *Aristotle* had executed more than two thousand years before.

When Nietzsche in section B of note 12 says without further justification that the highest values are "categories of reason," that characterization is once again the same as what Kant taught and Aristotle thought through. The expression "categories of reason" means reason, rational thinking, the judgment of understanding, *logos apophantikos,* "logic"—all things to which the categories stand related in a relationship that is distinctive and that co-determines their essence. The nature of the relationship between the categories and reason—judgmental thinking—is, of course, grasped differently by Aristotle, Kant, and Nietzsche, according to how they define the essence of "reason" and *logos*—that is to say, the essence of man—and how in conjunction with this they experience and explain the being as such, which reveals its articulation in the categories.

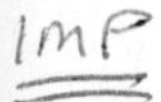

But throughout these differences what is essential and telling is preserved—that the determinations of beings as such are secured and grounded with respect to *logos,* assertory thinking. As determinations of the being as such, the categories say what the being as a being is. They say the "most universal" thing that can be said of beings: beingness, or Being. The Being of beings is grasped and comprehended on the guidelines of assertion, judgment, or "thinking." This way of defining the truth of beings as a whole, metaphysics, thinks beings by means of categories.

As an earmark of the essence of all metaphysics, therefore, we can inscribe the title *Being and Thinking* or, more specifically, *Beingness and Thinking,* a formulation which stresses that Being is conceived by way of thinking from beings and back to beings as *their* "most universal" element, whereby "thinking" is understood as assertory speech. Such thinking of beings, in the sense of *physei* and *technēi on,* "something present that rises up of itself or is produced," is the guiding thread for the philosophical thinking of Being as beingness.

The title *Being and Thinking* is also valid for irrationalist metaphysics, which is so called because it drives rationalism to its very peak—disburdening itself of it, however, least of all, just as every atheism must busy itself with God more than any theism does.

Because it is a question of the highest determinations of being as a whole in the matter Nietzsche calls "cosmological values," he is also able to speak of categories. That Nietzsche with no further explanation or justification calls these uppermost values "categories" and conceives of them as categories of reason shows how decisively he thinks along the path of metaphysics.

But whether Nietzsche strays from the path of metaphysics by conceiving the categories as *values,* and so describes himself correctly as an "antimetaphysician," or whether he merely brings metaphysics to its ultimate end and thereby himself becomes the last metaphysician, are questions to which we are still under way. The answers to those questions are most closely bound up with the *elucidation* of Nietzsche's concept of nihilism.

The second thing we must point out in our textual analysis of the last sentence in section A is the way in which Nietzsche summarily names the three categories by which beings as a whole have been interpreted. Instead of "meaning" he now says "purpose," instead of "totality" and "systematization" he says "unity," and, most decisively, instead of "truth" and "true world," here he says roundly "Being." Once again, he says all this without offering any explanation. We should not be amazed, however, at the lack of an explanation concerning the concepts and names used here. The sketch that lies before us in this fragment is not a section of a book meant for "publication," nor part of a textbook, but the dialogue of a thinker with himself. Here he is speaking not with his "ego" and his "person" but with the Being of beings as a whole and within the realm of what has already been said in the history of metaphysics.

We, however, his subsequent readers, must first penetrate the domain of metaphysics in order to gauge correctly the weight of the words, of each of their transformations and conceptual formulations, in order to be able to read his simple text *thoughtfully*. For now, we need only keep sight of the fact that Nietzsche grasps "truth" as a category of reason and equates "truth" with "Being." If in turn "Being" is the first and last word about beings as a whole, then Nietzsche's equation of "Being" and "truth" must be announcing something essential for the clarification of his basic metaphysical position, in which the experience of nihilism has its roots.

7. Nihilism and the Man of Western History

What does the final sentence of section A want to say? First, with the categories "purpose," "unity," and "Being" we have invested a *value* in the "world" (that is, in beings as a whole). Second, these categories invested in the world "will be *withdrawn* again by us." And, third, after this retraction of the categories—that is, of values—the world "now" appears *value-less.*

The state identified by the "now" is in no way thought of as final. The "now" does not mean to say that from now on matters shall rest with such value–lessness and such a valueless-aspect of the world. Of course, the title of the piece says simply "Decline of the Cosmological Values," and the first essential definition of nihilism runs "Devaluation of the Uppermost Values." But the concluding sentence, which we are now going to elucidate, not only reveals that the decline of the highest values hitherto does not betoken the end; the language of another perspective speaks within this final sentence. It tells of an investment of values in and a withdrawal of values from the universe of beings, which as it were exists in itself and permits such an investing and withdrawing of values. Values do not fall away of themselves; we withdraw values—first posited by us—from the world. We are actively engaged in valuation and devaluation. Who are "we"?

What is happening here? Nihilism is obviously not a mere unobtrusive collapse of values in themselves somewhere at hand. Nihilism is our deposition of values that are at our disposal with respect to their being posited. By "us" and "we," however, Nietzsche means the man of Western history. He does not mean to imply that the same men who posit values withdraw them again, but that those who posit and those who retract are men from *one* and the *same* Western history. *We* ourselves, the contemporary representatives of Nietzsche's era, belong to those who are once again withdrawing values that were posited earlier. The deposition of values does not arise from a mere thirst for blind destruction and vain innovation. It arises from the need and necessity to give the world *the* meaning that does not reduce it to a mere passage into the beyond. A world must arise that enables a man to develop his essence from his own fund of values. But for that we need a transition, a way through the predicament in which the world appears value-less but at the same time demands a new value. The passage through the intermediate state must perceive it as such with the greatest possible awareness. To achieve that, it is necessary to recognize the origin of the intermediate state and to bring to light the first cause of nihilism. The decisive will to overcome the intermediate state can only emerge from an awareness of it.

Nietzsche's exposition, which began as an enumeration of the conditions for the emergence of nihilism and as a mere description of its course, now suddenly sounds like a declaration of what we are acting out; indeed, must act out. It is not a question here of historical recognition of past events and their effects on the present. Something imminent is at stake, something barely under way, involving decisions and tasks whose transitional character is interpreted as investing values in and withdrawing values from the world.

But there is more than one kind of "nihilism." Nihilism is not only the process of devaluing the highest values, nor simply the *withdrawal* of these values. The very positing of these values in the world is already nihilism. The devaluation of values does not end with a gradual becoming worthless of values, like a rivulet that trickles into the sand. Nihilism is achieved in the withdrawal of values, in the aggressive removal of values. Nietzsche wants to make clear to us the inner richness of the essence of nihilism. Section B therefore must inspire us to adopt a decisive stance.

If we now review section A with a sharper focus, we are able to detect the various modes of introduction of the three conditions for the emergence of nihilism, which to all appearances are merely being enumerated. In the first paragraph Nietzsche is basically saying that nihilism "will have to enter on the scene" as a psychological state. Here he first names the fundamental condition for the possibility of nihilism—namely, the condition that in general something like a "meaning" is posited as what is sought.

In the second paragraph, he says that nihilism "arises" as a psychological state. Here he identifies the decisive condition that introduces the actual toppling of the highest values, and he arranges matters so that an encompassing, comprehensive totality, a "unity," is posited as meaning, a unity that works through man and establishes and secures human being amidst beings.

In the third paragraph, we find that "Nihilism as a psychological state has yet a *third* and *final* form." Here we preview the advent of something in which nihilism first finds its full essence. This is the positing of a true world beyond, in itself, as the goal and the paradigm of this illusory, earthly world.

The first paragraph names the fundamental condition of the possibility of nihilism, the second its actual beginning, and the third the necessary fulfillment of its essence. This in general is how the history of nihilism *as* history in its essential traits receives its first "portrayal."

Now we can no longer restrain the question touched on earlier as to whether and how the history of the essence of nihilism corresponds to the historical reality one is accustomed to regard historiologically. Nietzsche says nothing about it directly, just as he does not really describe his treatment as the essential history of nihilism. Everything here remains indeterminate. Nonetheless, there are indications that Nietzsche has "actual" history in view, above all where he is discussing the third form of nihilism.

By the positing of a "true world" over against a purely illusory world of becoming, Nietzsche is referring to Platonic metaphysics and in its wake the whole of subsequent metaphysics, which he understands as "Platonism." He takes Platonism to be a "doctrine of two worlds": above this earthly, mutable world, accessible to the senses, there stands a supersensuous, immutable world beyond. The latter is a world continually enduring in "Being," and so is a true world, while the former is illusory. The equation of "truth" and "Being" corresponds to this. As long as Christianity teaches that our world, as a vale of tears, is merely a temporal passage to eternal bliss beyond, Nietzsche can regard Christianity in general as Platonism (the doctrine of two worlds) for the people.

If the third form of the conditions for the emergence and essence of nihilism refers to Plato's philosophy, then we must search for the first and second in *pre*-Platonic philosophy in their corresponding historical forms. In point of fact, we can find the positing of a "unity" for being as a whole in Parmenides' doctrine *hen to on.* Nevertheless, because the first form of the conditions for emergence stands as the grounding condition for the *possibility* of nihilism, governing the whole history of nihilism, we can find no explicit historical testimony for it. But because what we have just said basically holds true for all three conditions, and because these conditions, even when they are correspondingly transformed, exercise some effect on every fundamental metaphysical position, the attempt to demonstrate a historiological correspondence for the three conditions designated does not have all the significance one could ask for, especially when we note that section A is merely the prelude to B.

8. The New Valuation

Section B reads as follows:

> Granted we realize to what extent the world may no longer be *interpreted* in terms of these *three* categories, and that after this insight the world begins to become valueless for us: we then have to ask *whence* our faith in these three categories comes—let us try to see if it is not possible to cancel our faith in *them!* Once we have *devaluated* these three categories, the demonstration that they cannot be applied to the universe is no longer any reason *for devaluating the universe.*
>
> Result: *Faith in the categories of reason* is the cause of nihilism—we have measured the value of the world according to categories *which relate to a purely fictitious world.*
>
> Final result: All the values by means of which we have so far tried to render the world estimable for ourselves and which, after they proved inapplicable, therefore *devaluated* the world—all these values are, psychologically reckoned, results of particular perspectives of utility, for the preservation and enhancement of human constructs of domination; and they have only been falsely *projected* into the essence of things. It is always and everywhere the *hyperbolic naiveté* of man, positing himself as the meaning and standard of value for things.

We have said that a different language is being spoken here, one that has, of course, already been intimated in section A, especially by its last sentence. Now no more is said about how nihilism as a psychological state "will have to enter on the scene"; no longer is there talk of nihilism as a phenomenon found only back in history, as it were. Now we ourselves are involved in the question. Therefore, we now read, "Granted we realize to what extent . . . may no longer be *interpreted*"; we read, "We then have to . . . "; the passage says, "Let us try . . . !"

When we have made the attempt, a wholly new relationship to the "universe" results, the "result" of history is first discerned. That "result" is gathered up in a "final result" by the concluding section.

There are "results" only where there is reckoning and calculation. In fact, Nietzsche's train of thought, as nihilistic, is reckoning. What kind of reckoning it is he specifies in the concluding section: "All these values are, psychologically reckoned, results" of this and that. It is a matter of the "psychological" reckoning and calculation of values, whereby, of course, we ourselves are included in the reckoning. But then to think psychologically means to think everything as a configuration of will to power. To reckon psychologically means to appraise everything on the basis of value and to calculate value on the basis of the fundamental value, will to power—to figure how and to what extent "values" can be evaluated in accord with will to power and so prove valid.

What is demanded in section B, and the purpose for which it is demanded, is the explicit, conscious, and consciously self-justifying attempt to devalue the uppermost values, to depose them as highest values. At the same time, this implies a decision to take seriously the intermediate state that the devaluation of the highest values produces, by simultaneously fixing on our earthly world as the only reality, and a decision *to be* in that decision as a historical one. Nihilism is now no longer a historical process that we as observers merely have before us, outside ourselves, or even behind us; nihilism reveals itself as the history of our era, which imposes its own effective limits on the age, and by which we are claimed. We do not stand in this history as in some uniform space in which any standpoint or position can be assumed at will. That history is itself the manner and mode in which we stand or move, in which we *are*. The devaluation of the highest values hitherto enters the state of deposition and overthrow. But even in an overthrow it is still a question of values that are to determine being as a whole. Through the decline of the highest values hitherto, being in the sense of what is real, what is accessible right here and now, does indeed become valueless. But instead of disappearing, what is accessible validates itself as what has been rendered needful of new values by the overthrow of prior values. Therefore the deposition of previous values is already inherently and necessarily on the path toward a new positing of values. By means of the deposition of prior values, the world, formerly the merely earthly world, becomes being as a whole as such. Now, as it were, being as a whole stands outside the difference between the earthly and the beyond. Thus the deposition of the highest values hitherto brings with it a change in being as a whole, such that it becomes questionable where and how one can still speak of beings and of Being. To put it another way, the new positing of values can no longer proceed simply by putting new values in the *same* places—which meanwhile have, of course, become empty—in lieu of the highest values hitherto.

With the downfall of the highest values also comes the elimination of the "above" and the "high" and the "beyond," the former *place* in which values could be posited. Such elimination means that the valuation in itself must become a different one. Even that *for* which the new values are supposed to be values is, after the downfall of the beyond, no longer something this-worldly. But this implies that the *way in which* the values are values, the essence of values, must be transformed. The earth-shaking change behind the devaluation of the highest values hitherto is revealed in the fact that a *new principle of valuation* becomes necessary. But because the devaluation of uppermost values is a conscious deposition of former values, arising from unequivocally known phenomena, the new valuation must have its origin in a new and enhanced consciousness (reckoning).

Hence the principle of a new valuation can become valid only if a new knowledge about the essence of values and the conditions for estimating values is awakened and propagated. The revaluation of all prior values must be accomplished and maintained by the highest awareness of one's own consciousness of essential value and valuation. The decline of prior values first *completes* itself in the new valuation understood in this way.

Nihilism first becomes classical through the revaluation of all values. What distinguishes it is knowledge of the origin and necessity of values, and along with that an insight into the essence of prior values. Here valuation and valuative thought first come to themselves, not simply in the way that an instinctive act also knows and casually observes itself, but rather in such a way that this consciousness becomes an essential moment and a driving force in the whole of behavior. What we describe with the ambiguous name *instinct* now comes to be not merely something of which we were formerly unconscious but now know; consciousness, "psychological reckoning," and calculation now become *instinct proper.*

Whereas in section B nihilism is experienced as a transitional state and made into a standard for thinking and acting, the concluding part of note 12 arrives at the position of classical nihilism. The "final result" is recounted in which being as a whole is newly reckoned and the knowledge of the essence of values and of valuation is expressed without obfuscation. Let us repeat the main sentence of the concluding section:

> All these values are, psychologically reckoned, results of particular perspectives of utility, for the preservation and enhancement of human constructs of domination; and they have only been falsely *projected* into the essence of things. It is always and everywhere the *hyperbolic naiveté* of man, positing himself as the meaning and standard of value for things.

Thus Nietzsche is saying that the essence of values has its ground in "constructs of domination." Values are essentially related to "domination." Dominance is the being in power of power. Values are bound to will to power; they depend on it as the proper essence of power. What is untrue and untenable about the highest values hitherto does not lie in the values themselves, in their content, in the fact that in them meaning is sought, unity posited, and truth secured. Nietzsche sees what is untrue in the fact that these values have been mistakenly dispatched to a realm "existing in itself," within which and from which they are supposed to acquire absolute validity for themselves, whereas they really have their origin and radius of validity solely in a certain kind of will to power.

If we think back from the concluding section of note 12 to its title, "Decline of Cosmological Values," then it becomes clear that the title corresponds to the whole of the note only if we first conceive of nihilism in Nietzsche's sense as history—that is, at the same time conceive of it positively as a preliminary stage of a "new" valuation, so decisively that we experience precisely the most extreme nihilism not as a complete downfall but as the transition to new conditions of human existence. Nietzsche preserves this overall insight into the essence of nihilism in a note composed about the time note 12 was written:

> *Overall insight.* All major growth is in fact accompanied by a tremendous *disintegration* and *passing away:* suffering, the symptoms of decline, *belong* to the times of tremendous advance; every fertile and powerful movement of humanity has also *created at the same time* a nihilistic movement. It could turn out to be the sign of crucial and most essential growth, of transition to new conditions of existence, that the *most extreme* form of pessimism, *nihilism* proper, comes into the world. *This I have grasped.* (WM, 112; spring–fall, 1887)

The following note stems from the same period:

> Man is *beast* and *Overbeast:* the higher man is Nonman and Overman: these belong together. With every growth of man in greatness and height, there is also growth in depth and terribleness: one should not will the one without the other—or rather: the more radically we will the one, the more radically we achieve precisely the other. (WM, 1027)

9. Nihilism as History

Following our first elucidation of note 12, the proper task of pondering and thinking through Nietzsche's concept of European nihilism has taken on greater definition. What at the beginning of our reflections was tentatively adumbrated can now be combined for the proper discussion of the essence of nihilism into two lines of questioning—as posed in the following statements. First, nihilism, as Nietzsche thinks it, is the history of the devaluation of the highest values hitherto, as the transition to the revaluation of all prior values, a revaluation that comes to pass in the discovery of a principle for a new valuation, a principle Nietzsche recognizes as the will to power. Second, Nietzsche conceives of the essence of nihilism solely on the basis of valuative thought, and in that form alone does it become an object of his critique and his attempt at an overcoming. But because the valuation has its principle in the will to power, overcoming nihilism by fulfilling it in its classical form develops into an interpretation of being as a whole as will to power. The new valuation is a metaphysics of will to power.

We comprehend the phrase "metaphysics *of* will to power" in a double sense, because the genitive case has the twofold meaning of the objective and subjective genitive. Nietzsche's metaphysics is for one thing metaphysics that has the will to power as the truth of being as a whole for its "object," inasmuch as will to power constitutes the overall character of being as a whole. As the fundamental trait of being as a whole, however, will to power is at the same time the essential definition of man. As such, it lies at the basis of the human coinage of the truth of being as a whole—that is, metaphysics—it is the *subiectum* of metaphysics. For another thing, therefore, Nietzsche's metaphysics is the one in which the will to power is brought to dominance. Such metaphysics itself belongs in the realm of power governed by the will to power and is one of its conditions. The will to power is the object and the subject of a metaphysics thoroughly dominated by valuative thinking. In this univocal sense, the expression "metaphysics *of* will to power" is equivocal.

First, it is necessary to understand nihilism in a unified way as the history of valuations. We are using the term *valuation* here in a broad sense. It includes the positing of the uppermost values, the devaluation of these values as their deposition, and the revaluation of these values as the new positing of values.

Taking up our first line of questioning, we note once again that nihilism is a history. By that we do not mean merely that what we call *nihilism* "has" a "history" inasmuch as it can be traced historically in its temporal course. Nihilism *is* history. In Nietzsche's sense it co-constitutes the essence of Western history because it co-determines the lawfulness of the fundamental metaphysical positions and their relationships. But the fundamental metaphysical positions are the ground and realm of what we know as world history, and especially as Western history. Nihilism determines the historicity of this history. Consequently, for a comprehension of the essence of nihilism there is little to be gained by recounting the history of nihilism in different centuries and depicting it in its various forms. First of all, everything must aim at recognizing nihilism as the lawfulness of history. If one wants to consider this history a "decline," reckoning it in terms of the devaluation of the highest values, then nihilism is not the cause of the decline but its *inner logic,* the lawfulness of events that goes further than mere decline and so also points beyond decline. Hence an insight into the essence of nihilism does not consist in the knowledge of phenomena that can be historically documented as nihilistic—it rests in an understanding of the steps, gradations, and transitions from the initial devaluation up to the inevitable revaluation.

If the highest values are devalued and the feeling arises that the world does not and never did correspond to what we ideally expected of it—if, indeed, the feeling is aroused that everything is going awry, turning into nothing, and that this world is therefore the worst of worlds, a *pessimum*—then there emerges the attitude that in the modern age is usually called "pessimism," the belief that in this worst of worlds life is not worth living or affirming (Schopenhauer). Nietzsche therefore explicitly describes "pessimism" (WM, 9; 1887) as the "prototype of nihilism" (see WM, 37: "Development of *Pessimism into Nihilism*"). But, like nihilism, pessimism too is ambiguous. There is a pessimism of strength and *as* strength; but there is also a pessimism of weakness and *as* weakness. The former does not delude itself, sees the danger, wants no obfuscation: it gazes soberly at the forces and powers that betoken danger. But it also recognizes those conditions that in spite of everything would establish control over things. The pessimism of strength therefore has its position in "analysis." By "analysis," Nietzsche does not mean a disentangling, as a dissecting and unraveling, but the scrutinizing of what "is," a depiction of the grounds for a being's being the way it is. In contrast, pessimism as weakness and decline sees only the dark side of everything, is ready with a reason for each new failure, and fancies itself the attitude that knows in advance how it will all turn out. The pessimism of weakness seeks to "understand" everything and explain it historically, to excuse it, and let it pass. For everything that happens, it has already ferreted out some corresponding precedent. Pessimism as decline takes refuge in "historicism" (see WM, 10).* The pessimism that has its strength in "analysis" and the pessimism that is caught up in "historicism" are opposed to each other in the most extreme way. There is more than one kind of "pessimism." Through pessimism and its ambiguity, therefore, the "extremes" come to appear and preponderate. Thus the "transitional state" that the devaluation of the highest values hitherto produces becomes clearer and more compelling.

From one point of view, it seems that the fulfillment of prior values

---

* Note 10 of *The Will to Power* reads thus:

> A. Pessimism as strength—*in what?* in the energy of its logic, as anarchism and nihilism, as analytic.
>
> B. Pessimism as decline—*in what?* as effeteness, as a sort of cosmopolitan fingering, as *tout comprendre* and historicism.
>
> —*The critical tension:* the extremes come to the fore and become predominant.

Actually, WM, 10 is a composite of two notes; the concluding sentence belongs to another page in the notebooks; cf. CM, WII 1 [126] and [128].

is *not* to be attained; the world seems valueless. From the other point of view, the waxing analytical consciousness of the origin of value estimations in will to power guides the inquisitive eye toward the source of new value estimations, although of course without the world gaining in value thereby. With regard to the shaken validity of prior values, however, there could just as well be an attempt to retain their "place," and to fill that old place—the transcendent—with new ideals. According to Nietzsche's treatment, this is what happens in "doctrines of universal happiness," for example, and in "socialism," as well as in "Wagnerian music," the Christian "ideal," and there "where the dogmatic form of Christianity has been abandoned" (WM, 1021). "Incomplete nihilism" arises in this way.

> *Incomplete* nihilism; its forms: we live right in the midst of it.
> Attempts to circumvent nihilism *without* revaluating prior values produce the opposite, make the problem more acute. (WM, 28)

With this it becomes clearer to what extent the "revaluation of all values" belongs to perfected, complete nihilism, and how a peculiar state of uncertainty precedes and accompanies the revaluation. The condition of uncertainty, in which prior values are deposed and new values not yet posited, consists in the fact that there is no truth in itself, although there is still truth. But truth has yet to be newly defined. In the "analytic," the suspicion was already awakened that the "will to truth," as the claim of something binding and authoritative, is a claim of *power,* and as such is sanctioned only by will to power as a configuration of will to power itself. The transitional state being described is "extreme nihilism," which recognizes and expressly states that there is no truth in itself. Again, such nihilism is ambiguous:

> A. Nihilism as a sign of *enhanced power of spirit: active nihilism.*
> B. Nihilism as *decline* and *recession of the power of spirit: passive nihilism.* (WM, 22; spring–fall 1887)

Passive nihilism says there is no truth in itself, and lets it go at that. For passive nihilism there is no truth at all. Active nihilism, however, sets out to define truth in its essence on the basis of that which lends all things their determinability and definition. Active nihilism acknowledges truth as a configuration of will to power and as a value of determinate rank.

If will to power is expressly and fully experienced as the ground of the possibility of truth, and if truth is conceived and portrayed as a function of will to power (as justification), then extreme nihilism, as active, is transformed into classical nihilism. But because active nihilism already recognizes and acknowledges will to power as the fundamental trait of beings, nihilism in general is not merely "contemplation" (WM, 24),* is not the mere "no" of judgment. It is the "no" of deed: "one lays his hand to," "one executes." One does not simply regard something as null, he sets it aside, overturns it, and creates an open field. Hence classical nihilism is itself the "ideal of supreme powerfulness" (WM, 14).

Such nihilism emerges from "life" as it used to be, cuts a path "for a new order," and grants whatever wants to die off its "longing for the end." In this way, nihilism makes a clean sweep and at the same time introduces new possibilities. Therefore, referring to the nihilism of a wholly new valuation, a nihilism which makes room by placing all being out into the clear, Nietzsche speaks of "ecstatic nihilism" (WM, 1055). Insofar as the supreme powerfulness of the classic-ecstatic, active-extreme nihilism knows nothing outside itself, recognizes no limits over it, and acknowledges nothing as a measure, classical-ecstatic nihilism could be a *"divine way of thinking"* (WM, 15). In such a form, nihilism is no longer simply a powerless "yearning for nothingness" (WM, 1029), but is the very opposite (see WM, 1010, 1023, 1025).† This reveals the essential fullness of nihilism as articulated in itself: ambiguous early forms of nihilism (pessimism), incomplete nihilism, extreme nihilism, active and passive nihilism, and active-extreme, ecstatic-classical nihilism.

When, how, and to what extent—whether recognized or not—*one*

* That is, not merely contemplation of the "In vain!" (cf. WM, 24).

† WM, 1025 invokes that kind of strength that can transmute apparent evil into good, can press everything frightful into its service. WM, 1023 identifies such strength with "pleasure," "felicity," and "progress." WM, 1010 speaks of a new conception of the world's "perfection," one that could even sanction prior misconceptions: "Whatever does *not* correspond to our logic, our 'beautiful,' our 'good,' our 'true,' could be perfect in a *higher* sense than even our ideal."

of these modes of nihilism dominates, or whether they all reign at the same time and produce a thoroughly ambiguous historical condition for an age: these are questions that can be asked only from a position of action and meditation, questions that must be asked here. For us, an indication of the interwoven modes of nihilism suffices to clarify the movement of its essence and its historical character, and at the same time to impress on us anew that by nihilism we do not mean something merely present or, indeed, "contemporary" to Nietzsche's time. The name *nihilism* points to a historical movement that extends far behind us and reaches forward far beyond us.

10. Valuation and Will to Power

Nihilism, however, considered by Nietzsche as the history of valuations, can be understood only if valuation as such is recognized in its essence; that is, in its metaphysical necessity. Therefore, *the primary emphasis of our reflections* shifts to the second line of questioning.

The principal points in this area of inquiry are, first, that Nietzsche thinks nihilism in its origin, development, and overcoming solely in terms of valuative thought; second, that thinking in values belongs to that reality that is defined as the will to power; third, valuative thought is a necessary constituent of the metaphysics of will to power.

But in what does such metaphysics have its historically essential ground? Or, to ask it another way, Where does valuative thinking have its "metaphysical" source? If metaphysics is the truth of beings as a whole and therefore speaks about the Being of beings, from what interpretation of being as a whole does value thinking originate? Our answer is that it originates from a determination of beings as a whole through the basic trait of will to power. It is a correct answer. But how do we arrive at *this* interpretation of beings, if we insist that it is not an arbitrary and exaggerated opinion occurring only in the head of the eccentric Herr Nietzsche? How do we arrive at a projection of the world as will to power, granted that in such an interpretation of the world Nietzsche must be talking about that toward which the long history of the West, especially the history of the modern age, has been pressing in its most concealed course? What occurs essentially and reigns in Western metaphysics, that it should finally come to be a metaphysics of will to power?

With that question, we move from what is seemingly mere summary and exposition to a "confrontation" with Nietzsche's metaphysics. Presuming that Nietzsche's metaphysics is the fulfillment of Western metaphysics, a confrontation with it will be adequate only if it concerns itself with Western metaphysics in general.

In a thoughtful confrontation with a thinker, it is not a question of opposing one "outlook" to another or of one "standpoint" being "refuted" by another. All that is extraneous and inessential. For us, a confrontation does not mean supercilious "polemic" or vain "critique." Confrontation means meditation on the truth that is up for decision, for a decision not made by us, but one that Being itself, as the history of Being, makes for our own history. Our sole alternatives are either to root about among "outlooks" and adopt "standpoints," among which we must also count the ostensible "freedom from standpoints," or, on the contrary, to break with all adherence to standpoints and outlooks and to take leave of all current opinions and ideas, in order to commend ourselves solely to an original knowing.

Even in our first elucidation of nihilism, we took our impetus from the fact that the name and concept *nihilism* intends thought about Being, although Nietzsche consistently understands nihilism in terms of valuative thought. Although the question about the being as such and as a whole was and is the guiding question of all metaphysics, thinking about values came to predominate *decisively* in metaphysics only recently, and did so only through Nietzsche, in such a way that metaphysics henceforth took a decisive turn toward the fulfillment of its essence.

Partly as a result of Nietzsche's influence, the academic philosophy of the later nineteenth and early twentieth centuries became a "philosophy of value" and a "phenomenology of value." Values themselves appeared to be things in themselves, which one might arrange into "systems." Although tacitly rejecting Nietzsche's philosophy, one rummaged through Nietzsche's writings, especially *Zarathustra,* for such values. Then, "more scientifically" than the "unscientific philosopher-poet" Nietzsche, one organized them into an "ethics of value."

When we discuss valuative thought in this lecture course, we are referring exclusively to Nietzsche's metaphysics. Around the turn of the century, one branch of neo-Kantianism, associated with the names Windelband and Rickert, described itself as "philosophy of value" in a rather narrow and academic sense.* The lasting service of the movement is not its "philosophy of value" but its attitude—remarkable for its time—which preserved and handed down a trace of authentic knowledge about the essence of philosophy and philosophical inquiry against the onslaught of scientific "psychology" and "biology," supposedly the only valid "philosophies." But this stance, which was "traditional" in a good sense, nonetheless prevented the "philosophy of value" from thinking through valuative thought in its metaphysical essence; that is, prevented this movement from really taking nihilism seriously. The movement believed it could elude nihilism by means of a return to Kantian philosophy, but this return was merely a retreat before nihilism and a refusal to look into the abyss it covers.

If Nietzsche's philosophy executes the fulfillment of Western metaphysics, and if for the first time and more originally than in the tardigrade "philosophy of value" valuative thought becomes decisive in Nietzsche's philosophy, then such thinking cannot accidentally and

---

* Wilhelm Windelband (1848–1915), professor of philosophy in Heidelberg from 1903 until his death, and Heinrich Rickert (1863–1936), who taught in Freiburg until assuming Cohen's chair at Heidelberg in 1916, were co-founders of the "Baden" or "Southwest German" School of neo-Kantian philosophy. (Rickert was co-director of Heidegger's doctoral dissertation in 1912–13, and Heidegger dedicated his *Habilitationsschrift* of 1915–16 to him "in most grateful homage.") Although there were differences of emphasis in the work of Windelband and Rickert, both understood philosophy to be the critical-scientific search for values (*Werte*) of universal validity (*Geltung*), primarily in the realm of "culture." In his first logic course at Marburg, in the winter semester of 1925–26, Heidegger discussed the neo-Kantian *value* philosophy of Windelband and Rickert in the context of Rudolf Hermann Lotze's philosophical logic of *validity*. He roundly castigated the former as "the outermost station in the decline of the question concerning truth" and as "the most wrongheaded formulation of the problem." See Martin Heidegger, *Logik: Die Frage nach der Wahrheit,* sections 9–10, especially pp. 82–83 and 91–92. The incipient and gingerly implied criticism of value philosophy in the Foreword to Heidegger's *Habilitationsschrift* had thus after a decade's time become a sardonic total rejection of his former teacher's work. For example, after citing Eduard Spranger's account of Rickert's thought, published in the house journal of neo-Kantian value philosophy (*Logos,* 1923, *12,* 198), Heidegger remarked, "One could almost wax sentimental over such profundity." His discussion here in the Nietzsche lectures is far milder than the earlier caustic treatment, and even includes words of praise for the Baden School. However, it seems clear that Heidegger's confrontation with Nietzsche was delayed throughout the 1920s by Nietzsche's reputation as a "philosopher of value" and by Heidegger's aversion to *Wertphilosophie.*

superficially have forced its way into metaphysics. The question about the origin of valuative thought in metaphysics becomes a question about the essence of values *and* about the essence of metaphysics. Insofar as the latter reaches its fulfillment, our question becomes a decisive question about what defines philosophy in its necessity and grants it its ground.

What is the source of valuative thought, that thinking which gauges everything in terms of values, conceives of itself as an estimation of values, and takes upon itself the task of a new valuation? Nietzsche himself posed the question about the origin of valuative thought and readily answered it, as well. We need only recall the course of his reflections in note 12. There, in section B, Nietzsche explicitly asks where our belief in cosmological values comes from. His answer: From the will of man to secure a value for himself. But how is he supposed to accomplish that if the world in which he belongs does not for its part have value, meaning, purpose, unity, and *truth*—if man cannot subordinate himself to an "ideal"? The concluding part of note 12 expresses the inner connection between valuation and will to power clearly enough. Of course, we have not really grasped the relation by pointing out the reference. However, we may surmise that if a distinctive consciousness is required for the revaluation of values, and thereby a knowledge of what values are all about, Nietzsche must have already brought that inner connection to light in his own way.

Every kind of value positing, including especially the new valuation by which a revaluation of values is to be accomplished, must be related to the will to power. Nietzsche expresses the connection in the first sentence of note 14: "*Values, and their alteration,* are related to the *growth in power of the one positing the values.*" In accord with the essential definition of will to power provided at the outset, "growth in power" is nothing but power enhancement in the sense of the self-overpowering of power. But therein lies the essence of power. The statement therefore means: Values and their changes, and hence valuation—be it devaluation, revaluation, or the new positing of values—are in every instance determined by the respective nature of the will to power, which for its part defines the one positing—that is, man—in the nature of his human being. Values stem from valuation; valuation corresponds to the will to power. But why and to what extent is the will to power a value positing? What does Nietzsche understand by *value?*

The Will to Power, which is a very confused book with respect to its organization of the posthumous notes, contains under note 715 (dated 1888) a notation of Nietzsche's that answers our question: "The viewpoint of 'value' is the viewpoint of *conditions of preservation* and *enhancement* with regard to complex constructs of relative life-duration within becoming."

According to this note, "value" is a "viewpoint." "Value" is indeed "essentially" the "viewpoint for" (see note 715*). We are not yet asking *for what* value is a point of view; let us first consider *that* "value" is "viewpoint" in general—the sort of thing that, once viewed, becomes a gauge for a seeing that has something in view. Such envisioning is a *reckoning* on something that also must reckon with something else. Thus we immediately place "value" too into conjunction with a "how much" and "so much," with quantity and number. Thus "values" are related to a "*numerical* and *mensural scale*" (WM, 710). There remains only the question of what this scale of increase and diminution is itself related to.

The characterization of value as a "viewpoint" yields one thing that is essential for Nietzsche's concept: as a viewpoint, value is always posited by a seeing. Through the positing, it first comes to be a "point" for the envisioning of something, a point that belongs in the purview of the envisioning of something. Thus values are not from the outset and inherently at hand in themselves, so that they can also occasionally serve as viewpoints. Nietzsche's thinking is lucid and open enough to specify that the viewpoint is "pointed" to the kind of thing it is only through the "punctuation" of the seeing. What is valid does not have validity because it is in itself a value; rather, a value *is* a value because it has validity. It has validity because it has been posited as valid. It is thus posited by an envisioning of something that *through* the envisioning first receives the character of a thing with which one can reckon and that therefore has validity.

Once valuative thought has come on the scene, it must also be

* The fourth paragraph of WM, 715 begins, "Value is essentially the viewpoint for the increase or decrease of these centers of domination." Cf. p.66 of the present volume.

admitted that values "are" only where there is reckoning, just as there are "objects" only for "subjects." To speak about "values in themselves" is either thoughtlessness, or counterfeiting, or both. "Value," according to its essence, is "viewpoint." There are viewpoints only for a seeing that points and reckons by means of "points."

But what is viewed with value as a gauge? What is that with which we reckon in any given case? What does reckoning essentially envision? Nietzsche says that "the viewpoint of 'value' is the viewpoint of *conditions of preservation* and *enhancement.*" Insofar as we reckon *on* something, there must be something we reckon *with,* something on which preservation and enhancement depend, that promotes or restricts preservation, that provides or denies enhancement. In other words, we must reckon with the sort of thing that conditions. After all we have said thus far, we may suppose that by preservation and enhancement are meant preservation of power and enhancement of power. Power is the "something"; that is, the "thing" that matters, as it were, the thing whose preservation and enhancement is conditioned.

"Values" are the conditions with which power as such must reckon. To reckon on enhancement of power, on the overpowering of the respective stages of power, is the *essence* of will to power. "Values" are in the first place the conditions of enhancement that the will to power has in view. As self-overpowering, will to power is never at a standstill.

In Nietzsche's metaphysics, will to power is a richer name for the overused and vacuous term *becoming.* That is why Nietzsche says that "the viewpoint of 'value' is the viewpoint of *conditions of preservation* and *enhancement* . . . within becoming." But, in the definition of the essence of value as *condition, what* the values condition still remains undetermined—what sort of thing they make into a thing, if we employ the word *thing* here in the broad sense of "something," which does not compel us to think of tangible things and objects.* But *what*

* Heidegger is now taking the verb "to condition" (*bedingen*) quite literally: *be-dingen* would be the making of something into a "thing" (*Ding*). If values are conditions for the preservation and enhancement of power, Heidegger now wants to ask what sorts of things value and power are; that is to say, he wishes to inquire into the ontological status of both the "viewpoint of value" and the "will to power." If the latter is Nietzsche's name for the Being of beings, how can value "be-thing" will to power?

values condition is the will to power. Yes, of course; but will to power, as the fundamental trait of the "real," is not some simple sort of matter, as its name already suggests. Nietzsche is not speaking casually when he says that "value" is the *condition of preservation* and *enhancement* set forth in reckoning. In the real, one is necessarily dealing equally with preservation *and* enhancement; because in order for the will to power as overpowering to be able to surpass a certain stage, that stage must not only be reached, it must also be inwardly, even *powerfully* secured. Otherwise the *over*powering could not be an over*powering.* Only what already has stability and a firm footing can "think" about enhancement. A stage must first be secured in itself before it can be used as a staging area.

Thus what is required for the real in its character as will to power are those values that establish its stability and continuance. But, just as necessarily, it requires the sort of conditions that guarantee an out-beyond-itself, a superelevation of what is real (what is living); it requires values as conditions of enhancement.

In accord with its inmost essence, therefore, the will to power must always and especially posit values of preservation *and* enhancement. Following these two mutually related outlooks, the will to power must look out and beyond, and, so looking, point to view*points,* posit values. The outlook on viewpoints belongs to valuation. What pertains to the will to power as vista and "perspect" Nietzsche calls its "perspectival" character. Will to power is thus *in itself* an envisioning of more power. The "envisioning of" is the path of *perspect* and *purview:* the per-spective belongs to will to power. That is why, in the fragment that is serving as our guide (note 12, concluding section), Nietzsche says, "All these values are, psychologically reckoned, results of particular perspectives." We could also say that all these values are as *values* particular viewpoints of particular purviews of a particular will to power. But insofar as each real thing is real by virtue of the fundamental character of will to power, a single and individual "perspective" belongs to every individual thing. *Beings as such are perspectival.* What we call reality is defined by its perspectival character. Only by keeping this fact constantly in mind can we think the "being" proper within Nietzsche's metaphysics. In the perspectival character of the being, Nietzsche is only expressing what has formed a covert basic trait of metaphysics since Leibniz.

According to Leibniz all being is defined by *perceptio* and *appetitus,* by the representing urge which presses for the *placing-before,* the "representation," of the whole of beings, presses for their *being* first of all and only in such *repraesentatio* and as such *repraesentatio.* In each case, the representing has what Leibniz calls a *point de vue*—a viewpoint. That is what Nietzsche says, too: it is "perspectivism" (the perspectival constitution of the being), "by virtue of which every center of force—and not only man—construes all the rest of the world *from its own viewpoint;* that is, measures, touches, shapes, according to its own force" (WM, 636, from the year 1888; see XIV, 13, from 1884–85: "If one wished to escape from the world of perspectives, he would be going to his doom.") But Leibniz does not yet think these viewpoints as values. Value thinking is not yet so essential and explicit that *values* could be thought as viewpoints of perspectives.

The real that is defined in its reality by the will to power is in every instance an interweaving of perspectives and valuations, a construct of a "complex kind." But it is so because the will to power itself has a complex nature. The complex unity of its essence should once again be brought into view.

If the essence of the power of will is more power, and if power is therefore empowered as overpowering, then something that is overcome as a particular stage of power, and at the same time something that overcomes, both belong to power. What is to be overcome can only be such a thing if it posits a resistance and stands firm and secure, sustaining and preserving itself. In contrast, the overcoming must be able to go up and over to higher stages of power; it requires the possibility of enhancement. The necessary interconnection of preservation and enhancement belongs to the essence of overpowering. The essence of power is itself something intricate. Reality thus defined is permanent and at the same time impermanent. Its permanence is therefore *relative.* Thus Nietzsche says, "The viewpoint of 'value' is the viewpoint of *conditions of preservation* and *enhancement* with regard to complex constructs of relative life-duration within becoming." Gathered together in these constructs are the products of the will to power, whose essence consists in being master and being able to command. That is why Nietzsche also calls these constructs succinctly "constructs of domination" or "centers of domination" (WM, 715): " 'Value' is essentially the viewpoint for the increase or decrease of these centers of domination." It is made explicit in this definition that values as *conditions* of preservation and enhancement are always related to a "becoming" in the sense of waxing and waning power. In no respect are values primarily something "for themselves," having only a subsequent and occasional relation to the will to power. They are what they are—that is, they are conditions—only *as conditioning,* and are therefore posited by the will to power itself as its own conditions of possibility. Thus they provide a standard of measure for the appraisal of degrees of power of a construct of domination and for judging its increase and decrease. When Nietzsche says at the conclusion of note 12 that values are "results of particular perspectives of utility, for the preservation and enhancement of human constructs of domination," use and utility are understood here in their unique relation to power. "Value" is essentially use-value; but "use" must here be equated with the condition of the preservation of power; that is, always at the same time, with the condition of the enhancement of power. According to their essence, values are conditions, and therefore never something absolute.

Values are conditions of "constructs of domination" within becoming; that is, within reality as a whole, whose fundamental character is will to power. The constructs of dominance are configurations of will to power. Nietzsche often calls not only the conditions of these constructs of domination, but even the constructs themselves, *values,* and rightly so. Science, art, the state, religion, and culture all pass as values insofar as they are conditions by virtue of which the classification of becoming—as what alone is real—is carried out. For their part, these values further posit definite conditions for securing their own continuance and development. But becoming itself—that is, reality as a whole—"has no value at all." That is clear now from the definition of the essence of value just given. There is nothing outside of being as a whole that might serve as a condition for it. What is lacking is something whereby it (becoming as a whole) might be measured. "*The overall value of the world cannot be evaluated;* consequently, philosophical pessimism belongs among comical things" (WM, 708, from the years 1887–88).

When Nietzsche says that being as a whole "has no value at all," he does not mean to deliver a disparaging judgment about the world. He merely wants to fend off every evaluation of the whole as a misunderstanding of its essence. The statement "being as a whole has no value at all," thought in the sense of a metaphysics of will to power, is the sharpest rejection of the belief that "values" are something in themselves, hovering over being as a whole and validating it. To say that being as a whole is value-less means that it stands outside every valuing, because through valuing the whole and the absolute would only be made dependent on parts and conditions that are what they are only in terms of the whole. The world of becoming, as will to power, is the un-conditioned. Only *within becoming,* only in relation to individual constructs of power, posited by them and for them, are there conditions; that is, viewpoints of the preservation and enhancement of degrees of power; that is, values. Do values therefore arise from will to power? Certainly. But we would be committing another error in thought if we now wished to understand values as if they were something "alongside" the will to power, as if there were at first the latter, which then posited "values" that would from time to time be pressed into service by it. Values, as *conditions* of preservation and enhancement of power, exist only as something conditioned by the *one* absolute, will to power. *Values are essentially conditioned conditions.*

But values can obviously be conditions of the will to power only if they themselves have the character of power, only if they represent power quanta for reckoning the enhancement of power, in terms of the conscious efforts of the will to power. Hence values, as conditions of the enhancement and preservation of power, are essentially related to man. As viewpoints, they are incorporated into *human* perspectives. Thus Nietzsche says (WM, 713, from 1888),

> *Value* is the highest quantum of power a man is able to incorporate—a man: *not* mankind! Mankind is much more a means than an end. It is a question of the type: mankind is merely the experimental material, a monstrous excess of failures, a field of ruins.

Value is always a quantum of power, posited and measured by the will to power.

Will to power and value positing are *the same,* insofar as the will to power looks toward the viewpoints of preservation and enhancement. Thus valuation cannot be referred back to the will to power as something different from it. The clarification of the essence of value and of valuation only yields a sketch of the will to power. The question of the origin of valuative thought and the essence of value is in no way answered when we demonstrate the inner coherence of valuation and the will to power. It is relegated to the question of the essential origin of will to power. Why is the latter something that inherently posits values? Why does the thought of will to power become dominant *along with* valuative thought in metaphysics? How and why does metaphysics become a metaphysics of the will to power?

11. Subjectivity in Nietzsche's Interpretation of History

In order to survey the scope of this question, we must consider what the dominance of valuative thought in metaphysics signifies. First of all, it leads to the fact that Nietzsche conceives the task of future metaphysics to be the revaluation of all values. At the same time, with no further explanation or rationale, the dominance of valuative thought presupposes as self-evident the fact that all prior metaphysics—that is, all metaphysics that historically preceded the metaphysics of the will to power—has been, even if only tacitly, metaphysics of the will to power. Nietzsche conceives the whole of Western philosophy as a thinking in values and a reckoning with values, as value positing. Being, the beingness of beings, is interpreted as will to power. In a covert yet utterly comprehensible way, the history of metaphysics appears in the light of valuative thought in all of Nietzsche's writings and notes.

We are inclined simply to disregard this fact, or to designate his interpretation of the history of metaphysics as that historiological view that was most available to Nietzsche. Then we would have before us merely one historiological view among others. Thus, in the course of the nineteenth and twentieth centuries, the scholarly discipline of history represented the history of philosophy sometimes within the horizon of Kant's or Hegel's philosophy, sometimes within the philosophy of the Middle Ages. But of course they still *more* frequently represented it within a horizon that, by means of a mixture of radically different philosophical teachings, pretended to a catholicity and universal validity by virtue of which all puzzles vanished from the history of thinking.

But the fact that Nietzsche explains the history of metaphysics from the horizon of will to power arises from his metaphysical thought and is not simply a subsequent historiological insertion of his own "views" into the teachings of earlier thinkers. Rather, the metaphysics of will to power, as a *revaluating* stance toward previous metaphysics, first determines the latter in the sense of valuation and valuative thought. Every confrontation is conducted on the basis of a predetermined interpretation that is banished from all discussion. The metaphysics of will to power does not exhaust itself in the fact that new values are posited over against former ones. It lets everything that has been thought and said in prior metaphysics concerning the totality of being as such appear in the light of valuative thought. For the very essence of history is defined in a new way through the metaphysics of will to power, something that we learned from Nietzsche's doctrine of the eternal recurrence of the same and its innermost relationship with the will to power. Any form of academic history is always only the consequence of a previously posited definition of the essence of history as such.

Hence, Nietzsche speaks of unity, totality, and truth as "highest values"—as if that were the most self-evident thing in the world. That these should be "values" is not simply Nietzsche's belated interpretation. It is the first decisive step of the "revaluation" itself. Properly thought, the revaluation carried out by Nietzsche does not consist in the fact that he posits new values in the place of the highest values hitherto, but that he conceives of "Being," "purpose," and "truth" *as values and only* as values. Nietzsche's "revaluation" is at bottom the rethinking of all determinations of the being on the basis of values. In note 12, "purpose," "unity," "totality," "truth," and "Being" are also called "categories of reason." At all events, that is what they *are* for Kant and Fichte, Schelling and Hegel. Even for Aristotle, and for him first of all, the determinations of the being as such are categories, although not "categories of reason"—granted that "reason" here, as with Kant and with German Idealism, is to be understood as the essence of *subjectivity*. Thus, when Nietzsche treats of the determinations of the being, which he conceives as "cosmological values," then what is speaking in this conception is the modern metaphysical interpretation of the definition of the Being of beings as categories of reason. The modern interpretation, however, is transformed by Nietzsche once again, so that now the categories of reason appear as the uppermost values. This interpretation of the definition of the Being of beings, stemming from the most recent times and from recent metaphysics, is traced back to Greek philosophy, because the whole history of Western metaphysics appears as the history of valuations. The earlier fundamental metaphysical positions are not expressed in their own proper truth. They speak the language of a philosophy of will to power understood as valuation.

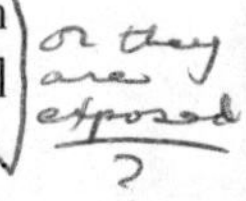

Moreover, if we consider the demonstration of the essential relatedness between valuation and will to power, then it becomes clear that Nietzsche's interpretation of all metaphysics in terms of valuative thought is rooted in the basic definition of being as a whole as will to power. The latter expression is the key word of *Nietzsche's* metaphysics. Neither Hegel nor Kant, neither Leibniz nor Descartes, neither Medieval nor Hellenistic thought, neither Aristotle nor Plato, neither Parmenides nor Heraclitus knew of will to power as the fundamental character of beings. If, then, Nietzsche sees metaphysics as such and its entire history within the horizon of valuation, that history thereby shifts into a one-sided perspective, and the historiological observation guided by it becomes untrue.

But is there anything at all like an observation of history that is not one-sided but omni-sided? Must not every particular period always examine and interpret the past in terms of *its own* horizon? Won't its historical knowledge be more "alive" the more decisively the given horizon of that particular period is taken as a guide? Did not Nietzsche himself in one of his early writings, the second essay of the *Untimely Meditations,* entitled "On the Use and Disadvantage of History for Life,"* demand and argue with great forcefulness and in detail that history must serve "life," and that it can only do so if it first of all

* There are some indications that during the winter semester of 1938–39 Heidegger conducted an informal seminar or "exercise" on the basis of this text. (See the notes on pp. ix–x and 235–36 of the present volume.) In any case, Heidegger was thoroughly familiar with this text even before he wrote *Being and Time,* published in 1927. (See Volume I, p. 247, n. 25.)

frees itself from the illusion of a supposed historiological "objectivity in itself"? If so, then our comment to the effect that on the basis of the questions he poses Nietzsche interprets the history of metaphysics as a history of valuation can scarcely function as an objection or a caution, because it merely confirms the genuineness of his historical thinking. It could even be that by means of Nietzsche's interpretation of metaphysics in terms of valuative thought, prior metaphysics is "comprehended better" than it has been able to comprehend itself, in that his interpretation first lends metaphysics the words to say what it has always wanted to say but could not. If that were how matters stood, then Nietzsche's conception of categories and categories of reason as the highest values and as "values" generally would not be a distortion of historical reality, but would be the release of earlier metaphysical values to their properly creative import, or indeed an enrichment of such import. Finally, if the basis for Nietzsche's conception of all metaphysics, the interpretation of the whole of beings as will to power, moved in the direction of prior metaphysical thinking and brought the fundamental thoughts of metaphysics to completion, then Nietzsche's "image of history" would be justified in every respect and proven to be the only possible and necessary one. In that case, there would be no escaping the opinion that the history of Western thought is running its course as a devaluation of the highest values and, in keeping with the nullification of values and decline of goals, is and must be "nihilism."

One result of such reflections is that the observation that Nietzsche reads his own basic metaphysical position—will to power as the fundamental character of being, valuation, and the origin of valuation within the will to power—back into the prior history of metaphysics may not be used as facile grounds for accusing him of distorting the image of history, or, indeed, for rejecting the legitimacy of valuative thought. Even if we must admit that Nietzsche's interpretation of metaphysics does not coincide with what earlier metaphysics taught, this admission requires substantiation that goes beyond a purely historiological demonstration of the difference between Nietzsche's metaphysics and earlier metaphysics.

It is necessary to show that valuative thought was and had to be alien to earlier metaphysics because such metaphysics could not yet conceive of the being as will to power. If we are to demonstrate this, then we must of course encounter the deeper source of valuative thought, because that is how we remove the illusion that thinking has always already taken place in metaphysics through valuations. If it should be shown to what extent the interpretation of the being as will to power first becomes *possible* on the basis of the fundamental positions of modern metaphysics, then as far as the question of the origin of valuative thought is concerned we would have achieved the important insight that Nietzsche has not and cannot have given an answer to the question of origins.

The reference to note 12 (B) where Nietzsche discusses the origin of our belief in the highest values hitherto, does not advance us any farther. For Nietzsche's account presupposes that valuations stem from the will to power. For Nietzsche, will to power is the ultimate *factum* to which we come. What seems certain to Nietzsche is questionable to us. In a similar way, Nietzsche's derivation of valuative thought is also questionable to us.

In his own way, Nietzsche merely shows that according to their essence values are conditions of the will to power, which the latter posits for itself for its own preservation and enhancement; that is, for the fulfillment of the essence of power. Valuation is included in will to power. But the will to power itself—where does it originate, this projection of beings as a whole that depicts them as will to power? *With this question, we are for the first time thinking about the roots of the origin of valuation within metaphysics.*

If however we now attempt to demonstrate that metaphysics before Nietzsche did *not* interpret the being as will to power and that as a result valuative thought was alien to it, then our plan will be subject to the same objection that was leveled against Nietzsche's interpretation of history. We too must observe and interpret past thought within the horizon of a particular thinking: that is to say, our own. No more than Nietzsche or Hegel can we step out of our history and "times" and, from an absolute standpoint, without any definite and therefore necessarily one-sided point of view, observe what-has-been in itself. The same limitation holds for us as it did for Nietzsche and Hegel, with one additional factor; namely, that perhaps the compass of our thinking does not even have the essentiality—and certainly not the greatness—of the questions posed by these thinkers, so that our interpretation of history even at its best falls short of the heights they attained.

With this thought we are approaching the circle of genuine decisions. The question about the truth of the "image of history" goes farther than the question of historiological correctness and accuracy in employing and interpreting sources. It touches on the question of the truth of our historical situation and the relationship to history prescribed by it. If European nihilism is not simply *one* historical movement among others, if it is *the* fundamental impulse of our history, then the interpretation of nihilism and our stance with respect to it depend on how and whence the historicity of human Dasein is determined for us.

A meditation on that theme can go in several directions. We will choose one suggested by the task of the lecture course. We will follow the path of a historical meditation before we develop a "philosophy of history"; in this way, perhaps, such a philosophy will automatically become superfluous. The path we are constrained to follow, no matter how right or wrong it is on particular points, tends to demonstrate that *prior to* Nietzsche valuative thought was and had to be alien to metaphysics, that nonetheless the emergence of valuative thought was prepared *by metaphysics* in those ages prior to him. But the extent to which we are simply losing ourselves in the distant past by taking this path, or are rather in fact preparing ourselves for the future, are questions we do not need to reckon with either before or after we are on the path, as long as we actually do follow the path. Of course, this inevitably and repeatedly puts in our way an obstacle that arises from the objections we have already cited, objections that have today become clichés: that every observation of history is determined by and related to the present, thus is "relative," thus is never "objective," thus is always "subjective"; that one must resign himself to such subjectivity, and would be better off if he made a virtue out of this lack of "reality," transforming acquiescence in subjectivity into the superiority of one who forces everything past into the service of his own present.

But in order to make the proper contrast between the history of metaphysics as it must first be experienced and Nietzsche's conception of metaphysics, we must on the basis of what has already been said first place his interpretation of the history of metaphysics before us in a comprehensible form. Until now, we have learned only that for Nietzsche valuations have their ground and their necessity in the will to power. Thus in Nietzsche's opinion a definite will to power must also have been definitive for the first positing of the highest values hitherto; that is, for the beginning of metaphysics. The first positing of the highest values has its particularity in the fact that according to Nietzsche the values "purpose," "unity," "truth," have been falsely "projected" into the "essence of things." How did the "projection" come to be? In the sense of Nietzsche's interpretation of history, the question asks, What configuration of the will to power was at work here?

12. Nietzsche's "Moral" Interpretation of Metaphysics

If "truth"—that is, the true and the real—is transposed upward and beyond into a world in itself, then the being proper appears as that to which all human life must be subordinated. The true is what is inherently desired, what ought to be. Human life is therefore worth something, is determined by the correct virtues, only when these virtues exclusively urge and enable us to realize what is commanded and desired—to comply with, and so be subjected to, "ideals."

The man who humbles himself before ideals and strives assiduously to fulfill them is the virtuous, the worthwhile—in a word, the "good man." Understood in Nietzsche's sense, this means the man who wills himself as the "good man" erects transcendent ideals above himself, ideals that offer him something to which he can submit himself, so that in the fulfillment of these ideals he will secure himself an aim for his life.

The will that wills the "good man" is a will to submission beneath ideals that exist in themselves and over which man may no longer have any power. The will that wills the "good man" and his ideals is a will to the power of these ideals and is therefore a will to the impotence of man. The will that wills the good man is of course also will to power, but in the form of the impotence of man's power. The highest values hitherto have this impotence of man's power to thank for their projection into the transcendent and their ascent to a world "in itself" as the only true world. The will that wills the "good man" and in that sense wills "the good" is the "moral" will.

By "morality," Nietzsche usually understands a system of evaluations in which a transcendent world is posited as an idealized standard of measure. Nietzsche consistently understands morality "metaphysically"; that is, with a view to the fact that in morality something is decided about the whole of beings. In Platonism, this occurs through the division of beings into two worlds—the transcendent world of ideals, of what ought to be, the true in itself—and the sensible world of unending toil and self-submission to what is valid in itself, which, as absolute, conditions everything. Therefore, Nietzsche can say (WM, 400),

> Thus in the *history of morality* a *will to power* expresses itself, through which the slaves and the oppressed, then the misfits and those who suffer from themselves, and then the mediocre attempt to make those value judgments prevail that are favorable to *them*.

Accordingly, he says (WM, 356), "Modest, industrious, benevolent, temperate: is that how you would have man? the *good man?* But to me that seems simply the ideal slave, the slave of the future." And, further (WM, 358),

> The *ideal slave* (the "good man"). —Whoever cannot posit *himself* as a goal, nor posit any goals for himself at all, bestows honor upon *selflessness*—instinctively. Everything persuades him to this: his wits, his experience, his vanity. And faith too is a form of selflessness.

Instead of selflessness, we could also say a refusal to posit oneself as the one in command and that means impotence to power, "turning one's back on the will to existence" (WM, 11). But impotence to power is merely a "special instance" of the will to power, and that implies that "the highest values hitherto are a special instance of the will to power" (XVI, 428). The positing of these values and their transposition into a transcendent world in itself, to which man is supposed to submit, arises from a "dwarfing of man" (WM, 898). Every metaphysics of the sort that posits a transcendent world as true *above* a sensible world as a world of appearances springs from morality. Hence the statement "It is no more than a moral prejudice that truth is worth more than semblance" (*Beyond Good and Evil,* section 34; VII, 55). In the same book, Nietzsche defines the essence of morality in this fashion: "Morality understood as the doctrine of the relations of dominance under which the phenomenon 'life' comes to be" (section 19; VII, 31). And in *The Will to Power,* note 256: "I understand by 'morality' a system of evaluations that touches on the conditions of a creature's life."

Here Nietzsche understands morality "metaphysically" too, of course, in relation to being as a whole and the possibility of life in general, and not "ethically" with regard to the "conduct of life." But he is no longer thinking about *that* "morality" that conditions Platonism. There is more than one kind of "morality," in Nietzsche's view, and these kinds vary, even in their metaphysical significance. On the one hand, morality in its broadest formal sense means *every* system of evaluations and relationships of dominance; morality here is conceived so broadly that even the new valuations might be called *moral,* simply because they posit conditions of life. On the other hand, and as a rule, Nietzsche means by morality the system of *those* evaluations that are contained in the positing of the absolutely highest values in themselves —in the sense of Platonism and Christianity. Morality is the morality of the "good man," who lives by and within the opposition to "evil," and not "beyond good and evil." To the extent that Nietzsche's metaphysics stands "beyond good and evil," and first fashions that standpoint and occupies it as a fundamental position, he can describe himself as an "immoralist."

This sobriquet in no way means that thinking and pondering are immoral in the sense that they take a stance *against* "good" and *for* "evil." "Without" morality means beyond good and evil. This in turn does not mean outside all law and order, but rather within the necessity of a *new* positing of a different order against chaos.

The morality of the "good man" is the origin of the highest values hitherto. The good man posits these values as unconditioned. In that form, they are the conditions of his "life," which, as impotent in power, demands for itself the possibility of being able to look up to a transcendent world. On this basis we now comprehend also what Nietzsche means in the final section of note 12 by the *"hyperbolic naiveté"* of man.

From a metaphysical point of view, the "good man" of "morality" is the sort of man who suspects nothing of the origin of the values to which he submits himself as to absolute ideals. This *not suspecting* the origin of value therefore prevents a person from any *explicit* reflection on the provenance of values, about the fact that they are conditions of will to power, posited by the will to power itself. "Naiveté" is equivalent to "psychological innocence." According to what was said earlier, this means being untouched by any reckoning of beings and thus of life and its conditions in the will to power. Because the provenance of these values in the power-based evaluation of man remains hidden to the psychologically innocent ("naive") person, the *naive* one takes the values (purpose, unity, totality, truth) as if they had descended to him from elsewhere, from heaven, and stood over against him as something to which he has only to bow. Naiveté as ignorance of the origin of value in human will to power is thus in itself "hyperbolic" (from *hyperballein*). Without knowing it, the "good man" casts values upward beyond himself to something that is "in itself." What is conditioned solely by man himself he takes instead for an absolute that taxes him with demands. Therefore, Nietzsche concludes his assessment of the origin of belief in the highest values and categories of reason, concludes the whole of note 12, with the sentence "It is always and everywhere the *hyperbolic naiveté* of man, positing himself as the meaning and standard of value for things."

In spite of the present discussion of the expression "hyperbolic naiveté," the danger still persists that we might totally misunderstand the important concluding sentence of note 12. It contains the all-too-compressed and therefore easily misinterpreted synopsis of an important thought. By appealing to this statement of Nietzsche's, one could raise the objection that according to its literal meaning Nietzsche is saying the opposite of what *we* have explained as the *essence* of hyperbolic naiveté. If naiveté consists in ignorance of the origin of values in the proper power-based valuation of man, how can it still be "hyperbolic naiveté" to "posit oneself as the meaning and standard of value for things"? The latter is anything but naiveté. It is the supreme consciousness of self-reliant man, explicit will to power, and certainly not in any way impotence to power. If we were forced to understand the statement in this way, then Nietzsche would be saying that "hyperbolic naiveté" consists in being thoroughly *not* naive. We should not attribute such a vacuity to Nietzsche. What, then, does the sentence say? According to Nietzsche's definition of the essence of values, the values posited in ignorance concerning the origin of value must also arise from human positing, which is to say, in the manner in which man posits himself as the meaning and measure of value. Naiveté does not consist in the fact that man posits values and functions as their meaning and as the measure of value. Man remains naive to the extent that he posits values as an "essence of things" that devolves upon him, without knowing that it is *he* who posits them and that the positing is a will to power.

Man remains mired in naiveté as long as he does not really act on the knowledge that he alone is the one who posits values, that only through him can values ever be the conditioned conditions of the preservation, securing, and enhancement of his life. A superficial reading of the statement seduces one to the opinion that Nietzsche—in opposition to the process of naive valuation, which often imposes human values on things and so humanizes all beings—is demanding an experience and definition of beings in which every anthropomorphism would be avoided. But precisely that interpretation of the statement would be erroneous; because the fault in naiveté is not the humanization of things, but the fact that the humanization is not *consciously* carried out. Naiveté is in itself a deficiency in will to power, because it lacks knowledge of the fact that the positing of the world according to the image of man and through man is the only true mode of any interpretation of the world, and therefore something toward which metaphysics must finally, resolutely, and without reservation set its course. The highest values hitherto were able to attain to their rank and validity because man posited himself as the meaning and measure of value for things, but did so unconsciously, believing instead that what had been posited by him was a gift given by the things, a gift that things offered him of their own accord. Of course, the will to power governs in naive valuation, as it does in every valuation. But here the will to power is still impotence to power. Here power does not yet empower as explicitly known, and in control of itself.

That in the positing of the highest values human positings are imposed on things is for Nietzsche something quite correct. The humanization of beings, however, is still innocent and therefore not unconditioned. Because the proper, power-based origin of the highest values hitherto *at first* remains hidden, although with the awakening and expansion of the self-consciousness of man it cannot remain permanently hidden, belief in it must weaken with the growing insight into the origin of values. But insight into the origin of values, of human valuation, and of the humanization of things cannot stop short with the realization that after the unveiling of the origin of value, and after the decline of values, the world seems valueless. In that case, we would be lacking every kind of "value," and therefore the conditions of life, so that life could not *be*. But, in view of the apparent valuelessness of the world, that which has to happen, that in which the revaluation of prior values must consist, is already decided and prescribed by the insight into the origin of values. Nietzsche summarized this new task in a note, stemming from the year 1888, which exhibits the very opposite of hyperbolic naiveté:

> All the beauty and sublimity we have bestowed upon real and imaginary things I will reclaim as the property and product of man: as his fairest apology. Man as poet, as thinker, as God, as love, as power: O, with what regal liberality he has lavished gifts upon things, only to *impoverish* himself and make *himself* feel wretched! His most unselfish act hitherto was to admire and worship and to know how to conceal from himself that it was *he* who created all that he admired. (WM, Introduction to Book II, Part One; XV, 241)

What the note is saying is clear enough. Man should no longer be borrower or lender, nor should he submit himself to what is dispensed by him alone as if it were something foreign to him, as if it were something that man in his misery needed. Instead, man ought to claim everything for himself as his own, something he can do only if first of all he no longer regards himself as a wretch and slave before beings as a whole, but establishes and prepares himself for absolute dominance. But this means that he himself is unconditioned will to power, that he regards himself as the master of such domination, and so consciously decides in favor of every exhibition of power; that is, decides for the continuous enhancement of power. Will to power is the *"principle of a new valuation."* Will to power is not simply the way in which and the means by which valuation takes place; will to power, as the essence of power, is the one basic value according to which anything that is supposed to have value, or that can make no claim to value, is appraised. "All events, all motion, all becoming, as a determination of degrees and relations of force, as a *struggle*" (WM, 552; spring–fall, 1887). What loses the struggle is—because it has lost—untrue and in the wrong. What emerges victorious is—because it has won—true and in the right.

What is being contested, if we want to think of it as a specific substantive goal, is always of less significance. All the aims and slogans of battle are merely the means for waging war. What is being contested is decided in advance: power itself, which requires no aims. It is aim-less, just as the whole of beings is value-less. Such aim-lessness pertains to the metaphysical essence of power. If one can speak of aim here at all, then the "aim" is the aimlessness of man's absolute dominance over the earth. The man of such dominance is the Over-man. It is quite usual to remonstrate with Nietzsche that his image of the Overman is indeterminate, that the character of this man is incomprehensible. One arrives at such judgments only if one has failed to grasp that the essence of the Over-man consists in stepping out "over" the man of the past. The latter needs and seeks ideals and idealizations "above" himself. Overman, on the contrary, no longer needs the "above" and "beyond," because he alone wills man himself, and not just in some particular aspect, but as the master of absolute administration of power with the fully developed power resources of the earth. It is inherent in the essence of this man that any particular substantive aim, any determination of such kind, is always a nonessential and purely incidental means. The absolute determination of Nietzsche's thought about the Overman lies precisely in the fact that he recognizes the essential indeterminateness of absolute power, although he does not express it in this fashion. Absolute power is pure overpowering as such, absolute supersedence, superiority, and command—the singular, the most high.

The sole reason for the inadequate portrayals of the Nietzschean doctrine of the Overman lies in the fact that until now it has not been possible to take the will to power seriously as a metaphysics, to comprehend *metaphysically* the doctrines of nihilism, Overman, and above all the *eternal recurrence of the same* as essentially *necessary* constituents; that is, to think them from within the history and the essence of Western metaphysics.

Nietzsche's note (XV, 241) belongs among the most lucid and in its way most beautiful of his notes. Here he speaks from the noonday brightness of a magnificent attunement by which modern man will be determined as the absolute center and sole measure of beings as a whole. Of course, the note is located in an impossible place in the book of posthumous writings we are using as a text (*The Will to Power*), and, furthermore, is omitted from the consecutive enumeration of aphorisms, and is therefore difficult to find. It stands as the preface to chapter one ("Critique of Religion") of Book II (*Critique of the Highest Values Hitherto*). The insertion of the note in this location is perhaps the clearest evidence for the altogether dubious nature of the book *The Will to Power.* The note we are referring to traverses Nietzsche's basic metaphysical position with simple, confident steps, and therefore ought to have been placed at the front of the entire work, *if* it is appropriate to use it as a foreword at all.

Exactly why we have cited the note will become clear as soon as we give a clearer account of our path of inquiry. In contrast to what *Nietzsche* has revealed as the history of metaphysics, it is necessary to take a *more original look* into the history of metaphysics. The first purpose of such a plan ought to be to make Nietzsche's description and conception of metaphysics clearer. It is a "moral" conception. "Morality" here means a system of evaluations. Every interpretation of the world, be it naive or calculated, is a positing of values and thus a forming and shaping of the world according to the image of man. In particular, that valuation which acts on the basis of insight into the origin of human value and so completes nihilism must explicitly understand and will man as the lawgiver. It must seek the true and the real in the *absolute humanization* of all being.

Metaphysics is anthropomorphism—the formation and apprehension of the world according to man's image. Therefore, in metaphysics as Nietzsche interprets it and above all demands it as future philosophy, *the relationship of man to being as a whole* is decisive. Thus we surmount valuative thought toward a relation that metaphysics as will to power almost forces on us; such metaphysics, to which the doctrine of the Overman belongs, thrusts man as no metaphysics before it into the role of the absolute and unique measure of all things.

hyperbolic naivete of Platonism + Christ has been narcissistic — supreme values treated as if given + objective which are in fact 1) projections 2) sourced in desires that belie their content (spirit of revenge)

∴ self-serving of slave to remain narcissistic precisely by advocating 'selflessness'

- to break w/ narcissism is not just a) to own up to one's own respon for values but also b) to confess the dark side of one's own will
  - not that darkness is innate (e.g. destruc instincts that must be repressed) BECAUSE spirit of revenge is a reactive formation
    - by nature one would have discharged or expressed oneself 'vitally' (avengingly, if need be) in the first place

prior metaphysics. Thus it sounds almost like a cliché if, for example, we mention that the metaphysics of the modern age is characterized by the special role which the human "subject" and the appeal to the subjectivity of man play in it.

At the beginning of modern philosophy stands Descartes' statement: *Ego cogito, ergo sum,* "I think, therefore I am." All consciousness of things and of beings as a whole is referred back to the self-consciousness of the human subject as the unshakable ground of all certainty. The reality of the real is defined in later times as objectivity, as something that is conceived *by* and *for* the subject as what is thrown and stands over against it. The reality of the real is representedness *through* and *for* the representing subject. Nietzsche's doctrine, which makes everything that is, and as it is, into the "property and product of man," merely carries out the final development of Descartes' doctrine, according to which truth is grounded on the self-certainty of the human subject. If we recall here that in Greek philosophy before Plato another thinker, namely Protagoras, was teaching that man was the measure of all things, it appears as if all metaphysics—not just modern metaphysics—is in fact built on the standard-giving role of man within beings as a whole.

Thus today *one* thought is common to everyone, to wit, an "anthropological" thought, which demands that the world be interpreted in accordance with the image of man and that metaphysics be replaced by "anthropology." In such a demand, a definite decision has already been rendered concerning the relationship of man to beings as such.

What is the position of metaphysics and its history with regard to the relationship? If metaphysics is the truth concerning beings as a whole, certainly man too belongs within them. It will even be admitted that man assumes a special role in metaphysics inasmuch as he seeks, develops, grounds, defends, and passes on metaphysical knowledge—and also distorts it. But that still does not give us the right to consider him the measure of all things as well, to characterize him as the center of all beings, and establish him as master of all beings. It might be thought that the saying of the Greek thinker Protagoras concerning man as the measure of all things, Descartes' doctrine of man as the "subject" of all objectivity, and Nietzsche's thought concerning man as the "producer and possessor" of all beings are perhaps merely exaggera-

13. Metaphysics and Anthropomorphism

Nietzsche's first sustained discussion of his doctrine of will to power in the book *Beyond Good and Evil* (1886) already shows the standard-giving role of the human experience of self and the preeminence of man's self-givenness in every interpretation of the world:

> Granted that nothing else is "given" as real except our world of desires and passions, that we could not descend or ascend to any other "reality" besides the reality of our drives—for thinking is merely a way these drives behave toward one another—: is it not permitted to make the experiment and to ask the question whether this "given" does not *suffice* to understand—on the basis of this kind of thing—the so-called mechanistic (or "material") world? (*Beyond Good and Evil,* section 36)

Nietzsche makes this attempt in his metaphysics of the will to power. When he thinks the material, lifeless world on the basis of man and according to human drives, then he is really giving a "human" interpretation of the living and historical world. We begin to suspect how decisively *valuative thinking,* as the reckoning of all beings according to the basic value of will to power, already has at its essential foundation *this* fact, that in general the being as such is interpreted *after the fashion of* human Being, and not only that the interpretation is fulfilled "through" man.

Thus we shall now temporarily set valuative thinking aside in order to reflect on the relationship of man to beings as such and as a whole, to reflect on the manner and the form *in which* the relationship is defined in the history of metaphysics. Hence we come to an area of questioning that is in fact suggested to us by Nietzsche's own metaphysics and his elucidation of metaphysics but that at the same time leads us into more primordial regions. The latter were known also to

tions and extreme examples of particular metaphysical standpoints, and not the temperate and well-balanced thoughts of an authentic knowing. Thus these exceptional cases ought not to be made the rule according to which the essence of metaphysics and its history are defined.

Such an opinion might also aver that the three doctrines that stem from the age of Greek culture, from the beginning of the modern period, and from the present age, are subtle indications that in totally different periods of time and in differing historical situations the doctrine reappears ever more intensely, the doctrine according to which every being is what it is solely on the basis of a humanization by man. Such an opinion might finally pose the question, "Why shouldn't metaphysics affirm once and for all, without reservation, man's unconditional role of dominance, make him into the definitive principle of every interpretation of the world, and put an end to all relapses into naive views of the world?" If matters stand this way, if this expresses the sense of all metaphysics, then Nietzsche's "anthropomorphism" is merely asseverating as undisguised truth what in earlier times was being thought repeatedly, throughout the history of metaphysics, and what was demanded as the principle of all thinking.

With respect to this opinion, and with a view to getting a more unobstructed view of the essence of metaphysics and its history, we would do well first of all to think through the basic features of the doctrines of Protagoras and Descartes. In doing so we must delineate that area of inquiry which in a more original way brings the essence of metaphysics as the truth concerning beings as a whole closer to us and lets us see in what sense the question "What is the being as such and as a whole?" is the guiding question of all metaphysics. The very title of Descartes' major work indicates what it is about: *Meditationes de prima philosophia* (1641), or *Meditations on First Philosophy.* The expression "first philosophy" derives from Aristotle and describes what primarily and properly constitutes the function of what has been given the name *philosophy. Prōtē philosophia* is concerned with the highest-ranking and all-pervasive question of what a being is insofar as it is a being: thus, for example, an eagle insofar as it is a bird; that is, a living creature; that is, something that comes to presence of itself. What distinguishes the being as a being?

In the meantime, of course, the question of what the being is appears to have been conclusively answered by Christianity, and the question itself is set aside, from a position essentially superior to arbitrary human opinion and error. Biblical revelation, which according to its own report rests on divine influence ("inspiration"), teaches that the being was created by a personal creator God and is preserved and guided by Him. Through the truth of revelation, promulgated in church doctrine as absolutely binding, the question of what the being is has become superfluous. The Being of a being consists in its being created by God (*Omne ens est ens creatum*). If human knowledge wishes to know the truth concerning beings, the only reliable path left open to it is to adopt and preserve diligently the doctrine of revelation and its transmission by the doctors of the church. Genuine truth is mediated only by the *doctrina* of *doctores.* Truth has the essential character of "doctrinality." The medieval world and its history are constructed on this *doctrina.* The only appropriate form in which knowledge as *doctrina* can express itself is the *Summa,* the collection of doctrinal writings in which the whole content of traditional doctrine is arranged and various scholarly opinions are examined, accepted, or rejected on the basis of their conformity to church doctrine.

Those who treat of beings as a whole in this manner are "theologians." Their "philosophy" is philosophy in name only, because a "Christian philosophy" is even more contradictory than a square circle. Square and circle are at least compatible in that they are both geometrical figures, while Christian faith and philosophy remain fundamentally different.* Even if one wished to say that truth is taught in both, what is meant by truth is utterly divergent. Medieval theologians' having studied Plato and Aristotle in their own way, that is to say, by reinterpreting them, is the same as Karl Marx's using the metaphysics of Hegel for his own political *Weltanschauung.* Viewed correctly, however, the *doctrina Christiana* does not intend to mediate knowledge about beings, about what the being is; rather, its truth is

* In a lecture course presented in 1935, Heidegger had employed a different oxymoron, "wooden iron," but his treatment of the issue there is quite similar: cf. Martin Heidegger, *Einführung in die Metaphysik* (Tübingen: M. Niemeyer, 1953), p. 6; see the English translation, *An Introduction to Metaphysics,* tr. Ralph Manheim (Garden City, N.Y.: Doubleday-Anchor, 1961), p. 6.

throughout the truth of salvation. It is a question of securing the salvation of individual immortal souls. All knowledge is tied to the order of salvation and stands in service to securing and promoting salvation. All history becomes the history of salvation: creation, the fall, redemption, last judgment. This itself determines the manner in which (that is, the method by which) what is alone worth knowing is to be defined and mediated. *Schola* ("schooling") corresponds to *doctrina,* and the teachers of the doctrine of faith and salvation are therefore "scholastics."

What is new about the modern period as opposed to the Christian medieval age consists in the fact that man, independently and by his own effort, contrives to become certain and sure of his human being in the midst of beings as a whole. The essential Christian thought of the certitude of salvation is adopted, but such "salvation" is not eternal, other-worldly bliss, and the way to it is not selflessness. The hale and the wholesome are sought exclusively in the free self-development of all the creative powers of man. Thus the question arises as to *how* we can attain and ground a certitude sought by man himself for his earthly life, concerning his own human being and the world. While in the medieval world it was precisely the path to salvation and the mode of transmitting truth (*doctrina*) that was firmly established, now the *quest* for new paths becomes decisive.

The question of "method"—that is, the question about *"finding the way,"* the question about attaining and grounding a certainty secured by man himself—comes to the fore. "Method" here is not to be understood "methodologically," as a manner of investigation or research, but metaphysically, as the way to a definition of the essence of truth, a definition that can be grounded only through man's efforts.

The question of philosophy can therefore no longer simply be "What is the being?" In the context of man's liberation from the bonds of revelation and church doctrine, the question of first philosophy is "In what way does man, on his own terms and for himself, first arrive at a primary, unshakable truth, and what is that primary truth?" Descartes was the first to ask the question in a clear and decisive way. His answer was *Ego cogito, ergo sum,* "I think, therefore I am." And it is no accident that the title of Descartes' chief philosophical works indicate the priority of "method": *Discours de la méthode, Regulae ad directionem ingenii, Meditationes de prima philosophia* (not simply "Prima philosophia"), *Les Principes de la philosophie* (*Principia philosophiae*).

In Descartes' principle *ego cogito, ergo sum,* which we shall discuss with more precision later on, the precedence of the human ego is expressed generally, and with it a new status for man. Man does not simply accept a doctrine on faith, but neither does he procure knowledge of the world merely by following a random course. Something else comes to the fore: man knows himself absolutely and certainly as that being whose Being is most certain. Man comes to be the self-posited ground and measure for all certitude and truth. If initially we think through Descartes' principle no farther than this, then we are immediately reminded of the saying of the Greek sophist Protagoras, Plato's contemporary. According to that saying, man is the measure of all things. Scholars habitually connect Descartes' principle with Protagoras' saying and see in this saying and in Greek sophistic thought in general the anticipation of the modern metaphysics of Descartes; in both instances, the priority of man is almost palpably expressed.

In its general form, the observation is also correct. Nevertheless, Protagoras' fragment says something very different from the import of Descartes' principle. Only the difference of both affords us a glimpse into the *selfsame* that they utter. That selfsame matter is the footing on the basis of which we first get an adequate grasp of Nietzsche's doctrine of man as lawgiver of the world and come to know the origin of the metaphysics of will to power and the value thinking ensconced in it. [For the following, see also *Holzwege,* pp. 94 ff.]*

* The remark in brackets was added in 1961. It refers to the eighth appendix to Heidegger's "Die Zeit des Weltbildes," composed prior to the lecture course on nihilism; see *Holzwege* (Frankfurt am Main: V. Klostermann, 1951), p. 344. Section 14 below is a reworking of that appendix, improving it in various details—e.g., the repetition of the four "moments" that determine a metaphysics—and generally sharpening the focus. For an English translation of the earlier text, see Martin Heidegger, *The Question Concerning Technology and Other Essays,* tr. William Lovitt (New York: Harper & Row, 1977), pp. 143–47.

14. The Statement of Protagoras

Protagoras' saying (according to its transmission by Sextus Empiricus) runs thus: *Pantōn chrēmatōn metron estin anthrōpos, tōn men ontōn hōs esti, tōn de mē ontōn hōs ouk estin* (see Plato, *Theaetatus,* 152). An accepted translation reads, "Man is the measure of all things, of things that are, that they are, and of things that are not, that they are not."

One might suppose that it is Descartes who is speaking here. Indeed, the sentence quite clearly betrays the frequently stressed "subjectivism" of the Greek sophists. In order not to confuse matters by bringing modern thoughts into play when interpreting the saying, let us first of all attempt a translation that will be more in keeping with Greek thought. The "translation," of course, already contains the interpretation.

> Of all "things" [of those "things," namely, which man has about him for use, customarily and even continually—*chrēmata, chrēsthai*], the [respective] man is the measure, of things that are present, that they are *thus* present as they come to presence, but of those things to which coming to presence is denied, that they do not come to presence.

The talk here is of beings and their Being. What is meant is the being that comes to presence of itself in the purview of man. But who is "man" here? What does *anthrōpos* mean here? Plato provides an answer to the question in the passage where he is discussing the saying by having Socrates ask the following question (as a rhetorical one):

> *Oukoun houtō pōs legei, hōs hoia men hekasta emoi phainetai toiauta men estin emoi, hoia de soi, toiauta de au soi; anthrōpos de su te kagō?*
> Does he [Protagoras] not somehow understand it *thus:* that each thing which

shows itself respectively to me [also] is for me of such an aspect, but that what shows itself to you is such as it is for you? But are you not a man even as I?

"A man" here is therefore "respective" (I and you and he and she, respectively); everyone can say "I"; the respective man is the respective "I." Thus it is certified in advance—and almost in so many words—that it is a question of man conceived "*ego*istically," that the being as such is determined according to the standard of man so defined, that therefore the truth concerning beings, both with Protagoras and later with Descartes, is of the same essence, gauged and measured by means of the "ego."

Nonetheless, we would be falling prey to a fatal illusion if we wished to presume a similarity of fundamental metaphysical positions here on the basis of a particular similarity in the words and concepts used. The import of these words has been obscured and flattened into the indeterminateness of quite general "philosophical" concepts precisely for purposes of traditional historical comparison with a stock of doctrinal tenets.

But because our path has led us to ask in a fundamental way the question about the relationship of man to the being as such and as a whole, and about the role of man in the relation, we must also establish proper guidelines for distinguishing between Protagoras' saying and Descartes' principle. The guidelines according to which we must differentiate can only be those that determine the essence of a fundamental metaphysical position. We shall single out four of them. A fundamental metaphysical position may be determined:

1. By the way in which man as man is *himself* and thereby knows himself;
2. By the projection of beings on Being;
3. By circumscribing the essence of the truth of beings; and
4. By the way in which each respective man takes and gives "measure" for the truth of beings.

Why and to what extent the selfhood of man, the concept of Being, the essence of truth, and the manner of standard giving determine in advance a fundamental metaphysical position, sustain metaphysics as such, and make it the articulation of beings themselves, are questions that cannot be asked by and through metaphysics. None of the four essential moments of a fundamental metaphysical position just cited can be conceived apart from the others; each of them characterizes the whole of a basic metaphysical position from a single perspective.

Protagoras' statement says unequivocally that "all" being is related to man as *egō* (I) and that man is the measure for the Being of beings. But what is the nature of the relation of beings to the "I," granted that in our retrospective understanding of the saying we are thinking it *in a Greek way* and are not unwittingly inserting representations of man as "subject" into it? Man perceives what is present within the radius of his perception. What is present is from the outset maintained as such in a realm of accessibility, because it is a realm of unconcealment. The perception of what is present is grounded on its lingering within the realm of unconcealment.

We today, and many generations before us, have long forgotten the realm of the unconcealment of beings, although we continually take it for granted. We actually think that a being becomes accessible when an "I" as subject represents an object. As if the open region within whose openness something is made accessible *as* object *for* a subject, and accessibility itself, which can be penetrated and experienced, did not already have to reign here as well! The Greeks, although their knowledge of it was indeterminate enough, nonetheless knew about the unconcealment in which the being comes to presence and which the being brings in tow, as it were. In spite of everything that lies between the Greeks and us by way of metaphysical interpretations of the being, we might still be able to recollect the realm of unconcealment and experience it as that in which our human being has its sojourn. By paying sufficient attention to unconcealment, we can accomplish such recollection even without being or thinking in the Greek way. By lingering in the realm of the unconcealed, man belongs in a fixed radius of things present to him. His belonging in this radius at the same time assumes a barrier against what is not present. Thus, here is where the self of man is defined as the respective "I"; namely, by its *restriction* to the surrounding unconcealed. Such restricted belonging in the radius of the unconcealed co-constitutes the being-oneself of man. By means of the restriction, man becomes an *egō,* but not through delimitation of *such* a kind that the self-representing ego vaunts itself as the midpoint and measure of all that is representable. For the Greeks, "I" is the name for *that* man who joins *himself* to this restriction and thus is *he* himself by himself.

Experienced in a Greek way, the man of the basic relationship with beings is *metron,* "measure," in that he lets his confinement to the restricted radius (restricted for each respective self) of the unconcealed become the basic trait of his essence. That also implies the recognition of a concealment of beings and the admission of an inability to decide about presence and absence, about the outward aspect of beings pure and simple. Therefore Protagoras says (Diels, *Fragmente der Vorsokratiker,* Protagoras, B4), *Peri men theōn ouk echō eidenai, outh' hōs eisin, outh' hōs ouk eisin outh' hopoioi tines idean;* "To know [in a Greek sense this means to 'face' what is unconcealed] something about the gods I am of course unable, neither that they are, nor that they are not, nor how they are in their outward aspect." *Polla gar ta kōluonta eidenai hē t'adēlotēs kai brachys ōn ho bios tou anthrōpou;* "For many are the things which prevent beings as such from being perceived; both the not-openness [that is, the concealment] of beings and also the brevity of the history of man."

Should we be surprised that Socrates says with respect to this prudent remark of Protagoras' (Plato, *Theaetatus,* 152b): *Eikos mentoi sophon andra mē lērein?* "It is to be presumed that he [Protagoras], as a thoughtful man [in his words involving man as *metron pantōn chrēmatōn*], was not simply talking foolishly." The way Protagoras defines the relationship of man to the being is merely an emphatic restriction of the unconcealment of beings to the respective radius of man's experience of the world. The restriction *presupposes* that the unconcealment of beings reigns. Even more, it presupposes that unconcealment was already experienced as such and was long ago taken up into knowledge as the basic character of beings. That occurred in the fundamental metaphysical positions of those thinkers who stand at the beginning of Western philosophy: Anaximander, Heraclitus, and Parmenides. Sophistic thought, whose leading thinker Protagoras is reckoned to be, is only possible on the basis of and as a variation of *sophia*—that is, of the Greek interpretation of Being as presence, and of the Greek definition of the essence of truth as *alētheia* (unconcealment). Man is in each case the measure of presence and unconcealment through his measuredness and restriction to that most intimate open region, without denying the remotest closure and without presuming to make a decision about presence and absence. There is no trace here of the thought that the being as such has to be oriented toward the self-posited ego as subject, that the subject is the judge of all beings and their Being, and that by virtue of this judgeship the subject may with absolute certitude decide about the objectivity of objects. Here, finally, there is no hint of Descartes' procedure, which attempts to prove the very essence and existence of God as absolutely certain. If we think of the four "moments" that determine the essence of metaphysics, we can now say the following about the saying of Protagoras:

1. The "I" is for Protagoras determined by the always limited belonging to beings in the unconcealed. The being-oneself of man is grounded in the reliability of the unconcealed being and its radius.
2. Being has the essential character of presence.
3. Truth is experienced as unconcealment.
4. "Measure" has the sense of the measuredness of unconcealment.

For Descartes and his fundamental metaphysical position, all these moments have a different meaning. His metaphysical position is not independent of Greek metaphysics, but it is essentially removed from it. Because the dependence and distance have as yet never been clearly distinguished, the illusion could easily creep in that Protagoras is, as it were, the Descartes of Greek metaphysics; in the same vein, one was able to assert that Plato is the Kant of Greek philosophy and Aristotle its Thomas Aquinas.

15. The Dominance of the Subject in the Modern Age

By interpreting Protagoras' saying about man as the measure of all things "subjectively"—that is, as if all things were dependent on man as the "subject"—one is misplacing the Greek import of the saying in a fundamental metaphysical position that conceives of man in an essentially different way from the way the Greeks did. But neither is the modern definition of man as "subject" quite so unequivocal as the current application of the concepts "subject," "subjectivity," "subjective," and "subjectivistic" would like to pretend.

We are asking, How do we arrive at an emphatic positing of the "subject"? Whence does that dominance of the subjective come that guides modern humanity and its understanding of the world? The question is justified because up to the beginning of modern metaphysics with Descartes, and even within Descartes' own metaphysics, *every being,* insofar as it is a being, is conceived as a *sub-iectum. Sub-iectum* is the Latin translation and interpretation of the Greek *hypo-keimenon* and means what under-lies and lies-at-the-base-of, what already lies-before of itself. Since Descartes and through Descartes, man, the human "I," has in a preeminent way come to be the "subject" in metaphysics. How does man come to play the role of the one and only *subject* proper? Why is the human subject transposed into the "I," so that subjectivity here becomes coterminous with I-ness? Is subjectivity defined through I-ness, or the reverse, I-ness through subjectivity?

According to the concept of its essence, *subiectum* is in a distinctive sense that which already lies-before and so lies at the basis of something else, whose ground it therefore is. We must at first remove the concept "man"—and therefore the concepts "I" and "I-ness" as well—from the concept of the essence of *subiectum*. Stones, plants, and animals are subjects—something lying-before of itself—no less than man is. We ask, For what is the *subiectum* a lying-at-the-base-of, if man becomes *subiectum* in an emphatic way at the beginning of modern metaphysics?

With that, we once again turn to a question we have already touched on: What ground and basis is sought in modern metaphysics? The traditional guiding question of metaphysics—"What is the being?"—is transformed at the beginning of modern metaphysics into a question about method, about the path along which the absolutely certain and secure is sought by man himself for man himself, the path by which the essence of truth is circumscribed. The question "what is the being?" is transformed into a question about the *fundamentum absolutum inconcussum veritatis,* the absolute, unshakable ground of truth. This transformation *is* the beginning of a new thinking, whereby the old order passes into the new and the ensuing age becomes the modern.

We have gathered from these introductory remarks on the distinction between Protagoras' saying and Descartes' principle that man's claim to a ground of truth found and secured by man himself arises from that "liberation" in which he disengages himself from the constraints of biblical Christian revealed truth and church doctrine. Every authentic liberation, however, is not only a breaking of chains and a casting off of bonds, it is also and above all a new determination of the essence of freedom. To be free now means that, in place of the certitude of salvation, which was the standard for all truth, man posits the kind of certitude by virtue of which and in which he becomes certain of himself as the being that thus founds itself on itself. The nature of such a transformation implies that the transformation often pursues its course within the very "language" and representations of what is left behind by the transformation. On the other hand, an unequivocal characterization of the transformation cannot avoid speaking in the language of what is first attained in the transformation. If we say pointedly that the new freedom consists in the fact that man himself legislates, chooses what is binding, and binds himself to it, then we are speaking Kant's language; and yet we hit upon what is essential for the beginning of the modern age. In its unique historical form, this essence is wrought into a fundamental metaphysical position for which freedom becomes essential in a peculiar way (see Descartes, *Meditationes de prima philosophia,* Med. IV). Mere license and arbitrariness are always only the dark side of freedom. The bright side is the claim of something necessary as what binds and sustains. Of course, these two "sides" do not exhaust the essence of freedom, nor do they touch its core. For us, it remains important to see that the sort of freedom whose obverse is the liberation from faith in revelation does not simply lay claim to something generally necessary, but rather makes its claim in such a way that man in each case independently posits what is necessary and binding. But what is necessary here is co-determined by what man, founding himself on himself, requires; that is to say, by the direction and the level of the way man represents himself and his essence. Viewed metaphysically, the new freedom is the opening up of a manifold of what in the future can and will be consciously posited by man himself as something necessary and binding. The essence of the history of the modern age consists in the full development of these manifold modes of modern freedom. Because such freedom implies man's developing mastery over his own definition of the essence of mankind, and because such being master needs power in an essential and explicit sense, the empowering of the essence of power as fundamental reality can therefore become possible only in and *as* the history of the modern age.

Thus it is not the case that earlier epochs also displayed power and that roughly since Machiavelli power has been given one-sided and excessive preeminence; rather, "power" in its correctly understood modern meaning—that is, as will to power—first becomes metaphysically possible as modern history. What reigned previously was something different in its *essence*. But just as one takes "subjectivism" to be something self-evident and then searches history from the Greeks to the present looking for forms of it, so does one trace the history of freedom, power, and truth. That is how historiological comparison blocks the way into history.

That Christianity continues to exist in the development of modern history; has in the form of Protestantism abetted the development; has asserted itself successfully in the metaphysics of German Idealism and romanticism; was in its corresponding transformations, adaptations, and compromises in every instance reconciled with the spirit of the times, and consistently availed itself of modern accomplishments for ecclesiastical ends—all of that proves more forcefully than anything else how decisively Christianity is bereft of the power it had during the Middle Ages *to shape history.* Its historical significance no longer lies in what it is able to fashion for itself, but in the fact that since the beginning of and throughout the modern age it has continued to be that *against which* the new freedom—whether expressly or not—must be distinguished. Liberation *from* the revealed certitude of the salvation of individual immortal souls is in itself liberation *to* a certitude in which man can by himself be sure of his own definition and task.

The securing of supreme and absolute self-development of all the capacities of mankind for absolute dominion over the entire earth is the secret goad that prods modern man again and again to new resurgences, a goad that forces him into commitments that secure for him the surety of his actions and the certainty of his aims. The consciously posited binding appears in many guises and disguises. The binding can be human reason and its law (Enlightenment), or the real, the factual, which is ordered and arranged by such reason (Positivism). The binding can be a humanity harmoniously joined in all its accomplishments and molded into a beautiful figure (the human ideal of Classicism). The binding can be the development of the power of self-reliant nations, or the "proletariat of all lands," or individual peoples and races. The binding can be the development of humanity in the sense of the progress of universal rationality. The binding can also be "the hidden seeds of each individual age," the development of the "individual," the organization of the masses, or both. Finally, it can be the creation of a mankind that finds the shape of its essence neither in "individuality" nor in the "mass," but in the "type." The type unites in itself in a transformed way the uniqueness that was previously claimed for individuality *and* the similarity and universality that the community demands. But the uniqueness of the "type" consists in an unmistakable prevalence of the same coinage, which nonetheless will not suffer any dreary egalitarianism, but rather requires a distinctive hierarchy. In Nietzsche's thought of the Overman, man is not a particular "type"; rather, he is man for the first time prefigured in the essential shape of the "type." Precursors here are the Prussian soldiery and the Jesuit Order, which are characterized by a peculiar meshing of their essential natures, a meshing in which the inner content of the first historical emergence of each can be almost completely ignored.

Within the history of the modern age, and as the history of modern mankind, man universally and always independently attempts to establish himself as midpoint and measure in a position of dominance; that is, to pursue the securing of such dominance. To that end, it is necessary that he assure himself more and more of his own capacity for and means of dominance, and that he continually place these at the disposal of an absolute serviceability. The history of modern mankind, the inner workings of which only in the twentieth century emerged into the full and open space of something incontrovertible and consciously comprehensible, was *mediately* prepared by Christian man, who was oriented toward the *certitude* of salvation. Thus one can interpret certain phenomena of the modern age as a "secularization" of Christianity. In most decisive respects, such talk of "secularization" is a thoughtless deception, because a world toward which and in which one is made worldly already belongs to "secularization" and "becoming-worldly." The *saeculum,* the "world" through which something is "secularized" in the celebrated "secularization," does not exist in itself or in such a way that it can be realized simply by stepping out of the Christian world.

The new world of the modern age has its own historical ground in the place where every history seeks its essential ground, namely, in metaphysics; that is, in a new determination of the truth of beings as a whole and of the essence of such truth. Descartes' metaphysics is the decisive beginning of the foundation of metaphysics in the modern age. It was his task *to ground the metaphysical ground of man's liberation in the new freedom of self-assured self-legislation*. Descartes anticipated this ground in an authentically philosophical sense. That is to say, he thought it out in its essential requirements—not in the sense of a soothsayer who predicts what later occurs, but in the sense that his thought remains the ground for subsequent thought. Prophesying is not the prerogative of philosophy. But neither is philosophy a know-it-all attitude, limping along behind. Common sense has of course eagerly spread the view that philosophy's task is simply to follow up on an age, bringing its past and present to intellectual formulation on the basis of so-called concepts, or even to a "system." People think that with this specification of philosophy's task they are even paying it special homage.

That definition of philosophy does not hold even for Hegel, whose fundamental metaphysical position apparently embraces this conception of philosophy. Hegel's philosophy, which in one respect was a fulfillment, was so only as an anticipation of the areas in which the history of the nineteenth century moved. Thought in terms of metaphysics, the fact that this century took its stand against Hegel on a level beneath Hegelian metaphysics (that is, the level of positivism) is merely proof that it was thoroughly dependent on him and that this dependence was first transformed by Nietzsche into a new liberation.

16. The Cartesian *Cogito* as *Cogito Me Cogitare*

Descartes anticipated the metaphysical ground of the modern age—which is not to say that all subsequent philosophy is simply Cartesianism. But in what way did the metaphysics of Descartes preground the metaphysical ground of the new freedom in the modern age? What kind of ground must it have been? Of such a kind that man could by himself assure himself at all times of that which ensures the advance of every human intention and representation. On the basis of this ground, man must be certain of himself, that is, certain of the surety of the possibilities of his intentions and representations. The ground could not have been anything other than man himself, because the sense of the new freedom forbade him any bond or commitment that did not arise from his own positings.

Everything that is certain of itself must in addition guarantee as certainly given that being *for* which every representation and intention, and *through* which every action, is supposed to be assured. The ground of the new freedom must be what is secure about such security and certitude which, transparent in themselves, satisfy the essential conditions cited earlier. What is the certainty that fashions the ground of the new freedom and so constitutes it? It is the *ego cogito (ergo) sum.* Descartes asserts that the statement is clear and evident indubitable knowledge; that is to say, the first and highest in rank, by which all "truth" is grounded. Some have concluded from this that such knowledge must be clear to everyone in its proper import. But what is forgotten is that this is possible in Descartes' sense only if one simultaneously understands what is meant by "knowledge" here and if one considers that through this principle the essence of knowledge and of truth is newly defined.

What is "new" in the definition of the essence of truth consists in the fact that truth is now "certitude," the full essence of which becomes clear to us only in connection with Descartes' guiding principle. Because one always overlooks the fact that the guiding principle itself first posits the conditions of its understanding and cannot be interpreted according to just any notions, Descartes' principle falls prey to every possible misinterpretation.

Even Nietzsche's opposition to Descartes is entangled in these misinterpretations, something that has its basis in the fact that Nietzsche ineluctably stands under the law of this principle, and that means under Descartes' metaphysics, in a way that no other modern thinker does. We allow "history" to deceive us about this, because "history" can easily establish that between Descartes and Nietzsche lies a span of two-and-a-half centuries. History can point out that Nietzsche openly advocated different "doctrines," that he even criticized Descartes very sharply.

But we do not believe that Nietzsche teaches a doctrine identical to Descartes'. Rather, we are affirming something far more essential, to wit, that he is thinking the *selfsame* in the historical fulfillment of its essence. What begins metaphysically with Descartes initiates the history of its completion through Nietzsche's metaphysics. Naturally, the inception of the modern age and the beginning of its historical completion differ in the extreme, so that of itself, as well as for a historical account, it must appear—and rightly so—that in the face of the expiration of the modern age the most modern times begin with Nietzsche. This is thoroughly true in a quite profound sense, and merely says that the difference between the fundamental metaphysical positions of Nietzsche and Descartes, when described by historical disciplines, extrinsically, is for historical contemplation (that is, a meditation that thinks with a view to essential decisions), the keenest indication of sameness in what is essential.

The position Nietzsche adopts *against* Descartes has its metaphysical ground in the fact that Nietzsche can set about fulfilling its essence absolutely only on the basis of the fundamental Cartesian position, and so must consider Descartes' position to be conditional and imperfect, if not entirely impossible. Nietzsche's misunderstanding of the Cartesian principle is even necessary, for a number of metaphysical reasons. But we do not wish to begin with Nietzsche's misunderstanding of the Cartesian principle. Prior to that, we will attempt a meditation on a law of Being and its truth that governs our own history and survives us all. In the following portrayal of Cartesian metaphysics, we must bypass a great deal that a thematic discussion of the fundamental metaphysical position of this thinker would not dare overlook. It is simply a question of making a few basic features visible, to permit us insight into the *metaphysical* origin of *valuative thought.*

Ego cogito (ergo) sum—"I think, therefore I am." In a literal sense, the phrase is correctly translated. The correct translation also seems to furnish a correct understanding of the "principle." "I think"—with this assertion, one fact is established; "therefore I am"—with these words, it follows, from the established fact, that I am. On the basis of this logical deduction, I can now be satisfied and rest assured that my existence is thereby "proven." Of course, no thinker of Descartes' stature would need to exert himself to reach that conclusion. And, indeed, Descartes wants to say something else. Our thought can pursue what he wants to say only if we clarify for ourselves what he understands by *cogito, cogitare.*

We translate *cogitare* with "thinking" and thus persuade ourselves that it is now clear what Descartes means by *cogitare.* As if we immediately knew what "thinking" means.* And as if, with our concept of thinking, culled perhaps from some textbook on "logic," we were already certain of confronting *that which* Descartes wishes to assert in the word *cogitare.* In important passages, Descartes substitutes for *cogitare* the word *percipere* (*per-capio*)—to take possession of a thing,

* *"Was 'denken' heisst."*—Heidegger's first lecture course at Freiburg after his reinstatement following World War II had as its title *Was heisst Denken?* See the English translation by Fred D. Wieck and J. Glenn Gray, *What Is Called Thinking?* (New York: Harper & Row, 1968). Note that in the ensuing discussion of Cartesian thought "representation" tries to translate *Vor-stellen.* "Pro-pose" would be more literal, as would "pre-sent." But these would confuse *Vor-stellen* with other German expressions, such as *vorschlagen, ansetzen, vergegenwärtigen,* and so on, so that "representation" seems the best rendering.

to seize something, in the sense of presenting-to-oneself by way of presenting-before-oneself, *representing.* If we understand *cogitare* as representing in the literal sense, then we are already coming closer to the Cartesian concept of *cogitatio* and *perceptio.* Words that end with "-tion" often describe two things that belong together: representation in the sense of "representing," and representation in the sense of "something represented." *Perceptio* also has the same ambiguity: *perceptio* has the senses of *percipere* and *perceptum,* the bringing-before-itself and what-is-brought-before-itself and made "visible" in the widest sense. Thus, instead of *perceptio* Descartes often uses the Latin word *idea,* which as a consequence of its use can mean not only what is represented in a representing but also the representing itself, the act and its execution. Descartes distinguishes three kinds of "ideas":

1. *Ideae adventitiae:* something represented which impinges on us; something perceived in things;
2. *Ideae a me ipso factae:* something represented which we purely and arbitrarily imagine by ourselves (imaginings);
3. *Ideae innatae:* something represented in the essential constitution of human representation which accompanies it as already given.

When Descartes grasps *cogitatio* and *cogitare* as *perceptio* and *percipere,* he wants to emphasize that bringing something to oneself pertains to *cogitare. Cogitare* is the presenting *to* oneself of what is representable. In such presenting-to lies something definitive, namely, the necessity of a designation for the fact that the represented is not only generally pregiven but is also presented to us as available. The presented-to, the represented—*cogitatum*— is therefore something for man only when it is established and secured as that over which he can always be master unequivocally, without any hesitation or doubt, in the radius of *his own* power to enjoin. *Cogitare* is not only a general and indeterminate representing, but also something that posits itself under the condition that what is presented-*to* no longer permits any doubt about what it is and how it is.

The *cogitare* is always "thinking" in the sense of a "thinking over," and thus a deliberation that thinks in such a way as to let only the indubitable pass as securely fixed and represented in the proper sense. *Cogitare* is essentially a deliberative representing, a representing that examines and checks: *cogitare* is *dubitare.* If we take this "literally," we might easily fall into error. Thinking is not "doubting" in the sense that deliberative thought is everywhere brought to the fore, that every standpoint becomes suspect and all agreement prohibited. Doubting is rather understood as essentially connected with the indubitable, with the undoubted and its securement. What is always doubted in deliberative thinking is whether what is represented is in every instance securely established within the circle of the reckoning power to enjoin. That every *cogitare* is essentially a *dubitare* says nothing other than this: representing is securement. Thinking, which is *essentially* deliberating, accepts nothing as secured and certain—that is, as true—which is not proven before thinking itself to be the sort of thing that has the character of the doubt*less,* whereupon thinking as deliberative doubting is at the same time "finished," and the account is closed.

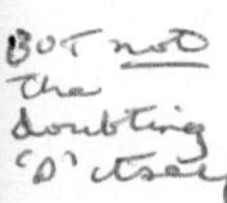

In the concept of *cogitatio,* there is a general stress on the fact that representing brings the represented *to* the one representing; that therefore the latter, *as* one who represents, in every case "presents" what is represented, calls it to account; that is, grasps it and appropriates it for itself, seizes and secures it. For what? For further representing, which is willed everywhere as securement and which seeks to establish the being as what is secured. But precisely what is to be *secured,* and for what purpose is it to be brought to certitude?

We will discover this when we inquire more essentially into the Cartesian concept of *cogitatio,* because we have *still not* grasped *one* feature of the essence of *cogitatio,* although we have actually touched on it and identified it. We encounter it when we consider that Descartes says that every *ego cogito* is a *cogito* me *cogitare;* every "I represent something" simultaneously represents a "myself," me, the one representing (for myself, in my representing). Every human representing is—in a manner of speaking, and one that is easily misunderstood —a "self-"representing.

The following objection might be raised: If we "represent" the Freiburg cathedral to ourselves—that is, in this case, make it present for ourselves, because at the moment we do not perceive it in the flesh; or if we represent it as standing immediately before us, in the manner of a perception—then we are representing the cathedral and only the cathedral. That is what is represented. We do not, however, represent ourselves, for otherwise we could never represent the cathedral itself, purely for itself, and let ourselves be released to what representing here sets up over against us, the ob-ject [*Gegen-stand*]. Nor in fact does Descartes, by defining the *cogito* as *cogito me cogitare,* mean that with every representing of an object "I" myself, the one representing, am represented as such into the bargain and so become an object. Otherwise every representing would ultimately have to flit constantly back and forth between our objects, between the representing of the properly represented object and the representing of the one who is doing the representing (*ego*). Is the "I" of the one representing therefore merely indistinctly and incidentally represented? No.

Rather, the representing I is far more *essentially* and necessarily co-represented in every "I represent," namely as something toward which, back to which, and *before* which every represented thing is placed. For this, I do not need an explicit turning toward and back to me, the one who is representing. In the immediate intuition of something, in every making-present, in every memory, in every expectation, what is represented in such fashion by representation is represented *to me,* placed before *me,* and in such a way that I myself do not thereby really become an object of a representing but am nonetheless presented "to me" in an objective representing, and in fact only in such representing. Since every representing presents the one who is representing and the represented object *to* the representing man, representing man is "co-represented" in a peculiarly unobtrusive way. But this characteristic of representing—that in it representation itself and the representing "I" are "co"-represented and represented "along with" the object—is easily misunderstood as long as we do not more sharply define the essential point on which everything depends. Because in every representing there is a representing person *to* whom what is represented in representation is presented, the representing person is involved with and in every representing—not subsequently, but in advance, in that he, the one who is placing *before,* brings what is represented before *himself.* Because the representing person has already come on the scene, along with what has been represented within representation, there lies in every representing the *essential* possibility that the representing itself take place within the scope of the one representing. Representation and the one who is representing are *co*-represented in human representing. This is not really to say that the I and its representing are, as it were—outside the representing, as additional objects for it—chanced upon and then subsequently introduced into the ambience of what is represented. In truth, the easily misunderstood talk about the *co*-representedness of the one representing and his representing in every act of representation wishes to express precisely the *essential* cohesion of the one representing with the constitution of representation.

That is primarily what the statement *"Cogito* is *cogito me cogitare"* says. Now—after this explanation—we can also describe matters thus: Human consciousness is essentially self-consciousness. The consciousness of my self does not accompany the consciousness of things, as if it traveled alongside the consciousness of things as its observer. The consciousness of things and objects is essentially and in its ground primarily self-consciousness; only as self-consciousness is consciousness of ob-jects possible. For representation as described, the *self* of man is essential as what lies at the very ground. The self is *sub-iectum.*

Even before Descartes, it was noticed that representation and what is represented in it are related to a representing I. What is decisively novel is the fact that this relation *to* the one who is representing and thereby the latter *as such* assumes a definitive role for what should and does come to pass in representation as the placing alongside of beings.*

Still, we have not yet fully surveyed the scope and import of the definition *"Cogito* is *cogito me cogitare."* All willing and asserting, all "affects," "feelings," and "sensations" are related to something willed, felt, or sensed. What relates them is, in the broadest sense, represented

* *"Was sich im Vorstellen als Bei-stellen des Seienden begibt und begeben soll."* The sense of the neologism *Bei-stellen* is not clear, but it may well be bound up with the existential structure of *Sein-bei,* the Being-alongside of beings that is characteristic of Dasein as "falling" in the present. See Martin Heidegger, *Being and Time,* sections 12 and 41. This is not to say that the sense of Being-alongside and that of placing-alongside are to be conflated: the first is an existential structure, the second an aspect of Cartesian thought. Their precise relationship poses a knotty problem.

and presented-to. All the modes of comportment mentioned, not just knowing and thinking, are therefore defined in their essence by presentational representation. All these ways of behaving have their Being in such representing; they are such representing; they are representations —*cogitationes.* Man's modes of acting are experienced as his own in and through *being carried out,* experienced as those in which he comports *himself* in such and such a manner. Now for the first time we are in a position to understand the brief answer that Descartes gives to the question *"Quid sit cogitatio?"* He says (*Principia philosophiae,* I, 9):

> *Cogitationis nomine, intelligo illa omnia, quae nobis consciis in nobis fiunt, quatenus earum in nobis conscientia est. Atque ita non modo intelligere, velle, imaginari, sed etiam sentire, idem est sic quod cogitare.*
>
> By the term *cogitatio,* I understand everything we are conscious of along with ourselves, everything which occurs in us for ourselves insofar as we have an accompanying knowledge of it in us. And thus not only are knowing, willing, and imagining, but also sensing, the same as what we call *cogitare.*

If one heedlessly translates *cogitatio* with "thinking" here, then one is tempted to believe that Descartes interpreted all modes of human behavior as thinking and as forms of thinking. This opinion fits in well with the current view concerning Descartes' philosophy, the view that it was "rationalism"—as if what rationalism is did not first have to be determined from a delineation of the essence of *ratio,* as if the essence of *ratio* did not first of all have to be illuminated by the already clarified essence of *cogitatio.* With respect to the latter, it has now been shown that *cogitare* is representing in the fullest sense, that we must conjoin in thought the following essentials: the relation to what is represented, the self-presentation of what is represented, the arrival on the scene and involvement of the one representing with what is represented, indeed in and through the representing.

We should not balk at the formal complexity with which the essence of the *cogitatio* is outlined here. What looks like formal complexity is an attempt to see the simple, unitary essence of representation. This essence reveals that representation places itself in the open region which it traverses as representing, for which reason one can also say—

although this is misleading: representing is a co-representing of oneself. But above all we must realize that for Descartes the essence of representation has shifted its weight to the presenting-itself-to [*das Sich-zu-stellen*] of what is represented, whereby the human being who is representing decides in advance and everywhere on his own what can and should be accepted as well placed and permanent.

If we heed the essential fullness of the equally essential relations that are there to be seen in Descartes' *cogitatio* and *cogito,* then the foundational role of representation as such *betrays itself* in our elucidation of the essence of *cogitare.* Here is announced *what* the underlying, the *subiectum,* is—namely, the representing—and *for what* the subject is a *subiectum*—namely, for the essence of truth. The essential role of representation—that is, of *cogitatio*—is explicitly expressed in the principle which for Descartes is the principle of all principles, and the founding principle of metaphysics: *ego cogito, ergo sum.* Of this principle he says (*Principia,* I, 7), *"Haec cognitio,* ego cogito, ergo sum, *est omnium prima et certissima, quae cui libet ordine philosophanti occurat";* "This insight, 'I represent, therefore I am' is [in terms of rank] the first and most certain of all, which rises up to meet everyone who duly [in an essentially fitting way] thinks metaphysically."*

The principle *ego cogito, ergo sum* is primary and most certain not in some vague and general way for just any opining and representing. It is primary and most certain *only* for *that* thinking which thinks in the direction of metaphysics and its primary and proper tasks, that is to say, which asks what the being is and in what the truth of beings is unshakably grounded.

* The word *metaphysically* is of course also a gloss, presupposing as it does Heidegger's understanding of *philosophanti* as inherently metaphysical inquiry. Cf. the translation by E. S. Haldane and G. R. T. Ross, *The Philosophical Works of Descartes,* 2 vols. (Cambridge, England: Cambridge University Press, [1911] 1967), I, 221: "And hence this conclusion *I think, therefore I am,* is the first and most certain of all that occurs to one who philosophises in an orderly way."

17. Descartes' *Cogito Sum*

Now that we have commented on the essence of *cogitatio,* we will venture an interpretation of the statement that for Descartes constitutes the principle of metaphysics. Recall what was said about *cogitatio: cogitare* is *per-cipere, cogitare* is *dubitare; cogito* is *cogito me cogitare.*

The greatest obstacle to the correct understanding of the principle is Descartes' formulation of it. Because of that formulation—because of the *ergo* ("therefore")—it appears as though the principle were a syllogism composed of a major premise, a minor premise, and a conclusion. Then the principle, separated into its component parts, must have gone as follows: major premise, *Is qui cogitat, existit* [he who thinks, exists]; minor premise, *Ego cogito* [I think]; conclusion, *ergo existo* (*sum*) [therefore I exist (I am)]. Quite gratuitously, Descartes even calls the principle a *conclusio.* On the other hand, we find a sufficient number of passages that clearly indicate that the principle is not to be thought of in the sense of a syllogism. In addition, many commentators agree that the principle is not "really" a syllogism. Not much is gained by the "negative" observation, however, for it simply gives rise to an equally untenable contrary supposition that the principle is *not* a syllogism but something that provides a sufficient elucidation for everything.

Of course, this supposition could insinuate itself only insofar as the principle has the character of a highest principle. "First principles" do not require a proof, nor are they amenable to being proven. They are said to be utterly transparent in themselves. Why, then, the argument about the principle? Why is this "supreme certitude" so uncertain and dubious in its import? Does it lie in the fact that Descartes thought with too little clarity and did not set to work carefully enough in constructing his "principle"? Or does the difficulty lie in the commentators? They have in the course of time adduced everything that Descartes himself said and everything his opponents said, and again everything that Descartes said in responding to his opponents, and all of it has been discussed endlessly, and yet we still remain in the dark so far as the principle is concerned.

Presumably the reason for this state of affairs is the very same difficulty that always blocks insight into essential philosophical principles: the fact that we do not think simply and essentially enough, that we are too facile and too hasty with our common presuppositions.

Thus we take even the "principle of contradiction" as a "fundamental principle" ("axiom") that is eternally valid in itself; we do not stop to consider that for the metaphysics of Aristotle this principle has an essentially different import and plays a different role from the role it plays for Leibniz, and has yet again a different kind of truth in Hegel's or in Nietzsche's metaphysics. The principle says something essential not only about "contradiction" but also about the being as such and about the kind of truth in which the being as such is experienced and projected. That is also true of Descartes' *ego cogito . . . sum.* But we dare not therefore conclude that everything here is immediately made crystal clear by the magic wand of "self-evidence." We must try to think the *ego cogito . . . sum* through, according to its own lineaments, on the basis of our foregoing commentary on *cogitatio.* In a literal sense, the principle points to the *sum,* "I am," and thus to the knowledge that I am. But if in general this is supposed to show with certainty that I—that is, "I" as *ego*—exist as the one representing in a representation, then there is no need for a syllogism that, from the certain existence of something known, concludes the existence of something previously unknown and uncertain. For in the human representation of an object, and through the object *as* something standing-over-against and represented, that "against-which" the object stands and "before which" it is presented—that is, the one representing—has already presented itself. It has done so in such a way that man, by virtue of such presenting himself to himself as the one representing, can say "I." The "I" in its "I am," or to be more specific, the one representing, is known *in* and for such representing no less than the represented object. The I—as "I am the one representing"—is *so* certainly presented to the representing that no syllogism, no matter how logical, can ever attain the certainty bound up with this presenting to himself of the one representing.

Hence we see at once why the *ergo* cannot be understood as the joining of two elements of a syllogism. The supposed major premise—*Is qui cogitat, est*—can never be the ground for the *cogito sum,* because that premise is first derived from the *cogito sum,* indeed in such a way that the *cogito sum* is thereby reproduced in its essential import, although in an altered form. The "I am" is not first deduced from the "I represent"; rather, the "I represent," according to its *essence,* is what the "I am"—that is, the one representing—has already presented to me. With good reason, we might now omit the confusing *ergo* from the formulation of the Cartesian principle. But if we do include it, then we must interpret it in a different sense. The *ergo* cannot mean "consequently." The principle is a *conclusio,* but not in the sense of a conclusion of a syllogism composed of major and minor premises and a conclusion. It is *conclusio* as the immediate joining together of what essentially belongs together and is securely fixed in such cohesion. *Ego cogito, ergo: sum;* I represent, "and this implies," "therein is already posited and presented by representing itself": I *as being.* The "therefore" does not express a consequence, but points toward that which the *cogito* not only "is" but also knows itself to be in accordance with its essence as *cogito me cogitare.* The *ergo* means nothing more than "and that of itself already says." We can most pointedly express what the *ergo* is supposed to say if we leave it aside, and furthermore if we remove the emphasis on "I" in the word *ego,* because the first-person pronoun is not essential here. Then the principle says: *cogito sum.*

What does the sentence *cogito sum* say? It almost seems to be an "equation." But here we are running a new risk of taking the formulations of one particular domain of knowledge—the equations of mathematics—and transferring them to a principle whose distinguishing feature is to be incommensurate in every way with everything else. The mathematical interpretation of the principle in the sense of an equation suggests itself because the "mathematical" is a standard of measure for Descartes' conception of knowledge and knowing. But it remains for us to ask here, Does Descartes simply take the already present and practiced form of "mathematical" knowledge as the model for all knowledge, or does he on the contrary newly define—in fact, metaphysically define—the essence of mathematics? The second is the case. Therefore we must try again to define more accurately the import of the principle, and above all to answer in this way the question as to what is posited as the *subiectum* "through" the principle.

Is the principle itself the *subiectum* that underlies everything? *Cogito sum* does not merely say that I think, nor merely that I am, nor that my existence follows from the fact of my thinking. The principle speaks of a connection between *cogito* and *sum.* It says that I am as the one representing, that not only is *my* Being essentially determined through such representing, but that my representing, as definitive *repraesentatio,* decides about the being present of everything that is represented; that is to say, about the presence of what is meant in it; that is, about its Being as a being. The principle says that representation, which is essentially represented to itself, posits Being as representedness and truth as certitude. That to which everything is referred back as to an unshakable ground is *the full essence of representation itself,* insofar as the essence of Being and truth is determined by it, as well as the essence of man, as the one representing, and the nature of the definitive standard as such.

The principle *cogito sum,* to the extent that it contains and expresses the essence of *cogitatio,* posits along with the essence of *cogitatio* the proper *subiectum,* which is itself presented only in the domain of *cogitatio* and through it. Because the *me* is implied in *cogitare,* because the relation to the one representing still belongs essentially to representing, because all representedness of what is represented is gathered back *to* it, therefore the one representing, who can thus call himself "I," is subject in an emphatic sense, is, as it were, the subject in the subject, back to which everything that lies at the very basis of representation refers. That is why Descartes can also construe the principle *cogito sum* in the following way: *sum res cogitans.*

This formulation is of course as easily misunderstood as the other. Literally translated, it says, "I am a thinking thing." In that case, man would be confirmed as an object at hand, with the simple result that the attribute "thinking" is assigned to him as a distinguishing property. But with this conception of the principle we would be forgetting that the *sum* is defined as *ego cogito.* We would be forgetting that *res cogitans,* in keeping with the concept of *cogitatio,* would at the same time mean *res cogitata:* what represents *itself.* We would be forgetting that such self-representing co-constitutes the Being of the *res cogitans.* Again, Descartes himself offers a superficial and inadequate interpretation of *res cogitans,* inasmuch as he speaks the language of the doctrines of medieval scholasticism, dividing being as a whole into *substantia infinita* and *substantia finita. Substantia* is the conventional and predominant name for *hypokeimenon, subiectum* in a metaphysical sense. *Substantia infinita* is God, *summum ens, creator.* The realm of *substantia f i n i t a* is *ens creatum.* Descartes divides the latter into *res cogitantes* and *res extensae.* Thus all being is seen from the point of view of *creator* and *creatum,* and the new delineation of man through the *cogito sum* is, as it were, simply sketched into the old framework.

Here we have the most palpable example of earlier metaphysics impeding a new beginning for metaphysical thought. A historiological report on the meaning and nature of Descartes' doctrine is forced to establish such results. A historical meditation on the inquiry proper, however, must strive to think Descartes' principles and concepts in the sense he himself wanted them to have, even if in so doing it should prove necessary to translate his assertions into a different "language." Thus *sum res cogitans* does not mean "I am a thing that is outfitted with the quality of thinking," but, rather, "I am a being whose mode *to be* consists in representing in such a way that the representing co-presents the one who is representing into representedness." The Being of that being which I am myself, and which each man as himself is, has its essence in representedness and in the certitude that adheres to it. But this does not mean that I am a "mere representation," a mere thought, and nothing truly actual; it means that the permanence of my self as *res cogitans* consists in the secure establishment of representation, in the certitude according to which the self is brought before itself. But because the *ego cogito,* the "I represent," is not meant as a particular process in an isolated "I," because the "I" is understood as the self, back to which representation as such is essentially referred and in that way is what it is—because of all this, the *cogito sum* in each case says something essentially more. The Being of the one who represents and who secures himself in the representing is the measure for the Being of what is represented as such. Therefore, every being is necessarily measured according to this measure of Being in the sense of certified and self-certifying representedness.

The certitude of the principle *cogito sum* (*ego ens cogitans*) determines the essence of all knowledge and everything knowable; that is, of *mathesis;* hence, of the mathematical. What can therefore be demonstrated and ascertained as a being is only the sort of thing whose placing-alongside guarantees the kind of surety that is accessible through mathematical knowledge and knowledge grounded on mathematics. The mathematically accessible, what can be securely reckoned in a being that man himself is not, in lifeless nature, is *extension* (the spatial), *extensio,* which includes both time *and* space. Descartes, however, equates *extensio* and *spatium.* In that way, the nonhuman realm of finite beings, "nature," is conceived as *res extensa.* Behind this characterization of the objectivity of nature stands the principle expressed in the *cogito sum:* Being is representedness. As one-sided and in many respects unsatisfactory as the interpretation of "nature" as *res extensa* may be, when it is nonetheless thought through in its metaphysical import and measured according to the breadth of its metaphysical project, then it is the first resolute step through which modern machine technology, and along with it the modern world and modern mankind, become metaphysically possible for the first time.

We today are witnesses to a mysterious law of history which states that one day a people no longer measures up to the metaphysics that arose from its own history; that day arrives precisely when such metaphysics has been transformed into the absolute. What Nietzsche already knew metaphysically now becomes clear: that in its absolute form the modern "machine economy," the machine-based reckoning of all activity and planning, demands a new kind of man who surpasses man as he has been hitherto. It is not enough that one possess tanks, airplanes, and communications apparatus; nor is it enough that one has at one's disposal men who can service such things; it is not even sufficient that man only master technology as if it were something neutral, beyond benefit and harm, creation and destruction, to be used by anybody at all for any ends at all.

What is needed is a form of mankind that is from top to bottom equal to the unique fundamental essence of modern technology and its metaphysical truth; that is to say, that lets itself be entirely dominated by the essence of technology precisely in order to steer and deploy individual technological processes and possibilities.

In the sense of Nietzsche's metaphysics, only the Over-man is appropriate to an absolute "machine economy," and vice versa: he needs it for the institution of absolute dominion over the earth.

Descartes, with his principle of the *cogito sum,* forced open the gates of the domain of such a metaphysically comprehended dominion. The principle that lifeless nature is *res extensa* is simply the essential consequence of the first principle. *Sum res cogitans* is the ground, the underlying, the *subiectum* for the determination of the material world as *res extensa.*

Thus the *principle* of the *cogito sum* is the *subiectum*—not the wording of the principle, or the principle considered as a grammatical construct, or taken in its supposedly neutral "meaningful content" that can be thought in itself, but rather the "principle" considered according to what is expressed as essentially unfolding there, and as what sustains it in its proper essence as a principle. What is that? It is *the full essence of representation.* Representation has in itself come to be the establishment and securement of the essence of the truth of Being. Representation presents itself here in its own essential space and posits such space as the standard of measure for the essence of the Being of beings and for the essence of truth. Because truth now means the assuredness of presentation-to, or *certitude,* and because Being means representedness in the sense of such certitude, man, in accordance with his role in foundational representation, therefore becomes the subject in a distinctive sense. In the realm of the dominion of the subject, *ens* is no longer *ens creatum,* it is *ens certum, indubitatum, vere cogitatum, "cogitatio."* *

Now for the first time we can clearly see in what sense the principle *cogito sum* is a "principle" and an "axiom." Following the more or less

* That is, "certain being, indubitable, truly thought, 'representation.'"

correct intuition that in Descartes' thought the "mathematical" *somehow* plays a special role, we recall in this connection that in mathematics certain highest principles or "axioms" occur. These highest principles are then equated with major premises in logical deductions, insofar as mathematical thinking thinks in a "deductive" manner. From here on one presumes without thinking any further about it that the principle *cogito sum,* which Descartes himself singled out as the "first and most certain," must be a highest principle and an "axiom" in the usual sense, the highest major premise, as it were, for all logical deduction. But with this formally correct consideration, which is partly supported by Descartes' own assertions, one overlooks what is essential, to wit, that a new definition of the essence of "ground" and *principium* is first given through the principle *cogito sum.* The *subiectum* is now the "ground" and *principium* in the sense of self-representing representation. Thus a new determination is made concerning the way in which the principle of the *subiectum* is *the* fundamental principle pure and simple. The essence of the fundamental principle now defines itself in and through the essence of "subjectivity." The "axiomatic" now has a different meaning in comparison to the truth of that *axiōma* which Aristotle proclaimed as the "principle of contradiction," applicable to the interpretation of beings as such. The "principial" character of the principle *cogito sum* consists in the fact that the essence of truth and of Being is newly defined, and indeed defined in such a way that the determination itself is addressed as the primary truth, which is also to say, addressed as a being in the proper sense.

Of course, Descartes did not explicitly commit himself concerning the principial character of this principle as the fundamental one. Nonetheless, he possessed a lucid knowledge of its uniqueness. But, through his many efforts to make what was new in his grounding of metaphysics intelligible to his contemporaries by responding to their doubts, Descartes was forced to discourse at the already prevailing level and so to explain his fundamental position superficially, that is, always inappropriately, a contingency that threatens *every essential thinking*—a contingency that is already the consequence of a hidden relationship. Correlative to it is the fact that a thinking also sets *its own* boundaries in *direct proportion* as it presses toward originality.

18. The Fundamental Metaphysical Positions of Descartes and Protagoras

At last we are able to describe Descartes' fundamental metaphysical position according to the four guidelines identified earlier [p.92], and to contrast it with the metaphysical position of Protagoras.

1. In Descartes' metaphysics, in what way *is* man himself, and as what does he know himself? Man is the distinctive ground underlying every representing of beings and their truth, on which every representing and its represented is based and must be based if it is to have status and stability. Man is *subiectum* in the distinctive sense. The name and concept "subject" in its new significance now passes over to become the proper name and essential word for man. This means that every nonhuman being becomes an *object for* this subject. From then on *subiectum* no longer serves as a name and concept for animals, plants, and minerals.

2. What projection of beings on *Being* pertains to such metaphysics? Asked in another way, how is the beingness of beings defined? Beingness now means the representedness of the representing subject. This in no way signifies that the being is a "mere representation" and that the latter is an occurrence in human "consciousness," so that every being evaporates into nebulous shapes of mere thought. Descartes, and after him Kant, never doubted that the being and what is established as a being is in itself and of itself actual. But the question remains what Being means here and how the being is to be attained and made certain through man as one who has come to be a subject. Being is representedness secured in reckoning representation, through which man is universally guaranteed his manner of proceeding in the midst of beings, as well as the scrutiny, conquest, mastery, and disposi-

tion of beings, in such a way that man himself can be the master of his own surety and certitude on his own terms.

3. How is the essence of *truth* circumscribed in such metaphysics? A basic trait of every metaphysical definition of the essence of truth is expressed in the principle that conceives truth as agreement of knowledge with beings: *Veritas est adaequatio intellectus et rei.* But according to what has been said previously we can now easily see that this familiar "definition" of truth varies depending on how the being with which knowledge is supposed to agree is understood, but also depending on how knowledge, which is supposed to stand in agreement with the being, is conceived. Knowing as *percipere* and *cogitare* in Descartes' sense has its distinctive feature in that it recognizes as knowledge only something that representation presents-to a subject as indubitable and that can at all times be reckoned as something so presented. For Descartes too, knowing is oriented toward beings, although only what is secured in the fashion we have described as representing and presenting-to-oneself is recognized *as* a being. That alone is a being which the subject can be certain of in the sense of his representation. The true is merely the secured, the certain. Truth is certitude, a certitude for which it is decisive that in it man as subject is continually certain and sure of himself. Therefore, a procedure, an advance assurance, is necessary for the securing of truth as certitude in an essential sense. "Method" now takes on a metaphysical import that is, as it were, affixed to the essence of subjectivity. "Method" is no longer simply a sequence arranged somehow into various stages of observation, proof, exposition, and summary of knowledge and teachings, in the manner of a scholastic *Summa,* which has its own regular and repetitive structure. "Method" is now the name for the securing, conquering proceeding against beings, in order to capture them as objects for the subject. It is *methodus* in the metaphysical sense that is meant when Descartes in his important posthumously published work *Regulae ad directionem ingenii* postulates as Rule IV: *Necessaria est methodus ad rerum veritatem investigandam.* "Method is necessary [essentially necessary] in order to come upon the trace of the truth [certitude] of beings and to follow this trace." If "method" is understood in this way, then all medieval thinking was essentially methodless.

4. How does man give and take *measure* for the truth of beings in

such metaphysics? This question has already been answered in the preceding. Because man essentially has become the *subiectum,* and beingness has become equivalent to representedness, and truth equivalent to certitude, man now has disposal over the whole of beings as such in an essential way, for he provides the measure for the beingness of every individual being. The essential decision about what can be established as a being now rests with man as *subiectum.* Man himself is the one to whom the power to enjoin belongs as a conscious task. The subject is "subjective" in that the definition of the being and thus man himself are no longer cramped into narrow limits, but are in every respect de-limited. The relationship to beings is a domineering proceeding into the conquest and domination of the world. Man gives beings their measure by determining independently and with reference to himself what ought to be permitted to pass as being. The standard of measure is the presumption of measure, through which man is grounded as *subiectum* in and as the midpoint of beings as a whole. However, we do well to heed the fact that man here is not the isolated egoistic I, but the "subject," which means that man is progressing toward a limitless representing and reckoning disclosure of beings. The new metaphysical position of man as *subiectum* implies that the discovery and conquest of the world, and all the fundamental changes these entail, must be taken up and accomplished by exceptional individuals. The modern conception of man as "genius" has as its metaphysical presupposition the definition of the essence of man as subject. Nevertheless, the cult of genius and its sundry degenerate forms are not what is essential about modern mankind—no more than are "liberalism" and the self-rule of states and nations in the sense of modern "democracies." That the Greeks should have thought of man as "genius" is inconceivable, just as the notion that Sophocles was a "man of genius" is unhistorical. All too infrequently do we reflect that modern "subjectivism" alone has discovered being as a whole, enabled it to be enjoined and controlled, and has made possible the forms and claims of domination that the Middle Ages could not know and that lay beyond the horizon of Greek culture.

We can now clarify what has been said by also distinguishing from each other the fundamental metaphysical positions of Descartes and Protagoras according to the same four guidelines. To avoid repetition, we can put it in the form of a postulation of four brief guiding principles:

1. For Protagoras, man in his selfhood is defined by his belonging in the radius of the unconcealed. For Descartes, man as self is defined by referring the world back to man's representing.

2. For Protagoras, the beingness of beings—in the sense of Greek metaphysics—is a coming to presence in the unconcealed. For Descartes, beingness means representedness through and for the subject.

3. For Protagoras, truth means the unconcealment of what is present. For Descartes, the certitude of self-representing and securing representation.

4. For Protagoras, man is the measure of all things in the sense of a measured restriction to the radius of the unconcealed and to the boundaries of the concealed. For Descartes, man is the measure of all things in the sense of the presumption of the de-limitation of representation for self-securing certitude. The standard of measure places everything that can pass as a being under the reckoning of representation.

If we correctly ponder the difference that has come to light in these fundamental metaphysical positions, then doubt might arise as to whether the same—something equally essential—holds true for both, which would justify our speaking about fundamental positions of *metaphysics* in both cases. But the intent of the contrast is precisely to make clear what is the same—although not identical—in the apparently dissimilar, and thus to make visible the covert unitary *essence* of metaphysics, and in this way to obtain a more *original* concept of metaphysics as opposed to the Nietzschean interpretation of metaphysics, which is merely moral, that is, determined by valuative thought.

But before we attempt the passage to a more original insight into the essence of metaphysics, we must refresh our memory concerning Nietzsche's fundamental metaphysical position, so that the historical connection—not the historiological dependence—between Nietzsche and Descartes may come to light. This we will do by means of a discussion of Nietzsche's position vis-à-vis Descartes.

19. Nietzsche's Position vis-à-vis Descartes

This reference to Nietzsche's position on Descartes' main principle is not intended to call Nietzsche to account for some failing in his interpretation of that principle. Rather, it is a question of our seeing that Nietzsche stands on the ground of metaphysics as laid out by Descartes, and seeing to what extent he must stand on that ground. We cannot deny that Nietzsche rejects the change that Descartes brought to metaphysics, but the question still remains as to why and how Nietzsche arrives at his rejection.

The most important of Nietzsche's notes dealing with Descartes' guiding principle belong among the sketches for his intended major work *The Will to Power.* The editors of the posthumous collection of notes, however, did not include them, which once again sheds some light on the thoughtlessness with which this book was compiled. Nietzsche's relation to Descartes is *essential* for Nietzsche's own fundamental metaphysical position. The *intrinsic* presuppositions of the metaphysics of will to power are determined by that relationship. Because it has gone unnoticed that behind Nietzsche's exceedingly sharp rejection of the Cartesian *cogito* stands an *even more rigorous commitment* to the subjectivity posited by Descartes, the essential historical relationship between these two thinkers—that is, the relationship that determines their fundamental positions—remains in obscurity.

The major part of Nietzsche's observations on Descartes is found in volumes XIII and XIV of the *Grossoktavausgabe,* which contain those notes which, for reasons that are not apparent, were excluded from the posthumous publication. First of all, we will list the passages on which the following discussion is based, by simply enumerating them: XIII, notes 123 (1885); XIV, first half, notes 5, 6, 7 (1885; from the same notebook as the preceding); XIV, second half, notes 160 (1885–86); also, from the posthumous book *The Will to Power,* notes 484, 485, and 533 (all dated spring–fall 1887); see also XII, Part I, note 39 (1881–82). From these notes, it again becomes clear that Nietzsche's confrontations with great thinkers were for the most part undertaken on the basis of philosophical literature *about* these thinkers and therefore, when it comes to particulars, are already questionable, so that it often simply would not pay us to discuss them more thoroughly.

On the other hand, even if we go back to the works of the great thinkers and refer to the full and exact text, that is still no guarantee that the thinking of these thinkers will now be thoughtfully reflected, rethought, and comprehended in a more original manner. The result is that the historian of philosophy, working with great precision, often reports the most incredible things about thinkers he has "researched," while a true thinker can nonetheless use such an inadequate historical report to recognize what is essential, for the simple reason that as a thinker and questioner he is from the start closer to what is to be thought and asked, in an intimacy that can never be achieved by historical inquiry no matter how exact it is. This is true also for Nietzsche's position with respect to Descartes. It is a mixture of mistaken interpretations and essential insights. This, plus the fact that Nietzsche is separated from the great thinkers by the highly complex nineteenth century, so that we lose track of the essential *simple line* running through the historical contexts, makes Nietzsche's relationship to Descartes a very complicated one. Here we restrict ourselves to what is most important.

At the outset, Nietzsche agrees with the familiar interpretation of the principle, which takes *ego cogito,* ergo *sum* as a logical deduction. Underlying the logical deduction is the intention of proving that "I" am, that a "subject" is. Nietzsche believes that Descartes assumes it is self-evident that man may be defined as "I" and that the "I" may be defined as "subject." But of all his arguments against the possibility of the conclusion, many were adduced already in Descartes' time and all have been repeatedly advanced since then: that, in order to be able to arrive at the logical deduction and posit the principle, I must already know what is meant by *cogitare, esse,* and *ergo,* and what "subject" signifies. According to Nietzsche, and others, because such knowledge is presupposed for and in the principle—granted that it is a conclusion —the principle itself cannot be primal "certitude" and indeed the ground of all certitude. The principle cannot bear the burden that Descartes places on it. Descartes himself answered the objection in his last comprehensive work, *Principia philosophiae* (*Les principes de la philosophie,* I, 10; published in 1644 in Latin, 1647 in the French translation of a friend; see *Oeuvres de Descartes,* Adam and Tannery, Paris, 1897–1910, VIII, 8). The passage has a direct connection with the previously cited characterization of the principle as *prima et certissima cognitio:*

> *Atque ubi dixi hanc propositionem* ego cogito ergo sum, *esse omnium primam et certissimam, quae cuilibet ordine philosophanti occurrat, non ideo negavi quin ante ipsam scire oporteat,* quid sit cogitatio, quid existentia, quid certitudo; *item* quod fieri non possit, ut id quod cogitet, non existat *et talia; se quia hae sunt simplicissimae notiones et quae solae nullius rei existentis notitiam praebent, idcirco non censui esse numerandas.*

> And where I have said that the principle "I think, therefore I am" is the first and most certain of all, which occurs to anyone who philosophizes in the proper manner, I have not thereby denied that one must "know" [*scire*] in advance of this principle what "thinking," "existence," and "certitude" are, and also that "it cannot be that something that thinks does not exist," and other such things; but because these are the simplest concepts which alone provide knowledge, without what is named in them actually existing as a being, therefore I have taken the position that these concepts are not explicitly to be enumerated [taken into account].*

* Heidegger's translation is actually more literal than most renderings. Cf. the translation by Haldane and Ross, I, 222:

> "And when I stated that this proposition *I think, therefore I am* is the first and most certain which presents itself to those who philosophise in orderly fashion, I did not for all that deny that we must first of all know *what is knowledge, what is existence, and what is certainty,* and that *in order to think we must be,* and such like; but because these are notions of the simplest possible kind, which of themselves give us no knowledge of anything that exists, I did not think them worthy of being put on record."

One can hardly resist the comment that Heidegger's labors from *Being and Time* (see section 10) through the present Nietzsche lectures represent the effort *to put these things on record.*

Thus Descartes unequivocally concedes that "before" the insight into the *cogito,* knowledge about Being, knowledge itself, and other such things are necessary. But the substantive question remains how this "before" is to be understood, in what the foreknowledge of what is most known is grounded, and on what basis the essence of such knownness of what is most known is to be defined. The passage just quoted is to be understood in this way: The principle, which is posited as an "axiom" and as primal certitude, represents the being as certain (certitude understood as the essence of representation and everything included in it) in such a way that what Being, certitude, and thinking mean is first co-posited through the principle. That these concepts are co-conceived in the principle merely says that they pertain to the import of the principle, but not as something *on which* the principle, along with what it posits, relies for support. Only with the principle—with it first of all—is it stipulated what character the *notissimum* (the most cognizable and recognizable) must possess.

Here we must pay heed to Descartes' preceding fundamental remark, which speaks entirely in Aristotle's idiom (*Physics,* B1) and yet still preserves its own modern tone:

> *Et saepe adverti Philosophos in hoc errare, quod ea, quae simplicissima erant ac per se nota, Logicis definitionibus explicare conarentur; ita enim ipsa obscuriora reddebant.*
>
> And I have often observed that philosophers err in that they have tried to make what was most simple and knowable through itself clearer by means of conceptual determinations of logic; for in this way they [merely] turned what is clear in itself into something more obscure.

Here Descartes is saying that "logic" and its definitions are not the highest tribunal for clarity and truth. These rest on a different ground —for Descartes, on the ground that is posited through his grounding principle. Above all, priority is given to what is secure and certain, in which the most universal determinations—Being, thinking, truth, and certitude—are of course included.

One could object against Descartes that he does not state clearly enough whether and to what extent the universal concepts that are thought together in the principle get their determination through the principle itself, and that any prior determination of these concepts is impossible if it does not rest on the fundamental certitude of the principle. But this objection—thought through in its implications—would be an objection that concerns *every* fundamental metaphysical position. For it is characteristic of the leading mode of metaphysical thought to take the concept and essence of Being for what is most known and therefore to ask which being is to be experienced, and experienced so that it may be interpreted in a particular way with respect to its Being.

As a preview of what is to come, we can formulate in a basic way what Descartes has to say in answer to the arguments raised: A being must first be established in its truth, after which Being and truth are also conceptually determined. Descartes' principle is such that it immediately expresses the inner ties of Being, certitude, and thinking all at once. In this lies its essence as an "axiom."

If in addition we consider that according to Descartes' own decisive explanations of it the principle ought not to be taken as a logical deduction, then it also becomes clear how the being it secures—representation in its complete essence—in keeping with the principial character of the principle grants certainty about Being, truth, and thinking. Again, what Descartes himself *seems* not to have emphasized sufficiently—that the principle as "axiom" must also be thought "principially," that is, *philosophically*—he actually does indicate by the phrase he has used more than once: *ordine philosophanti.* The principle can be fulfilled and its full content exhausted only if we think along the singular line taken by the search for a *fundamentum absolutum inconcussum veritatis.* This search necessarily ponders *fundamentum, absolutum, inconcussum,* and *veritas,* and in a definite sense thinks all these together with what satisfies the search as the being that is certain and therefore established. The provisional conceptions of Being, knowledge, and representation are also represented in the sense of what is certain and most known. The principle *cogito sum* merely states that they are already represented in such fashion. Nietzsche's objection that Descartes' principle makes use of unproven presuppositions and is therefore not a grounding principle misses the mark in two respects: that to which every principle and every act of knowledge appeal as their essential ground is expressly posited in the principle, first, if the principle is not at all a logical deduction which refers back to higher premises; second, and above all, if according to its essence the principle is itself precisely the *pre-supposing* which Nietzsche fails to notice.

There is another objection that Nietzsche lodges against the principle and that seems more essential, an objection that likewise rests on the presupposition that the principle is a logical deduction. But if we disregard this untenable presupposition, it becomes clear that Nietzsche really has hit on something essential. Nonetheless, his confrontation with Descartes remains opaque on the decisive points, because precisely where his deliberations could carry some weight—if they were adequately thought—they recoil directly on Nietzsche himself. It may be surmised from the start that at the most critical junctures Nietzsche views the Cartesian position from his own, that he interprets it on the basis of will to power. That is to say, in view of what we noted earlier, he "reckons it psychologically." So we should not be surprised if, because of the psychological interpretation of a fundamental position already "subjective" in itself, we fall into a tangle of positions that at first glance cannot be unraveled. We must nonetheless make such an attempt, *because everything depends on conceiving Nietzsche's philosophy as metaphysics; that is, in the essential context of the history of metaphysics.*

Nietzsche believes that through Descartes' principle the "I" and the "subject" are to be posited and secured as conditions of "thinking." But, as a result of the skeptical trend in modern philosophy, it has become easier to believe that contrary to Descartes' intention thinking is the condition of the "subject," which is to say, of the concepts of "subject," "object," and "substance." Nietzsche points to the "skeptical trend" of modern philosophy and in so doing is thinking of "British empiricism," according to which "essential concepts" (the categories) arise from associations and habits of thought.

Of course, Nietzsche knew that the doctrines of Locke and Hume merely represented a coarsening of Descartes' fundamental position, that they tended to obliterate philosophical thinking, and that they arose from a failure to comprehend the beginning of modern philosophy in Descartes. Descartes' observation, which we have cited concerning the universal "concepts" in the *cogito sum,* also contends that the most universal and most known concepts are not only produced as concepts *through* thinking, as all concepts as such are, but rather are attained and determined in their content *along the guideline of* thought and assertion. For Descartes, it is decisive that beingness means representedness, and that truth as certainty signifies establishment in representation.

What Nietzsche believes he must raise against Descartes as a supposedly new perspective, namely, that the "categories" emerge from "thinking," is indeed the decisive principle for Descartes himself. Of course, Descartes was striving for a uniform metaphysical grounding of the essence of thinking as *cogito me cogitare,* while Nietzsche, led on the leash of British empiricism, lapses into a "psychological explanation." By also explaining the categories on the basis of "thinking," Nietzsche agrees with Descartes on the very point on which he believes he must oppose him. Only his *way* of explaining the origin of Being and truth in thinking is different: Nietzsche gives the *cogito sum* a different interpretation.

Without being sufficiently aware of it, Nietzsche agrees with Descartes that Being means "representedness," a being established in thinking, and that truth means "certitude." In this respect, Nietzsche thinks in a thoroughly modern fashion. But he actually believes he is speaking *against* Descartes when he argues that Descartes' principle is *immediate* certitude; that is, is attained and secured through mere cognizance. Nietzsche says that Descartes' quest for unshakable certitude is a "will to truth": " 'will to truth' as an 'I will not be deceived' *or* as an 'I will not deceive' *or* an 'I will convince myself and be firm,' as forms of will to power" (XIV, second half, note 160).

What is happening here? Nietzsche refers the *ego cogito* back to an *ego volo* and interprets the *velle* as willing in the sense of will to power, which he thinks as the basic character of beings. *But what if the positing of this basic character became possible only on the basis of Descartes' fundamental metaphysical position?* Then Nietzsche's critique of Descartes would be a misunderstanding of the essence of metaphysics. That will come as a surprise only to someone who has not yet realized that such self-mistaking of metaphysics has become a necessity in the stage of its completion. The following sentence makes it clear just how far Nietzsche was thrown off the path of an *original* metaphysical meditation: "The *substance*-concept a consequence of the *subject*-concept: *not* the reverse!" (WM, 485; from the year 1887). Nietzsche understands "subject" here in a modern sense. The subject is the human "I." The concept of substance is never, as Nietzsche believes, a consequence of the concept of the subject. But neither is the concept of the subject a consequence of the concept of substance. The subject-concept arises from the new interpretation of the *truth* of the being, which according to the tradition is thought as *ousia, hypokeimenon,* and *subiectum,* in the following way: on the basis of the *cogito sum* man becomes what is properly foundational, becomes *quod substat,* substance. The concept of the subject is nothing other than a restriction of the transformed concept of substance to man as the one who represents, in whose representing both what is represented and the one representing are firmly founded in their cohesion. Nietzsche mistakes the origin of the "concept of substance" because, in spite of all his criticism of Descartes, and without an adequate knowledge of the *essence of a fundamental metaphysical position,* he takes the fundamental position of modern metaphysics as absolutely certain and stakes everything on the priority of man as subject. Of course, the subject is now conceived as will to power; consequently *cogitatio,* thinking, is also given a different interpretation.

The change is revealed in one of Nietzsche's remarks about the essence of "thinking," a remark that is not jotted down just anywhere, but stands in the context of his explanation of Cartesian certitude as a form of will to power (XIII, note 123): "Thinking is for us a means not of 'knowing' but of describing an event, ordering it, making it available for our use: that is what we think today about thinking: tomorrow perhaps something else."

Thinking is meant purely "economically" here, in the sense of "machine economy." *What* we think is, as something thought, "true" only insofar as it serves the preservation of will to power. But even *how* we think about thinking is measured solely by the same standard. On the basis of this conception of thinking, then, Nietzsche necessarily comes to the conclusion that Descartes was deluding himself when he supposed that an *insight* into the transparency of his principle would secure its certitude. According to Nietzsche, the principle *ego cogito, ergo sum* is only an "hypothesis" assumed by Descartes because it gave "him the greatest feeling of power and security" (WM, 533; from the year 1887).

Now Descartes' principle is suddenly a hypothesis, an assumption, and not primarily a logical deduction as it was when the first objections were raised! Nietzsche's position with respect to Descartes lacks a single, consistent focus. It becomes unequivocal only where Nietzsche no longer engages in a discussion of the substantive content of the principle, but reckons it "psychologically"; that is, understands it as a form of man's self-securing that arises from will to power.

Of course, it would be rash of us to want to conclude from Nietzsche's position that he has in the least abandoned or overcome Descartes' interpretation of Being as representedness, his definition of truth as certitude, and his determination of man as "subject." Descartes' interpretation of Being is adopted by Nietzsche on the basis of his doctrine of the will to power. The adoption goes so far that Nietzsche, without asking for reasons to justify it, equates Being with "representedness" and the latter with "truth." In the equation between "Being" and "truth," which was already apparent in *The Will to Power,* note 12, Nietzsche most unequivocally certifies the rootedness of his fundamental metaphysical position in the *cogito sum.* "Truth" and "Being" mean the same for Nietzsche: specifically, they mean what is established in representing and securing.

But Nietzsche does not acknowledge "Being" and "truth" and their equivalence as the basic truth. That is to say, in *his* interpretation they are not the "highest value"; he tolerates truth only as a necessary value for the preservation of the will to power. It is doubtful—in fact, it is to be denied—that what is represented in representation reveals anything at all about reality; for everything real is a becoming. Every representing, however, as a fixating, occludes becoming and shows it at a standstill, shows it in a way that it "is" *not.* Representation gives only the semblance of reality. What representation takes to be true and existent is therefore essentially in error when measured against the real taken as becoming. Truth is an error, but a necessary error. "*Truth is the kind of error* without which a certain kind of living being [namely man] could not live. The value for *life* ultimately decides" (WM, 493; see also Pascal, *Pensées,* note 18).*

Nietzsche adopts Descartes' fundamental position completely, although reckoning it psychologically; that is, by grounding certitude as "will to truth" on will to power. But does not Nietzsche argue against the concept of "subject" as Descartes thinks it? At any rate, Nietzsche says that the concept of the "I" as subject is an invention of "logic."

And what is "logic"?

Logic is "an imperative, *not* to knowledge of the true, but to the positing and tidying up of a world *which we shall then call true*" (WM, 516; from the year 1887). Here logic is conceived as command and a form of command; that is, as an "instrument" of will to power. Still more decisively, (WM, 512; from the year 1885): "Logic does *not* stem from the will to truth." That is surprising. According to Nietzsche's own conception, truth is indeed what is firm and fixed; but should not logic emerge from this will to fixate and make permanent? According to Nietzsche's own conception, it can only derive from the will to *truth.* If Nietzsche nonetheless says, "Logic does *not* stem from the will to truth," then he must unwittingly mean "truth" in another sense here: not in *his* sense, according to which truth is a kind of error, but in the traditional sense, according to which truth means agreement of knowledge with things and with reality. This concept of truth is the presupposition and principal standard of measure for the interpretation of truth as semblance and error. Then does not Nietzsche's own interpretation of truth as semblance become semblance? It becomes even less than semblance: Nietzsche's interpretation of "truth" as error, by appealing to the essence of truth as agreement with the real, leads to the reversal of his own thinking and thus to its dissolution.

---

* The first paragraph of Pascal's eighteenth "thought" reads as follows: "When we do not know the truth of a thing, it is of advantage that there should exist a common error which determines the mind of man, as, for example, the moon, to which is attributed the change of seasons, the progress of diseases, etc. For the chief malady of man is restless curiosity about things which he cannot understand; and it is not so bad for him to be in error as to be curious to no purpose" (Blaise Pascal, *Pensées* and *The Provincial Letters,* tr. W. F. Trotter, New York: Modern Library, 1941, p. 9).

But we would be taking the confrontation with Nietzsche's fundamental metaphysical position too lightly and leaving everything half-finished if we were to pursue the dissolution of Being and truth solely from this perspective. The tangles from which Nietzsche can no longer extricate himself are at first covered over by the basic notion that everything is sustained, necessitated, and therefore justified by the will to power. This is made explicit in the fact that Nietzsche can simultaneously say that "truth" is semblance and error, but that as semblance it is still a "value." Thinking in values veils the collapse of the essence of Being and truth. Valuative thinking is itself a "function" of the will to power. When Nietzsche says that the concept of the "I" and thus the "subject" is an invention of "logic," then he must have rejected subjectivity as "illusion," at least where it is claimed as the basic reality of metaphysics.

In Nietzsche's thought, however, the argument against subjectivity in the sense of the I-ness of conscious thought nonetheless accords with the absolute acceptance of subjectivity in the metaphysical sense of *subiectum,* an acceptance that is of course unrecognized. For Nietzsche, what underlies is not the "I" but the "body": "Belief in the body is more fundamental than belief in the *soul*" (WM, 491); and "The phenomenon of the *body* is the richer, clearer, more comprehensible phenomenon: to be placed first methodologically, without stipulating anything about its ultimate significance" (WM, 489). But this is Descartes' fundamental position, presupposing that we still have eyes to see; that is, to think metaphysically. The body is to be placed first *"methodologically."* It is a question of method. We know what that means: it is a question of a procedure for defining what everything determinable is referred back to. That the body is to be placed first methodologically means that we must think more clearly and comprehensibly and still more adroitly than Descartes, but do so wholly and solely in his sense. The method is decisive. That Nietzsche posits the body in place of the soul and consciousness alters nothing in the fundamental metaphysical position which is determined by Descartes. Nietzsche merely coarsens it and brings it to the edge—or even into the realm—of absolute meaninglessness. But meaninglessness is no longer an objection, provided only that it remain of some use to the will to power. "Essential: to set out from the *body* and to use it as guideline" (WM, 532). If we ponder this together with the passage already quoted from *Beyond Good and Evil* (note 36), where Nietzsche posits "our world of desires and passions" as the only definitive "reality," we discover clearly enough how decisively Nietzsche's metaphysics is developed as the fulfillment of Descartes' fundamental metaphysical position, except that here everything is transferred from the realm of representation and consciousness (*perceptio*) to the realm of *appetitus* or drives, and thought absolutely in terms of the physiology of will to power.

However, we must also think Descartes' position in a truly *metaphysical* way, and must consider in its complete *inner* scope the *essential* change of Being and truth in the sense of representedness and certainty. Nearly contemporaneous with Descartes, but essentially determined by him, Pascal sought to save man's Christianity, an attempt that not only made Descartes' philosophy seem to be a mere "theory of knowledge" but also caused it to appear as a mode of thought that only served "civilization," but not "culture." But in truth Descartes' thought was concerned with an essential transposition of all of mankind and its history from the realm of the speculative truth of faith for Christian man into the representedness of beings grounded in the subject, a representedness that serves as the essential ground of the possibility of modern man's position of dominance.

In 1637, as a prelude to the *Meditations,* appeared the *Discours de la méthode: Pour bien conduire sa raison et chercher la vérité dans les sciences.* After what has been said above about the modern metaphysical meaning of "method," the title needs no further commentary.

In the sixth part of the *Discourse on Method* Descartes speaks about the parameters of the new interpretation of beings, especially of nature in the sense of *res extensa,* which is represented as "shape and motion" (location and mobility); that is to say, which is supposed to be made predictable and thus controllable. The newly structured concepts, grounded on the *cogito sum,* open up a vista whose development the present age is only now experiencing in its full metaphysical absoluteness. Descartes says (Opp. VI, 61 ff.; see the edition by Etienne Gilson, 1925, p. 61 f.):

Car elles [quelques notions générales touchant la Physique] m'ont fait voir qu'il est possible de parvenir à des connaisances qui soient fort utiles à la vie, et qu'au lieu de cette philosophie spéculative qu'on enseigne dans les écoles, on en peut trouver une pratique, par laquelle connaissant la force et les actions du feu, de l'eau, de l'air, des astres, des cieux et de tous les autres corps qui nous environnent, aussi distinctement que nous connaissons les divers métiers de nos artisans, nous les pourrions employer en même façon a tous les usages auxquels ils sont propres, et ainsi nous rendre comme maîtres et possesseurs de la nature.

For they [the concepts which on the basis of the *cogito sum* determine the modern projection of the essence of nature] have opened for me the prospect that it is possible to attain to insights that are very useful for life, and that, instead of that scholastic philosophy which merely performs a belated conceptual analysis on a given truth, it is possible to find a philosophy that immediately advances to beings and against them, so that we gain knowledge about the power and effects of fire, water, air, the stars, the heavens, and all other bodily things that surround us; indeed, such knowledge [of the elementary, of the elements] will be just as precise as our knowledge of the various activities of our artisans. Thus we will be able to bring such knowledge into use and perfection in the same way for every purpose to which they are suited, so that such knowledge [the modern mode of representing] will in that way make us masters and proprietors of nature.*

* Heidegger's translation of this passage contains several glosses that are not placed in brackets. Cf. the translation by Haldane and Ross, I, 119:

For they caused me to see that it is possible to attain knowledge which is very useful in life, and that, instead of that speculative philosophy which is taught in the Schools, we may find a practical philosophy by means of which, knowing the force and the action of fire, water, air, the stars, heavens and all other bodies that environ us, as distinctly as we know the different crafts of our artisans, we can in the same way employ them in all those uses to which they are adapted, and thus render ourselves the masters and possessors of nature.

20. The Inner Connection Between the Fundamental Positions of Descartes and Nietzsche

Nietzsche's position with respect to Descartes' *cogito, ergo sum* is in all respects proof that he *misapprehends* the historically essential inner connection between his own fundamental metaphysical position and that of Descartes. The basis for the necessity of the misapprehension lies in the essence of the metaphysics of will to power, which—without being able to know it yet—obstructs an essentially correct insight into the essence of metaphysics. Of course, we learn that this is so only when a comparative review of the three fundamental metaphysical positions cited lets us see in *one* glance the *selfsame* that governs their essence and at the same time demands their respective uniqueness.

To extract the selfsame in the right way, it might also be advisable to contrast *Nietzsche's* fundamental metaphysical position with Descartes', according to our four guidelines.

1. For Descartes, man is subject in the sense of representing I-ness. For Nietzsche, man is subject in the sense of drives and affects present before us as the "ultimate fact"; that is, in short, the *body*. In such recourse to the body as the metaphysical guideline, all world interpretation is pursued.

2. For Descartes, the beingness of beings is equivalent to representedness through and for the I-subject. For Nietzsche too, "Being" is indeed representedness; but "Being," conceived as permanence, is not sufficient for grasping a proper "being," that is, something that becomes, in its reality as becoming. "Being" as the firm and fixed is merely the semblance of becoming, but a necessary semblance. The

proper character of the Being of the real as becoming is will to power. It requires an explicit and separate demonstration to show how far Nietzsche's interpretation of being as a whole as will to power is rooted in the previously mentioned subjectivity of drives and affects and at the same time is essentially co-determined through the projection of beingness as representedness.

3. For Descartes, truth means the same as secure conveyance of what is represented in self-representing representation; truth is certitude. For Nietzsche, truth is equivalent to taking-for-true. The true is defined by what man makes of the being and what he takes as being. Being [*Sein*] is permanence, fixedness. Taking-for-true is the making-fast of becoming, a fixation through which something permanent is secured for a living creature both in himself and in his surroundings. By virtue of it, he can be secure in his existence and his continuance and thus have control over the *enhancement* of power. For Nietzsche, truth as fixation is the semblance needed by the living creature; that is, by the power center of the "body" as "subject."

4. For Descartes, man is the measure of all beings in the sense of the presumption of the de-limitation of representing to self-securing certitude. For Nietzsche, not only is what is represented as such a product of man, but every shaping and minting of any kind is the product and property of man as absolute lord over every sort of perspective in which the world is fashioned and empowered as absolute will to power.

Therefore, Nietzsche says in his treatise *Toward the Genealogy of Morals,* which was joined to *Beyond Good and Evil* the following year (1887) as a "supplement and clarification" (note 12, section III):

> 'Objectivity'—the latter understood not as 'disinterested apprehending' (which is nonsense and an absurdity), but as the ability *to control* one's pro and con and to apply one or the other of them, so that one knows how to employ a *variety* of perspectives and affective interpretations for knowledge. There is *only* a perspectival seeing, *only* a perspectival 'knowing'; and the *more* affects we allow to express themselves concerning one thing, the *more* eyes, and different eyes, we can use to observe one thing, the more complete will our 'concept' of this thing, our 'objectivity' be.

The more easily one affect or another can be brought into play, the *more* one must look toward *need and utility*—the more one must foresee, reckon, and thus *plan*.

The particular emphasis of the change through which man becomes a "subject" at the beginning of modern metaphysics, and the role that then falls to subjectivity in modern metaphysics, might give rise to the notion that the innermost history of metaphysics and of the change in its basic positions is simply a history of the alteration in man's self-conception. This opinion would correspond completely to contemporary anthropological modes of thought. But it would be an erroneous notion, even though it may seemingly have been suggested and prompted by our earlier discussions; in fact it would be the one error it is necessary to overcome.

Thus at this juncture, having summarized the comparisons between Protagoras and Descartes on the one hand, and between Descartes and Nietzsche on the other, we must provisionally indicate the essential ground of the historicity of the history of metaphysics as a history of the truth of Being. Such an indication at the same time allows us to clarify a distinction that we have already employed several times: the distinction between conditioned and absolute subjectivity. This distinction is also tacitly presupposed by the following remark, presented here as more than a mere assertion: As the fulfillment of modern metaphysics, Nietzsche's metaphysics is at the same time the fulfillment of Western metaphysics in general and is thus—in a correctly understood sense—the end of metaphysics as such.

21. The Essential Determination of Man, and the Essence of Truth

Metaphysics is the truth of beings as such and as a whole. The fundamental positions in metaphysics therefore have their ground in the respective essence of truth and in their respective essential interpretations of the Being of beings. As a metaphysics of subjectivity, modern metaphysics, under whose spell our thinking too stands, or rather inevitably *seems* to stand, takes it as a foregone conclusion that the essence of truth and the interpretation of Being are determined by man as the subject proper. More essentially thought, however, it becomes clear that subjectivity is determined from the essence of truth as "certitude" and from Being as representedness. We saw how representation unfolds its full essence, and how only within it—as the essence of what underlies—man is transformed into the subject in a narrower sense, initially as "I." That man thereby becomes the executor and trustee and even owner and bearer of subjectivity in no way proves that man is the essential ground of subjectivity.

These discussions concerning the origin of subjectivity ought to have moved us closer to a question we must refer to at this point in our reflection. The question asks, Is not any interpretation of man and therefore of the history of human being always only the essential *consequence* of the respective "essences" of truth and of Being itself? If that is so, then the essence of man can never be *adequately* determined in its origin through *the prevailing*—that is, *the metaphysical*—interpretation of man as *animal rationale,* whether one prefers to give priority to *rationalitas* (rationality, consciousness, and spirituality) or to *animalitas* (animality and corporeality), or whether one merely seeks an acceptable compromise between these two.*

The insight into these relationships was the impetus for the treatise *Being and Time.* The essence of man is determined by Being itself from the essence (understood verbally†) of the truth of Being.

---

* The following passage, containing one of Heidegger's most forceful statements on his major work, *Being and Time,* appears as an inset in the Neske edition (cf. NII, 194–95). The typescript of the lecture course, completed in 1953, indents the passage and places it in brackets. A second set of brackets in red ink was later entered by hand on the typescript page. The implication is that the passage was not read as part of the 1940 Nietzsche lectures. Indeed, the extant holograph of the lecture course does not contain the inset passage. When it was written is therefore impossible to tell: the phrase "the past thirteen years" refers either to 1940 (if the 1953 *Abschrift* be taken as the starting point) or to 1927 (if the year 1940 be taken). The latter solution is probable, since 1927 is the year of publication of *Being and Time.* But when and where Heidegger first formulated the passage is a matter of conjecture. Certain turns of phrase are so reminiscent of Heidegger's "Letter on Humanism" that the late 1940s seems a likely conjecture. But Heidegger's own reference to "the past thirteen years" implies an intention to make the passage contemporaneous to his 1940 lecture course on nihilism.

† *Das Wesen* normally translates the Latin *essentia,* hence is rendered into English as "essence." It also forms the root of *Anwesen,* "coming to presence," which Heidegger takes to be the basic sense of Being (*Sein*) in philosophy. According to Hermann Paul's *Deutsches Wörterbuch* (pp. 591–92 and 796), however, the substantive derives from an Indogermanic root suggesting "to reside," "to dwell," or "to tarry," senses that the verb *wesen* preserves up to Luther and Goethe. As early as *Being and Time* (1927) Heidegger had stressed the verbal character of *Wesen;* for instance, in the phrase *"The 'essence' of Dasein lies in its existence"* (p. 42 of the German edition). Here "essence" suggests the radically temporalizing projection of Dasein as such, rather than some sort of property or even quiddity of being. During the summer semester of 1927 Heidegger commented at length on the problematic nature of the traditional distinction between *essentia* and *existentia.* See Martin Heidegger, *Grundprobleme der Phänomenologie* (Frankfurt am Main: V. Klostermann, 1975), ch. 2, esp. pp.169–71. In his 1935 lecture course, "Introduction to Metaphysics" (*Einführung in die Metaphysik,* p. 140), Heidegger emphasized the verbal sense of *wesen* as a "governing" or "effecting," while retaining the fundamental reference to "presencing." One of the most detailed statements appears in "The Question Concerning Technology," in Martin Heidegger, *Basic Writings,* ed. D. F. Krell (New York: Harper & Row, 1977), pp. 311–12:

> In the academic language of philosophy "essence" means *what* something is; in Latin, *quid. Quidditas,* whatness, provides the answer to the question concerning essence. For example, what pertains to all kinds of trees—oaks, beeches, birches, firs—is the same "treeness." Under this inclusive genus, the "universal," fall all real and possible trees. Is then the essence of technology, enframing, the common genus for everything technological? . . . Enframing, as a destining of revealing, is indeed the essence of

In *Being and Time,* on the basis of the question of the truth of Being, no longer the question of the truth of beings, an attempt is made to determine the essence of man solely in terms of his relationship to Being. That essence was described in a firmly delineated sense as *Da-sein.* In spite of a simultaneous development of a more original concept of truth (since that was required by the matter at hand), the past thirteen years have not in the least succeeded in awakening even a preliminary understanding of the *question that was posed.* On the one hand, the reason for such noncomprehension lies in our habituation, entrenched and ineradicable, to the modern mode of thought: man is thought as subject, and all reflections on him are understood to be anthropology. On the other hand, however, the reason for such noncomprehension lies in the attempt itself, which, perhaps because it really is something historically organic and not anything "contrived," evolves from what has been heretofore; in struggling loose from it, it necessarily and continually refers back to the course of the past and even calls on it for assistance, in the effort to say something entirely different. Above all, however, the path taken terminates abruptly at a decisive point. The reason for the disruption is that the attempt and the path it chose confront the danger of unwillingly becoming merely another entrenchment of subjectivity; that the attempt itself hinders the decisive steps; that is, hinders an adequate exposition of them in their essential execution. Every appeal to "objectivism" and "realism"

---

technology, but never in the sense of genus and *essentia.* If we pay heed to this, something astounding strikes us: it is technology itself that makes the demand on us to think in another way what is usually understood by "essence." But in what way? If we speak of the *Hauswesen* and *Staatswesen* we do not mean a generic type; rather we mean the ways in which house and state hold sway, administer themselves, develop, and decay—the way in which they essentially unfold [*wesen*]. . . . It is from the verb *wesen* that the noun is derived. *Wesen* understood as a verb is the same as *währen* [to last or endure], not only in terms of meaning, but also in terms of the phonetic formation of the word.

But such enduring is not permanent. *Währen* is the same as *gewähren,* the "granting" of Time and Being within the history and destiny of Being. The verbal *wesen* of the "truth of Being" is in fact history as such. See D. F. Krell, "Work Sessions with Martin Heidegger," in *Philosophy Today,* 1982, *26* (2–4), 126–38. In what follows, *wesen,* when used as a verb, will be rendered as "essentially unfold" or "occur essentially."

remains "subjectivism": the question concerning Being as such stands outside the subject-object relation.

In the prevailing Western interpretation of man as *animal rationale,* man is first experienced within the compass of *animalia, zōa,* living creature. Then *ratio, logos,* is attributed to the being that has thus come forward as the chief property and distinguishing feature of *its* animality, as opposed to that of mere animals. Of course, in *logos* lies the relation to beings, which we gather from the connection between *logos* and *katēgoria.* But this relation does not attain prominence as such. Rather, *logos* is conceived as a capability that makes higher and broader knowledge possible for the living creature "man," while animals remain "irrational" creatures, *a-loga.* Metaphysics knows and *can* know nothing about whether and how the essence of truth and of Being, and a relationship to that essence, define the essence of man in such a way that neither animality nor rationality, neither the body nor the soul, neither the spirit nor all these together suffice for a primordial conception of the essence of man.

If the appropriate "essence" of truth—rather than a conception of man—is decisive for the essential definition of subjectivity, then subjectivity in each case must allow itself to be defined in terms of the respective essence of truth by which it is measured. However, the appropriate essence of truth comes to be recognized by how untruth is determined in it and from it, and in what respect untruth is comprehended.

It is no accident, and has nothing to do with "theory of knowledge," that in Descartes' proper major work, the *Meditations on Metaphysics,** we find a meditation—the fourth—entitled *"De vero et falso"* ["On the True and the False"]. Untruth is conceived as *falsitas* (falsehood), and falsehood as *error, erring.* Error occurs when in representation something is presented-to the one representing that does not satisfy the conditions of presentability, that is to say, of indubitability and certitude. The fact that man errs and so is *not* in immediate, continuous, and full possession of the true certainly

* What is meant, of course, is the *Meditationes de prima philosophia.* Heidegger chooses the word *metaphysics* in order to emphasize that Descartes' major work on "first philosophy" is not a contribution to "epistemology" but an event in the history of Being.

signifies a limitation of his essence; consequently the subject, as which man functions within his representing, is also limited, finite, conditioned by something else. Man is not in possession of absolute knowledge; thought from a Christian point of view, he is not God. But insofar as he does know, he is also not simply a nullity. Man is a *medium quid inter Deum et nihil*—a definition of man that Pascal, in a different way and from another perspective, later appropriated and made into the kernel of his definition of the essence of man.

However, although being-able-to-err is a lack for Descartes, it is also a certification that man is free, is a being founded on himself. *Error* directly attests to the priority of subjectivity, so that from the viewpoint of subjectivity a *posse non errare,* an ability not to err, is more essential than a *non posse errare,* the inability to err at all. Where no possibility of error exists, there is either—as in the case of a stone—no relationship to truth at all, or—as in the case of an essence that is absolutely knowing, that is, creative—a binding into pure truth that excludes all subjectivity, that is, all reversion of a self back to itself. In contrast, the *posse non errare,* the possibility and the capacity of *not* erring, means *at one and the same time* the relationship to truth but also the factuality of error and thus entanglement in untruth.

In the further course of the development of modern metaphysics, untruth becomes (with Hegel) a stage and a mode of truth itself, which means that subjectivity, in its reversion of self back to itself, is the sort of essence that cancels and conducts [*aufhebt*] untruth into the unconditioned realm of absolute knowledge, a process through which untruth first comes to appear as something conditioning and finite. Here all error and everything false is but the one-sidedness of what in and for itself is true. The negative *belongs* to the positivity of absolute representation. Subjectivity is absolute representing, which in itself mediates, cancels, and conducts everything that conditions. It is absolute spirit.

For Nietzsche, subjectivity is likewise absolute, albeit in a different sense, one that is in keeping with his different determination of the essence of truth. Here truth itself is in its essence error, so that the distinction between truth and untruth falls away. The distinction is consigned to the command decision of will to power, which absolutely enjoins the respective roles of various perspectives according to the need for power. Because the power of disposing over the true and the untrue, the verdict concerning the respective roles of error, semblance, and the production of semblance for the preservation and enhancement of power remain solely with the will to power itself, the power-based essence of truth is, according to Nietzsche, "justification."* Of course, in order to grasp the Nietzschean sense of the word *justification* we must immediately put aside any ideas about "justice" that stem from Christian, humanistic, enlightenment, bourgeois, and socialist morality. "Justification as a constructive, exclusive, and annihilative way of thought, advancing beyond evaluations: *the supreme representative of life itself*" (XIII, note 98). And "*Justification,* as function of a perspicacious power which looks beyond the narrow perspectives of good and evil, thus has a wider horizon of *advantage*—the intention of preserving something that is *more* than any given person" (XIV, first half, note 158).

That "something" to whose preservation justification is exclusively tied, is the will to power. Such novel "justification" no longer has anything to do with deciding about right and wrong according to a true relationship of measure and rank that would subsist of itself. Rather, the new justification is active, and above all "aggressive"; it posits what is to be considered right and wrong solely from the viewpoint of its own power.

For example, when the British recently blew to smithereens the French fleet docked at Oran it was from *their* point of view "justified"; for "justified" merely means what serves the enhancement of power.†

---

* The word *Gerechtigkeit* is usually rendered as "justice" or "righteousness," especially as an attribute of the Judeo-Christian God. Nietzsche writes about it often, early and late, and always with ambivalence: *Gerechtigkeit* is the virtue closest to intellectual probity, which may be identified with "the grand righteousness" of philosophers (see *Beyond Good and Evil,* note 213); yet "justice" and "righteousness" have their origins in moralizing-reactionary will to power, they do the work of rancor. To emphasize the active, critical, genealogical aspect of Nietzsche's usage, *Gerechtigkeit* has been translated here as "justification." Heidegger regards it as one of the five fundamental terms of "Nietzsche's metaphysics" (see NII, 314–33, in Volume III of the present series).

† Heidegger is referring to the British ultimatum and attack of July 3, 1940, an event that had just occurred and which therefore should not be confused with the battle (November 7–8, 1942) that ensued upon the Allied landing in North Africa. Heidegger

At the same time, what this suggests is that *we* dare not and cannot ever justify that action; in a metaphysical sense, every power has *its own* right and can only come to be in the wrong through impotence. But it belongs to the metaphysical tactics of every power that it cannot regard any act of an opposing power from the *latter's* power perspective, but rather subjects the opposing activity to the standard of a universal human morality—which has value only as propaganda, however.

In accordance with the essence of truth as justification, the subjectivity of that will to power which justification "represents" is absolute. But absoluteness now has a different meaning than it does in Hegel's metaphysics, for example. The latter posits untruth as a stage of one-sidedness taken up into truth. Nietzsche's metaphysics directly posits untruth in the sense of error as *the* essence of truth. Truth—so qualified and conceived—fashions for the subject an absolute power to enjoin what is true and what is false. Subjectivity is not merely *de*limited from every limit, it is itself what now enjoins every kind of restriction and delimitation. It is not the subjectivity of the subject that first transforms the essence and the position of man in the midst of beings. Rather, being as a whole has already experienced a different interpretation through that in which subjectivity finds its origin; that is, through the *truth* of beings. By virtue of the transformation of the human being into the subject, the history of modern mankind does not merely receive new "contents" and areas of activity; rather, the course of history itself takes a different direction. To all appearances, everything is merely discovery of the world, research into the world, portrayal of the

found the event compelling for probably two reasons: first, the French forces were—and the British knew them to be—largely incapable of defending themselves in the event of an attack; second, the "moral status" of the French, a defeated ally caught in the shadowy realm of collaboration, was a delicate issue throughout Europe during the weeks following the fall of France. Nevertheless, whatever Heidegger's reasons, I am not inclined to temper my sardonic treatment of this ostensible example of Nietzschean *Gerechtigkeit* (in D. F. Krell, "Nietzsche and the Task of Thinking: Martin Heidegger's Reading of Nietzsche," unpublished doctoral dissertation, Duquesne University, 1971, pp. 62–63, 77–79), an example that remains alien to the letter and spirit of Nietzschean will to power. Otto Pöggeler also comments on Heidegger's reference, more equably than I, in his *Philosophie und Politik bei Heidegger* (Freiburg and Munich: K. Alber, 1972), pp. 33–34.

world, arrangement of the world, and dominion over the world in which man extends himself, and in such extension stretches his essence thin, flattens it, and loses it. In truth, however, these are matutinal appearances of those basic features with which the unconditioned subjectivity of mankind is stamped.

22. The End of Metaphysics

In order to grasp Nietzsche's philosophy as metaphysics and to circumscribe its place in the history of metaphysics, it is not enough to explain historiologically a few of his fundamental concepts as being "metaphysical." *We must grasp Nietzsche's philosophy as the metaphysics of subjectivity.* What was said concerning the expression "metaphysics of will to power" is also valid for the phrase "metaphysics of subjectivity." The genitive is ambiguous, having the sense of a subjective and objective genitive, in which the words *objective* and *subjective* maintain emphatic and rigorous significance.

Nietzsche's metaphysics, and with it the essential ground of "classical nihilism," may now be more clearly delineated as a *metaphysics of the absolute subjectivity of will to power.* We do not say merely "metaphysics of absolute subjectivity," because this determination also applies to Hegel's metaphysics, insofar as it is the metaphysics of the absolute subjectivity of self-knowing will; that is, spirit. Correspondingly, Hegel determines the nature of absoluteness from the essence of reason existing in and for itself, which he always thinks as the unity of knowing and willing, although never in the sense of a "rationalism" of pure understanding. For Nietzsche, subjectivity is absolute as subjectivity of the body; that is, of drives and affects; that is to say, of will to power.

The essence of man always enters into these two forms of absolute subjectivity in a way that is different in each case. The essence of man is universally and consistently established throughout the history of metaphysics as *animal rationale.* In Hegel's metaphysics, a speculatively-dialectically understood *rationalitas* becomes determinative for subjectivity; in Nietzsche's metaphysics, *animalitas* is taken as the guide.

Seen in their essential historical unity, both bring *rationalitas* and *animalitas* to absolute validity.

The absolute essence of subjectivity necessarily develops as the *brutalitas* of *bestialitas.* At the end of metaphysics stands the statement *Homo est brutum bestiale.* Nietzsche's phrase about the "blond beast" is not a casual exaggeration, but the password and countersign for a context in which he consciously stood, without being able to peer through its essential historical connections.

But to what extent metaphysics, when considered from the themes we have discussed, is brought to essential completion, and to what extent its essential history is at an end, require a separate discussion.

Here once again, we must emphasize the following: our talk of the end of metaphysics does not mean to suggest that in the future men will no longer "live" who think metaphysically and undertake "systems of metaphysics." Even less do we intend to say that in the future mankind will no longer "live" on the basis of metaphysics. The end of metaphysics that is to be thought here is but the beginning of metaphysics' "resurrection" in altered forms; these forms leave to the proper, exhausted history of fundamental metaphysical positions the purely economic role of providing raw materials with which—once they are correspondingly transformed—the world of "knowledge" is built "anew."

But then what does it mean, "the end of metaphysics"? It means the historical moment in which *the essential possibilities* of metaphysics are exhausted. The last of these possibilities must be that form of metaphysics in which its essence is reversed. Such a reversal is performed not only in actuality, but also *consciously*—although in different ways—in Hegel's and in Nietzsche's metaphysics. In the view of subjectivity, the *conscious* act of reversal is the only one that is *real;* that is, appropriate to subjectivity. Hegel himself says that to think in the manner of his system means to attempt to stand—and walk—on one's head. And Nietzsche very early describes his philosophy as the reversal of "Platonism."

The fulfillment of the essence of metaphysics can be very imperfect in its realization, and does not need to preclude the continued existence of previous fundamental metaphysical positions. Reckoning in terms of various fundamental metaphysical positions and their individual doctrines and concepts remains a likelihood. But such reckoning does not take place indiscriminately. It is guided by the *anthropological* mode of thinking which, *no longer comprehending the essence of subjectivity,* prolongs modern metaphysics while vitiating it. "Anthropology" as metaphysics is the transition of metaphysics into its final configuration: "world view" [*Weltanschauung*].

Of course, the question of whether and how all the essential possibilities of metaphysics can be surveyed at once has yet to be decided. Might not the future still be open to metaphysical possibilities of which we suspect nothing? Surely, we do not stand "above" history, least of all "above" the history of metaphysics, if it is really the essential ground of all history.

Were history a thing, then it might be plausible for one to insist that he must stand "above it" in order that he might know it. But if history is not a thing, and if we ourselves, existing historically, are implied along with history *itself,* then perhaps the attempt to stand "above" history is an effort that can never reach a standpoint for historical decision. The statement concerning the end of metaphysics is of course a historical decision. Presumably, our meditation on the more original essence of metaphysics brings us into proximity to the standpoint for the decision mentioned. Such meditation is equivalent to insight into the way European nihilism essentially unfolds in the history of Being.

23. Relations with beings and the Relationship to Being. The Ontological Difference

The comparison of the three fundamental metaphysical positions of Protagoras, Descartes, and Nietzsche has at least in part prepared us to answer the question we have been holding in check. What, in the fundamental metaphysical positions we have characterized, is the self-same—what is it that everywhere sustains and is indicative? It is obviously something that in each comparison of the three fundamental positions was seen to be that one-and-the-same regarding which we were interrogating the positions, in order to distinguish what was proper to each of them. We have already highlighted this one-and-the-same in naming the four guidelines that steered the entire comparison. They comprise:

1. The way in which man is himself.
2. The projection of the Being of beings.
3. The essence of the truth of beings.
4. The manner in which man takes and gives measure for the truth of beings.

Now the question arises: Have we just arbitrarily bound these four guidelines together, or do they themselves have an inner connection such that in each one the other three are already posited? If the second alternative applies, and if therefore the four guidelines do indicate a unified articulation, this gives rise to a further question: How does the articulation circumscribed by these four guidelines stand with respect to what we called the relations of man with beings?

The first guideline considers man as he himself is, as a being who knows himself and knowingly is *this* being who consciously distinguishes himself from every being he himself is *not.* Included in such being-himself is the fact that man stands within some kind of truth about beings, indeed about the being he himself is *and* the beings he himself is *not.* Thus the first guideline includes the third: the truth of beings. The second is already thought along with the third, for the truth of beings must uncover and represent these beings in what they are as beings; that is, in their Being. The truth of beings contains a projection of the Being of beings. But, insofar as man, himself a being, maintains himself in the projection of Being and stands in the truth of beings, he must either *take* the truth of beings as a measure for his being-himself, or must *give* a measure for the truth of beings out of his own being-himself. The first guideline contains the third, in which the second is included, but also at the same time embraces the fourth in itself. Correspondingly, one can show in terms of the second, and also in terms of the third, the cohesion of the remaining guidelines.

The four guidelines characterize the unity of an as yet nameless articulation. But how does the latter relate to what we have vaguely called the relation of man to beings? If we consider the relation more precisely, it becomes clear that it cannot subsist or be absorbed in the relation of man as subject to the being as object. For once the subject-object relation is restricted to the modern history of metaphysics, it no longer holds in any way for metaphysics as such, especially not for its beginning with the Greeks (specifically, with Plato). The relation in which we seek the more primordial essence of metaphysics does not at all concern the relation of man as a self and as a somehow self-existent being to the other remaining beings (earth, stars, plants, animals, fellow men, works, facilities, gods).

Metaphysics speaks of beings as such and as a whole, thus of the *Being* of beings; consequently, a relationship of man to the *Being* of beings reigns in it. Nonetheless, still unasked is the question of whether and how man comports himself to the *Being* of beings, not merely to *beings,* not simply to this or that thing. One imagines that the relation to "Being" has already been sufficiently defined by the explanation of man's relations with beings. One takes both the relations with beings and the relationship to Being as the "selfsame," and indeed with some justification. The fundamental trait of metaphysical thought is intimated in such an equivalence. Because the relationship to Being is scarcely thought beyond relations with beings, and even when it is, is always taken as their shadow, the essence of these very relations also remains obscure. According to the third guideline, metaphysics is the truth "of" beings as a whole. It likewise remains unasked in what relation man stands to truth and to its essence. Finally, in the fourth guideline, according to which man posits the measure for the determination of a being as such, there is concealed a question of how the being *as such* can be brought into view by man at all, can be experienced and preserved in its determinateness, no matter whether man here takes the role of subject or of some other essence.

Although unexpressed and at first perhaps even inexpressible, the one-and-the-same is already experienced and claimed in advance in the four guidelines: the relationship of man to Being. The unitary articulation indicated by the four guidelines is nothing other than man's relations with beings, the essential structure of these relations. Perhaps the primary and uniquely experienced relation of man to beings is what it is only because man as such stands in *relationship to Being.* How could man comport himself to beings—that is, experience beings as being—if the relationship to Being were not granted him?

Let us immediately try to clarify this with a specific illustration. Suppose that every trace of the essence of history were hidden and that every elucidation of what history as such *is* were missing: then the being that we call historical being would also remain concealed. Then not only would historiological inquiry, communication, and tradition never be able to come into play, there would never be any historical experience anywhere and, prior to it, no historical decision or action. Nonetheless, we experience historical events and acknowledge historiological reports as if they were self-evident.

The most essential aspect of all this, the fact that we operate within a perhaps quite indefinite and confused knowledge of the historicity of history, does not trouble us—nor does it need to trouble everyone. But *our* not being troubled does not deprive the *Being* of beings in the form of what is historical of anything essential. It becomes all the more strange when we recognize that *such* essentiality does not even require the general awareness of the public in order to radiate its essential fullness. Such strangeness increases the questionableness of what we are here pointing to, the *questionableness* of Being and thereby the questionableness of the relationship of man to Being.

Therefore, what we were pointing to with the vague expression "relations of man with beings" is in its essence the relationship of man to Being.

But what is this relationship itself? What "is" Being, granted that we can and must distinguish it from beings? How does it stand with the *differentiation* of Being from beings; how does man stand vis-à-vis the differentiation? Is man first of all man, and does he in addition "have" a relationship to Being? Or does the latter constitute the essence of man? If it does, then of what essence "is" man if his essence is defined in terms of that relationship? Has the essence of man ever yet been defined in terms of the relationship to Being? If not, why not? If so, why is the relationship as inconceivable to us, as incomprehensible and indiscernible, as Being itself? We can at any time encounter, pinpoint, and investigate beings—historical matters, for example. But "Being"? Is it an accident that we scarcely grasp it, and that with all the manifold relations with beings we forget the relationship to Being? Or is metaphysics and its dominance the reason for the obscurity that enshrouds Being and man's relationship to it? How would it be if it were the essence of metaphysics to establish the truth of beings, and thus necessarily to be sustained by the relationship of man to Being, but *not* to ponder the relationship itself, not even to be able to ponder it?

The relationship of man to Being is obscure. Nonetheless, we everywhere and continually stand within it wherever and whenever we comport ourselves toward beings. When and where would we—ourselves beings—*not* comport ourselves toward beings? We keep hold of beings and at the same time hold ourselves in the relationship to Being. Only in that way is being as a whole our foothold and halting place. This is to say that *we stand in the differentiation of beings and Being.* Such differentiation sustains the relationship to Being and supports relations with beings. It prevails, without our being aware of it. Thus it appears to be a differentiation whose differences are not differentiated by anyone, a differentiation for which no differentiator "is there" and no region of differentiation is constituted, let alone experienced. One might almost surmise and maintain correctly that with what we call the "differentiation" between Being and beings we have invented and contrived something that "is" not and that above all does not need "to be."

But a glance at metaphysics and into its history soon teaches us otherwise. The differentiation of beings and Being shows itself as that selfsame from which all metaphysics arises and also, in arising, inevitably escapes, that selfsame which it leaves behind as such, and outside its domain, which it never again expressly considers and no longer needs to consider. The differentiation of beings and Being makes possible every naming, experiencing, and conceiving of a being as such. In Greek, the being is called *to on;* addressing a being as being and, furthermore, grasping a being take place in *logos.* One can therefore circumscribe the essence of metaphysics, which explicitly brings beings as such to word and concept, in the name "onto-logy." The name, even though it is formed from Greek words, does not stem from the period of Greek thought, but was coined in the modern age; it was employed by the German scholar Clauberg, for example, who was a disciple of Descartes' and a professor in Herborn.*

Following the basic position of metaphysics and its scholastic formations, various opinions concerning the knowledge of beings and Being attach to the term *ontology.* Today *ontology* has once again become a fashionable term; but its time seems to be over already. We therefore ought to recall its simplest application, based on the Greek meaning of the words: *ontology*—addressing and grasping the Being of beings. With this name, we are not identifying a particular branch of metaphysics, nor a "direction" of philosophical thought. We take the title

* The term *ontology* apparently was coined by Goclenius in 1613, then taken up by the Cartesian philosopher Johannes Clauberg (1622–1665) into his *Metaphysica de ente sive Ontosophia* of 1656, and finally established in the German language around 1730 by the Leibnizian rationalist Christian Wolff (1679–1754). Attacked and eclipsed by Kant's transcendental philosophy, "ontology" emerged once again at the forefront of philosophical inquiry only with Martin Heidegger and his onetime Marburg colleague Nicolai Hartmann (1882–1950), author of *Zur Grundlegung der Ontologie* (1935) and *Neue Wege der Ontologie* (1942).

so broadly that it simply indicates an event, the event in which the being is addressed as such; that is, addressed in its Being.

"Ontology" is grounded on the differentiation of Being and beings. The "differentiation" is more appropriately identified by the word *difference,* in which it is intimated that beings and Being are somehow set apart from each other, separated, and nonetheless connected to each other, indeed of themselves, and not simply on the basis of an "act" of "differentiation." Differentiation as "difference" means that a *settlement* [Austrag] between Being and beings exists. We shall not say from where and in what way the settlement comes about; we mention the difference at this point merely as an occasion for and an impetus toward an inquiry concerning the settlement. The differentiation of Being and beings is intended as the ground of the possibility of ontology. But the "ontological difference" is introduced not in order to resolve the question of ontology but to identify what, as the heretofore unasked, first makes all "ontology," that is, metaphysics, fundamentally questionable. The reference to the ontological difference identifies the ground and the "foundation" of all onto-logy and thus of all metaphysics. The naming of the ontological difference is to imply that a historical moment has arrived in which it is necessary and needful to ask about the ground and foundation of "onto-logy." Thus in *Being and Time* there is talk of "fundamental ontology." Whether another "foundation" is to be laid under metaphysics as if under a building already standing, or whether other decisions about "metaphysics" are to result from meditation on the "ontological difference," need not be discussed here. The reference to the "ontological difference" wishes only to point out the inner connection of our present meditation on a more original concept of metaphysics to what we communicated earlier.

The differentiation of Being and beings—although taken for granted everywhere—is the unknown and ungrounded ground of all metaphysics. All enthusiasm for metaphysics and all efforts to produce "ontologies" as doctrinal systems, but also every critique of ontology within metaphysics—all these merely attest to an accelerating *flight* in the face of the unknown ground. For one who knows of it, however, the ground is so *worthy* of question that it even remains an open question whether the very thing we call *differentiation,* the settlement between Being and beings, can be experienced in an essentially appropriate way on the basis of such a designation.

Every designation is already a step toward interpretation. Perhaps we have to retrace this step once again. That would mean that the settlement cannot be grasped if we think it formally as "differentiation" and wish to search out an "act" of the differentating "subject" for such differentiation. Once again, however, our designation is perhaps at first the *only* possible *basis* for bringing the generalized selfsameness of all metaphysics into view, not as some neutral quality, but as the decisive ground that historically guides and shapes every metaphysical inquiry. The fact that metaphysics generally thinks Being in the same way, although the Being of beings is variously interpreted in the playspace of presencing, must have its ground in the essence of metaphysics.

But *does* metaphysics think Being in the same way? There are several pieces of testimony that say it does, pieces which at the same time are related to each other and thus display their provenance from what we first identified as the differentiation of Being and beings.

Even the name for Being that was already familiar at the beginning of metaphysics, in Plato—namely, *ousia*—betrays how Being is thought; that is to say, in what way it is differentiated from beings. We need only translate the Greek word in its literal *philosophical* meaning: *ousia* means being*ness* and thus signifies the universal in beings. If we simply assert of a being—for instance, of a house, horse, man, stone, or god—that it is in being, then we have said what is most universal. Being*ness,* therefore, designates the most universal of universals, the most universal of all, *to koinotaton,* the highest genus, the "most general." In contrast to what is most universal of all, in contrast to Being, a being is "particular," "individual," and "specified" in a certain way.

The differentiation of Being from beings appears here to depend on and consist in looking away from ("abstracting") all the particularities of beings, in order to retain the most universal as the "most abstract" (the most removed). With such differentiation of Being from beings nothing is said about the inner content of the essence of Being. It merely reveals the way in which Being is differentiated from beings, specifically, by way of "abstraction," which is also quite normal for our representing and thinking of ordinary things and connections among things, and is in no way reserved for the consideration of "Being."

It cannot surprise us, therefore, when we frequently encounter the assurance in metaphysics that of Being itself nothing further can be predicated. One can even prove this assertion with "rigorous logic." For if something were to be predicated of Being, then that predicate would have to be *still more* universal than Being. But, because Being is the most universal of all, such an attempt contradicts its essence. As if by calling it "the most universal" anything would be said about the essence of Being! At best, what this tells us is the way in which one thinks "Being"—namely, through a generalization concerning beings—but not what "Being" means. But by defining Being as what is most universal, all metaphysics nonetheless certifies the fact that it posits itself on the basis of a peculiar kind of differentiation of Being and beings. Furthermore, if metaphysics always affirms that Being is the most universal and therefore emptiest concept, and so a concept not to be determined any further, it remains true that every fundamental metaphysical position does think Being according to an interpretation all its own. Of course, this easily gives rise to the mistaken notion that, because Being is the most universal, the interpretation of Being also proceeds on its own and requires no further grounding. In the interpretation of Being as the most universal, nothing is said about Being itself, but only about the way in which metaphysics thinks about the *concept* of Being. That metaphysics thinks about it so remarkably thoughtlessly—that is, from the viewpoint and in the manner of everyday opinion and generalization—proves quite clearly how decisively every meditation on the differentiation of Being and beings is utterly remote to metaphysics, although metaphysics everywhere makes use of the differentiation. All the same, the differentiation also comes to appear everywhere within metaphysics, indeed, in an essential form which governs the articulation of metaphysics in all its fundamental positions.

Being, the beingness of beings, is thought as the *a priori*, the *prius*, the prior, the precursory. The *a priori*, the prior in its ordinary temporal significance, means an older being, one that emerged previously and came to be, and was, and now no longer comes to presence. If it were a question here of the temporal sequence of beings, then the word and its concept would need no special elucidation. But what is in question is the differentiation of Being and beings. The *a priori* and the prior are predicated of Being as words that distinguish Being. The Latin word *prius* is a translation and interpretation of the Greek *proteron.* Plato, and later Aristotle, first discussed the *proteron* with particular reference to the beingness of beings (*ousia*). Here we must forego an explicit presentation of Platonic and Aristotelian thoughts concerning *proteron* from the dialogues and treatises of these thinkers. A rather more general and freer commentary must suffice. Of course, even that cannot be done without at some point entering briefly into a few of the main features of Plato's doctrine of the Being of beings. Discussing the *a priori* with the intention of characterizing the differentiation of Being and beings ought at the same time to insure that nothing irrelevant is introduced in thinking about the *a priori,* but rather that something all-too-near is for the first time conceived and yet grasped only within definite limits, which are the limits of philosophy; that is, the limits of metaphysics. In terms of the matter, therefore, our foregoing discussions have already dealt with what will be brought to language in the following special treatment of the *a priori.*

24. Being as *A Priori*

If we compare two colored things with respect to their coloration and say that they are alike, then we are establishing the equality of the coloration. Such establishment mediates for us a knowledge of things that are. In the sphere of everyday cognition and treatment of things such establishment suffices. But if we meditate on the cognition of similar coloration with respect to what might be further revealed in such knowledge, then something remarkable takes place, something Plato first approached with measured steps.* We say that the coloration—or simply these colored things—are alike. With regard to the two similar things, we first of all—and for the most part continue—to overlook the likeness. We pay no heed to the fact that we can make out both colored things *as* alike, can examine them with respect to their being alike or different at all, only if we already "know" what likeness means. If we supposed with all seriousness that "likeness," equality, is not at all "represented" (that is, not "known") to us, then we might *perhaps* continue to perceive green, yellow, or red, but we could never come to know *like* or different colors. Likeness, equality, must previously have been made known to us, so that in the light of likeness we can perceive something like "similar beings."

Because it is made known *beforehand,* equality and likeness must be "prior" to what is alike. But we will now object that we really first—that is, previously—perceive like colors, and only afterward—if at all—recognize that we are thereby thinking likeness and equality. We cautiously add the "if at all" because many people establish many things as alike and never in all their "lives" consider, and do not need to consider, that with this perception and for its sake they are already "repre-

---

* See, for example, *Phaedo,* 74–76.

senting" likeness. Actually, then, likeness and equality are subsequent and not prior. In a certain sense, this is accurate, and nonetheless does not touch on the theme we are dealing with here, the *a priori.* We must therefore ask more precisely in what sense colored things are "prior" and "equality" is later, or in what sense likeness is prior and similarly colored things are "subsequent."

It is said that like things are *given* prior to likeness and equality, and that it takes a special reflection to bring the subsequent "givenness" to us. Only afterward can we "abstract" likeness from previously perceived like things. But this popular explanation remains superficial. The matter at hand cannot be sufficiently clarified as long as we do not bring it into an established radius of inquiry. We might with the same —indeed, with greater—justice say the reverse: Likeness and equality in general are "given" to us beforehand, and only in the light of such givenness can we first ask whether two things are alike in this or that respect. How could an investigation and a determination be initiated with respect to equality if equality were not somehow in view, thus given beforehand? The question remains: What do "given" and "givenness" mean here and in what we said earlier? If we think in Greek fashion, we obtain from the Greek thinkers a primal and lucid illumination of the matter under consideration. They tell us that similarly colored existing things are *proteron pros hēmas,* "they are prior, or previous, particularly with reference to us" who perceive them. What is meant, however, is not that the things must have already "existed" before us, but that when they are viewed in relationship to us, with reference to our everyday perception and observation, they are revealed prior; that is, in their explicit coming to presence as such. Prior to what? Prior to likeness and equality. In the sequence of steps in our perception, we first perceive similar existing things and then *afterward* perhaps, although not necessarily, explicitly perceive likeness and equality. But the unequivocal result is that likeness and equality and all Being are subsequent to beings, and so are not *a priori.* Certainly they are subsequent—that is, subsequent *pros hēmas*—with regard to us, in the manner and sequence in which we find our way to something that is expressly known, pondered, and investigated by us. In the temporal order of explicit comprehension and observation carried out by us, the beings—for example, similar existing things—are *proteron,* prior to likeness and equality. In the order indicated, beings are—now we can also say "with respect to us"—"prior" to Being. The order according to which the previous and the subsequent are determined here is the sequence of *our knowing.*

But the *a priori* is supposed to contain a distinctive determination of *Being.* In its ownmost essence, Being must be defined on its own terms, independently, and not according to what *we* comprehend it and perceive it to be. *Pros hēmas,* with reference to *our* approach to beings, beings are prior as what is known beforehand and often solely, in contrast to Being as the subsequent. If, however, we contemplate whether and to what extent beings and Being *essentially unfold* of themselves, according to their own proper essence, then we are not asking how it stands with Being *pros hēmas,* with regard to the way *we* explicitly grasp Being and beings. Instead, we are asking how it stands with Being insofar as Being "is." The Greeks primally and primordially conceived Being as *physis*—as rising forth from itself and thus essentially self-presenting in upsurgence, self-revealing in the open region. If we inquire into Being with regard to itself as *physis,* therefore *tēi physei,* then the result is: *tēi physei,* Being is *proteron,* before beings, and beings are *hysteron,* subsequent.

The *proteron* has a twofold sense: first, *pros hēmas*—in the order of temporal sequence in which *we* expressly grasp beings and Being; and second, *tēi physei*—in the order in which Being essentially unfolds and beings "are."

How are we to understand this? Basically, we have already provided an answer. In order to achieve clarity here, we need only continue our effort to think every Greek utterance about beings and Being in truly Greek fashion, so far as we can do so in retrospect. For the Greeks (Plato and Aristotle), Being means *ousia,* the presence of what endures in the unconcealed. *Ousia* is an altered interpretation of what initially was named *physis. Tēi physei,* from the point of view of Being itself—that is, viewed from the presence of what endures in the unconcealed, likeness, for example, or equality—is *proteron,* pre-vious [*vor-herig*] compared to things that are alike. Equality already unfolds essentially in the unconcealed; likeness "is" before we, with our perceiving, *ex-*

plicitly view, observe, and indeed consider like things as like. In our comportment toward similar things, equality has already come into view in advance. Equality, Being-alike, as Being—that is, as presence in the unconcealed—is what stands essentially in view, and in such a way that it first brings "view" and "the open" with it, holds them open, and grants visibility of similar beings. Plato therefore says that Being as presence in the unconcealed is *idea,* visibleness. *Because Being is presence of what endures in the unconcealed, Plato can therefore interpret Being,* ousia (*beingness*), *as* idea.* "Idea" is not the name for "representations" that we as "I-subjects" have in our consciousness. That is a modern thought, whereby moreover what is modern is diluted and distorted. *Idea* is the name for Being itself. The "ideas" are *proteron tēi physei,* the pre-vious as presencing.

In order to grasp the Platonic or Greek essence of *idea,* we must eliminate *every* reference to the modern determination of *idea* as *perceptio* and thus the relation of idea to the "subject." The most pertinent aid in doing so is the recollection that in a certain sense *idea* says the same thing as *eidos,* a name that Plato also uses frequently in place of *idea. Eidos* means the "outward appearance." But *we* understand the "outward appearance" of a thing in a modern sense as the perspective that we form for ourselves concerning a thing. Considered in a Greek sense, the "outward appearance" of a being, for example, a house, thus the houselike, is that wherein this being comes to appear; that is, to presence; that is, to Being. The "outward appearance" is not—as the "modern" sense would have it—an "aspect" for a "subject," but that in which the thing in question (the house) has its subsistence and from which it proceeds, because it continuously stands there; that is, *is* there. Viewed in terms of individually existing houses, then, the houselike, the *idea,* is the "universal" vis-à-vis the particular,

* See Martin Heidegger, "Plato's Doctrine of Truth," in *Wegmarken* (Frankfurt am Main: V. Klostermann, 1967), esp. pp. 130–31 and 135–36. The remarks on Plato in these Nietzsche lectures, along with those on Nietzsche in the Plato essay (e.g., pp. 133, 139, and 142), remind us that Heidegger concentrates on precisely these two thinkers during the decade—the 1930s—dedicated to the question of the essence of truth. See Heidegger's "Foreword to All Volumes" in Volume I of this series, p. xvi, and my "Analysis" to that volume, pp. 251–53.

and so *idea* immediately receives the characterization of *koinon,* something common to many individuals.

Because every individual and particular has its presence and subsistence, hence its Being, in its *idea,* the *idea,* as that which confers "Being," is for its part the proper being, *ontōs on.* In contrast, the individual house, and thus every particular being, merely lets the *idea* appear in a particular way, and thus appear in a limited and impaired way. Plato therefore calls individually existing things the *mē on:* that is, not simply nothing, but an *on,* a being, although in a way that it properly ought not to be, precisely the sort of thing to which the full designation *on* must, strictly speaking, be refused—the *mē on. Idea* and only *idea* always distinguishes the being as a being. Consequently, *idea* first and foremost makes its appearance in everything that comes to presence. According to its own essence, Being is the *proteron,* the *a priori,* the prior, although not in the order in which it is grasped by us, but with regard to what first *shows itself to us,* what first of all and on its own comes to presence toward us into the open.

In terms of our theme, the most appropriate German translation for *a priori* is obtained when we call the *a priori* the *Vor-herige* [previous]. *Vor-herige* in the strict sense says two things at once: the *vor* means "beforehand," and *her* means "from out of itself toward us"—the *Vor-herige.* If we think the authentic meaning of *proteron tēi physei,* the *a priori* as the *Vor-herige,* the word loses the misleading "temporal" significance of "prior" by which we understand "temporal" and "time" as ordinary time reckoning and temporal sequence, the succession of beings. But the *a priori,* when rightly conceived as the previous, first reveals its *time*-ly essence in a more profound sense of "time," which our contemporaries do not presently *wish* to see, because they do not see the concealed essential connection between Being and Time.

What is stopping them? Their own structures of thought and their covert entanglement in disordered habits of thought. They do not wish to see because otherwise they would have to admit that the foundations on which they continue to build one form of metaphysics after another *are no foundations at all.*

Through his interpretation of Being as *idea,* Plato was the first to identify Being with the character of the *a priori.* Being is the *proteron tēi physei;* consequently, the *physei onta;* that is, beings, are subsequent. Viewed from the standpoint of beings, Being as the previous not only accrues to the being but also reigns over it, and shows itself as something that lies above beings, *ta physei onta.* The being, as what is defined by Being in the sense of *physis,* can be comprehended only by a knowing and cognizing that thinks the character of such *physis.* The knowledge of beings, of *physei onta,* is *epistēmē physikē.* What becomes the theme of such knowledge of beings is therefore called *ta physika. Ta physika* thus becomes the name for beings. Being, however, in accord with its apriority, lies above beings. In Greek, "above" and "beyond" are called *meta.* Cognition and knowledge of Being is (*proteron tēi physei*) what is essentially *a priori*—the *Vor-herige*—and must therefore, when seen from beings or *physika,* surpass them; that is to say, the knowledge of Being must be *meta ta physika;* it must be metaphysics.

According to the meaning of the matter under consideration, the name *metaphysics* means nothing other than knowledge of the Being of beings, which is distinguished by apriority and which is conceived by Plato as *idea.* Therefore, *meta-physics begins* with Plato's interpretation of Being as *idea.* For all subsequent times, it shapes the essence of Western philosophy, *whose history, from Plato to Nietzsche, is the history of metaphysics.* And because metaphysics begins with the interpretation of Being as "idea," and because that interpretation sets the standard, all philosophy since Plato is "idealism" in the strict sense of the word: Being is sought in the idea, in the idea-like and the ideal. With respect to the founder of metaphysics we can therefore say that all Western philosophy is Platonism. *Metaphysics, idealism,* and *Platonism* mean essentially the same thing. They remain determinative even where countermovements and reversals come into vogue. In the history of the West, Plato has become the prototypal philosopher. Nietzsche did not merely *designate* his own philosophy as the reversal of Platonism. Nietzsche's thinking *was* and *is* everywhere a single and often very discordant dialogue with Plato.

The incontestable predominance of Platonism in Western philosophy ultimately reveals itself in the fact that philosophy *before* Plato, which as our earlier discussions have shown was not yet a metaphysics—that is to say, not a developed metaphysics—is interpreted with reference to Plato and is called pre-Platonic philosophy. Even Nietzsche adopts this point of view when he interprets the teachings of the early thinkers of the West. His remarks about the pre-Platonic philosophers as "personalities," together with his first book, *The Birth of Tragedy,* have strengthened the prejudice still current today that Nietzsche's thought is essentially determined by the Greeks. Nietzsche himself had a much clearer view, and in his final book, *Twilight of the Idols,* expressed himself concerning it in a segment called "What I Owe to the Ancients." Here he says, in section 2 (VIII, 167): "To the Greeks I do not by any means owe similarly strong impressions; and—to come right out with it—they *can* not be for us what the Romans are. One does not *learn* from the Greeks." Nietzsche by that time had clear knowledge of the fact that the metaphysics of will to power conforms only to Roman culture and Machiavelli's *The Prince.** For the thinker of will to power, the only essential figure among the Greeks was the historical thinker Thucydides, who reflects on the history of the Peloponnesian War; thus, in the passage cited earlier, which contains Nietzsche's sharpest words *against* Plato, Nietzsche says, "My *cure* for all Platonism was always Thucydides." But Thucydides, the thinker of *history,* was not able to overcome the Platonism reigning at the basis of Nietzsche's thought. Because Nietzsche's philosophy is metaphysics, and all metaphysics is Platonism, at the end of metaphysics, Being must be thought as value; that is, it must be reckoned as a merely conditioned conditioning of beings. The metaphysical interpretation of Being as value is prefigured in the beginning of metaphysics. For Plato conceives Being as *idea.* The highest of ideas, however—and that means *at the same time* the essence of all ideas—is the *agathon.* Thought in a Greek sense, *agathon* is what *makes suitable,* what befits a being and makes it possible for it to be a being. Being has the

* Cf. Heidegger's formulation in 1936 (Volume I, p. 7), which is more cautious. There he asserts that the "world of the Greeks" remains "decisive for the whole of Nietzsche's life, although in the last years of his wakeful thinking it had to yield some ground to the world of Rome."

character of making possible, is the condition of possibility. To speak with Nietzsche, Being is a *value.* Was Plato therefore the first to think in values? That would be a rash conclusion. The Platonic conception of *agathon* is as essentially different from Nietzsche's concept of value as the Greek conception of man is from the modern notion of the essence of man as subject. But the history of metaphysics proceeds on its path from Plato's interpretation of Being as *idea* and *agathon* to an interpretation of Being as will to power, which posits values and thinks everything as value. Because of it, we today think exclusively in "ideas" and "values." Because of it, the new order of metaphysics is not only intended as a revaluation of all values but is carried out and established as such.

But all these remarks are only descriptions of the fundamental fact that the differentiation of beingness and beings forms the proper framework of metaphysics. The characterization of Being as the *a priori* grants the differentiation a unique coinage. Thus in the various formulations of apriority that are reached in particular fundamental metaphysical positions by virtue of an interpretation of Being, which is at the same time an interpretation of ideas, there is also a guideline for a more accurate delineation of the role that the differentiation of Being and beings always plays, without really being thought as such. Of course, in order to grasp the formulations of the apriority of Being, especially in modern metaphysics, and to think them in the context of the origin of valuative thought, Plato's doctrine of *idea* as the essential character of Being must be more decisively thought through in yet another respect.

25. Being as *Idea,* as *Agathon,* and as Condition

The interpretation of Being as *idea* made immediately compelling the analogy between grasping beings and seeing. The Greeks, particularly since the time of Plato, also conceived knowledge as a kind of seeing and viewing, a state of affairs suggested by the expression "theoretical," an expression that is still common today. In it, the words *thea,* "view," and *horan,* "seeing" (compare with *theater* and *spectacle*) speak. One believes he has given the fact a profound explanation when he assures us that the Greeks were to a special degree visually oriented and were a "visual people." It is easily shown that this popular explanation cannot be an explanation at all. It is supposed to explain why the Greeks explicated the relationship to beings through seeing. But that can have its sufficient reason only in an interpretation of Being which was decisive for the Greeks. Because Being means presence and permanence, "seeing" is especially apt to serve as an explanation for the grasping of what is present and what is permanent. In seeing, we have the perceived "over against" us in a strict sense, provided that an interpretation of beings does not already underlie our seeing. The Greeks did not explain relations with beings through seeing because they were "visual people"; they were "visual people," so to speak, because they experienced the Being of beings as presence and permanence.

This would be the place to discuss the question of why no sense organ, taken separately, can have precedence over the others in the experience of beings. What would remain to be considered is that no sensation is ever able to perceive a being *as* a being. At the end of Book VI of his great dialogue *The Republic,* Plato attempts to elucidate the relationship of knowing to the being that is known by bringing that relationship into correspondence with seeing and being seen. Supposing that the eye is endowed with the capacity to see, and supposing that colors are present in things, the faculty of sight will nonetheless not see, and colors will not become visible, if a third thing is not introduced that according to its essence is destined to make both seeing and visibility possible. That third thing, however, is *to phōs,* light, and the source of light, the sun. It confers a brightness in which things become visible and eyes see.

A corresponding situation prevails in our knowing as grasping a being in its Being; that is, its *idea.* Knowing would not be able to know and the being could not be known—that is, perceived as unconcealed—if there were not some third element that granted to the one knowing his capacity to know, and granted unconcealment to what is known. That third element, however, is *hē tou agathou idea,* "the idea of the Good." The "Good" takes the sun as its image. But the latter not only expends light, which as brightness makes seeing and visibility and thus unconcealment possible. The sun also confers warmth, through which the capacity for seeing and the visible things first *become* "beings," or, in the Greek view, first become the kind of things that can each in its own way come to presence into the unconcealed. Correspondingly, the "idea of the Good" is not only something that confers "unconcealment," on the basis of which knowing and knowledge become possible, but is also what makes knowing, the knower, and beings as beings possible.

Thus it is said of *agathon, esti epekeina tēs ousias presbeiai kai dynamei.* "The Good is above and beyond even Being in worth and power; that is to say, in *basileia,* dominion"—not merely above and beyond unconcealment.

What does Plato mean here by *agathon,* the "Good"? There is much disagreement among commentators about this doctrine of Plato's. In the Christian era, Plato's *agathon* was taken to mean the *summum bonum;* that is, *Deus creator.* Plato, however, speaks of the *idea tou agathou.* He thinks the *agathon* as *idea,* as the idea of ideas, in fact. It is a Greek thought—and here all theological and pseudotheological tricks of interpretation shatter. But now, to be sure, the substantive difficulties of Platonic thought begin to appear: *idea* means Being; beingness, *ousia,* is *idea.* At the same time, however, we hear that *hē idea tou agathou* is *epekeina tēs ousias,* "beyond even beingness." That can only mean that if the *agathon* remains rooted in the basic character of *idea,* then it constitutes the proper essence of beingness.

In what does the essence of beingness consist; that is to say, in what does the essence of the visuality of the idea consist? The "idea" itself gives the answer when Plato calls it *agathon.* We say "the Good" and think of "good" in Christian-moral fashion as meaning well-behaved, decent, in keeping with law and order. For the Greeks, and for Plato too, *agathon* means the suitable, what is good for something and itself makes something else worthwhile. It is the essence of *idea* to make suitable; that is, to make the being as such possible, that it may come to presence into the unconcealed. Through Plato's interpretation of *idea* as *agathon* Being comes to be what makes a being fit *to be* a being. Being is shown in the character of making-possible and conditioning. Here the decisive step for all metaphysics is taken, through which the *a priori* character of Being at the same time receives the distinction of being a condition.

However, we now know that Nietzsche conceives *values* as conditions of the possibility of the will to power; that is, as conditions for the basic character of beings. Nietzsche thinks the beingness of beings essentially as condition, making possible, making suitable, *agathon.* He thinks Being in a thoroughly Platonic and metaphysical way—even as the subverter of Platonism, even as the antimetaphysician.

Then are all those correct who conceive of Plato's *agathon* and the "ideas" in general as values? By no means. Plato thinks Being as *ousia,* as presence and permanence, and as visuality—not as the will to power. It might be tempting to equate *agathon* and *bonum* with value (see *Duns Scotus' Doctrine of Categories and Meaning,* 1916).* The

* Heidegger's *Habilitationsschrift* appears now in Martin Heidegger, *Frühe Schriften* (Frankfurt am Main: V. Klostermann, 1972), pp. 131–353. Heidegger's reference to the work here is mysterious. For the problem of the Good (*bonum*), mentioned only on pp. 158 and 174, is expressly left out of account. The decisive reference—not listed in the volume's index of topics—is the following parenthetical remark on p. 207, n. 1: "In *this* investigation, which has to do solely with *theoretical* objectivity, the *bonum* remains outside of consideration." Heidegger's admission betrays the principal shortcoming of his

equation bypasses in thought what lies between Plato and Nietzsche; bypasses, that is, the entire history of metaphysics. To the extent that Nietzsche conceives of values as conditions—indeed, as conditions of "beings" as such (or, better, as conditions of the actual, of becoming)—he is thinking Being Platonically as beingness. Of course, that still does not explain why Nietzsche thinks these conditions of the being as "values" and thus gives the *a priori* character of Being a different significance as well. With Plato's interpretation of Being as *idea,* philosophy as metaphysics begins. Through Plato's determination of the *essence* of *idea* in the sense of *agathon,* Being and its apriority become explicable as what makes possible, as the condition of possibility. The prototype of valuative thought is completed at the beginning of metaphysics. Value thinking becomes the carrying through of the completion of metaphysics. But valuative thought was every bit as foreign to Plato as the interpretation of man as "subject."

The *a priori* is not a quality of Being, but is itself the pre-vious [*Vor-herige*] in its essence, insofar as the latter must be understood in reference to the *alētheia* that belongs to it, however much it is to be thought in its own terms. But already at the beginning, with Parmenides and Heraclitus, *alētheia* is thought in terms of *noein.* Thus the *a priori* shifts into the differentiation between the previous and the subsequent in knowledge; that is, in perception. At the same time, Being is in a certain sense necessarily experienced as the utmost being [*das Seiendste*]; Being is *ontōs on,* while "beings" become *mē on.*

With regard to such true being (Being taken as a being), the *a priori* immediately becomes a property; that is to say, the truth of the essence

---

second dissertation, a shortcoming intimated in the Introduction and Conclusion of the work itself: although that work falls under the influence of Rickert and Cohen's *Wertphilosophie* (see pp. 200–07 and 352), it does not explore the realms of medieval mysticism, moral theology, and asceticism—that is, the realms of the "Good"—which alone would enable the work to advance from the gray-on-gray of epistemology to the full palette of "the living spirit" in *cultural history* and in *metaphysics* (pp. 147–48 and 347–53). Such an advance would in fact lead back to Aristotle, and thence to Plato and the *agathon,* thus closing the circle of *theoretical* inquiry into *the Good.* The problem of theory, apriority, and the Good later receives prolonged and intense treatment in Martin Heidegger, *Metaphysische Anfangsgründe der Logik im Ausgang von Leibniz,* a lecture course taught during the summer semester of 1928 at Marburg (Frankfurt am Main: V. Klostermann, 1978), pp. 183–87, 235–38, and 284.

of Being as *physis, alētheia,* withdraws into concealment. The "ideas" are installed in "God's" thought and ultimately in *perceptio.* The *idea,* then, is itself something placed in a sequence relative to which it is distinguished as *proteron.* The sequence is determined as the *differentiation* of Being and beings. With regard to the differentiation, and from the viewpoint of Being, Being is prior to beings, because as *idea* it is *what conditions.* Within the differentiation, through which Being has become "visible," beings at the same time become conceptually "prior" with respect to knowledge and cognition.

More essentially thought, however, Being as *physis* does not at all require a "sequence" by which one can decide about its before and after, its previous and subsequent; because it is in itself a pro-ceeding [*Her-vor-gehen*] into its lighting; as going forth it is the fore-going [*Vor-herige*]; it is what essentially unfolds of itself into the lighting and what through the lighting first comes toward man.

This* would be an opportunity to define the fundamental metaphysical position of Aristotle, for which the traditional contrast with Plato is quite insufficient. For Aristotle once again attempted—although by passing through Platonic metaphysics—to think Being in the primordial Greek way and, as it were, to retrace the step Plato had taken with the *idea tou agathou,* whereby beingness receives the character of what conditions and makes possible, *dynamis.* As opposed to that, Aristotle thinks Being in a more Greek way—if such an expression is permissible—by thinking it as *entelecheia* (see "On the Essence and the Concept of *Physis:* Aristotle, *Physics B 1*"). † What this signifies cannot be said in a few words. We can only note that Aristotle is neither a Platonist gone wrong nor a precursor

---

* The present passage appears as an inset in the Neske edition (NII, 228). In the 1953 typescript, which shows some variations of the text as reproduced in Neske, the passage is indented, although without brackets. In the holograph of the 1940 lecture course, the passage appears on a loose sheet inserted into the lecture text, and appears there in brackets. The implication is that the passage was not read as part of the lecture course but is a contemporaneous reference to Heidegger's then recently completed work on Aristotle's concept of *physis.*

† Heidegger adds in brackets the bibliographical reference to "Biblioteca 'Il Pensiero,' 1960." The essay, composed in 1939, appears now in *Wegmarken,* pp. 309–71. See the English translation by Thomas J. Sheehan, "On the Being and Conception of *Physis* in Aristotle's *Physics* B, 1," *Man and World,* 1976, 9(3), 219–70.

of Thomas Aquinas. Nor is his philosophical accomplishment summed up in the nonsense often ascribed to him, that he fetched Plato's ideas from their being-in-themselves and lodged them in the things themselves. Despite its distance from the beginning of Greek philosophy, Aristotle's metaphysics is in essential respects a kind of swing back toward the beginning within Greek thought. That Nietzsche never—apart from his thoughts about the essence of tragedy—established an intimate relationship with Aristotle's metaphysics that would be equivalent to his perdurant relationship with Plato, is something that would merit our thinking it through in its essential grounds.

26. The Interpretation of Being as *Idea*, and Valuative Thought

According to Plato's doctrine, Being is *idea,* visuality, presence as outward appearance. What stands in such outward appearance becomes and is a being insofar as it comes to presence there. However, because the highest of ideas is at the same time conceived as *agathon,* the essence of all such ideas undergoes a decisive interpretation. The idea as such, that is, the Being of beings, receives the character of *agathoeides,* of what makes something suitable for . . . ; namely, what makes the being suitable to be a being. Being receives the essential trait of what makes possible. From that point on—that is, from the beginning of metaphysics—a peculiar ambiguity enters into the interpretation of Being. In a certain sense, Being is pure presence, and yet it is at the same time the making possible of beings. Thus as soon as the being itself presses forward and draws all human comportment to itself and claims it, Being must retreat in favor of beings. Of course, Being still remains what makes possible, and in that sense is the previous, the *a priori.* But the *a priori,* although it cannot be denied, by no means has the weight of *what* it continually makes possible, the beings themselves. The *a priori,* in its beginning and essence the pre-vious, thus becomes an addendum, which in view of the hegemony of beings is barely tolerated as the condition for the possibility of beings.

The ambiguity of Being as Idea (pure presence and making-possible) also announces itself in the fact that through the interpretation of Being (*physis*) as *idea* the reference to "seeing" evokes human knowing. As the visual, Being is presence, but at the same time is what man brings before his eyes.

How is it, then, if there comes a moment when man frees himself to himself, as to the one being who represents by bringing everything before himself, as the tribunal of continuance? Then the *idea* becomes the *perceptum* of a *perceptio;* becomes what the representing of man brings before itself, precisely as what makes the to-be-represented possible in its representedness. Now the essence of *idea* changes from visuality and presence to representedness for and through the one who is representing. Representedness as beingness makes what is represented possible as the being. Representedness (Being) becomes the condition of the possibility of what is represented and presented-to and thus comes to stand; that is, the condition of the possibility of the object. Being—Idea—becomes a condition over which the one representing, the subject, has disposal and must have disposal if objects are going to be able to stand over against him. Being is conceived as a system of necessary conditions with which the subject, precisely with regard to the being as the objective, must reckon in advance on the basis of his relations with beings. *Conditions* with which one must necessarily *reckon*—how could one not eventually call them "values," "the" values, and account for them *as* values?

The essential origin of valuative thought in the original essence of metaphysics, and of the interpretation of Being as *idea,* and *idea* as *agathon,* has now been clarified.

We see that in the history of the provenance of valuative thought the transformation of *idea* into *perceptio* becomes decisive. Only through the metaphysics of subjectivity is the at first largely veiled and reserved essential trait of *idea*—the trait of being something that makes possible and conditions—transposed into the free region and then put into uninhibited play. What is innermost in the history of modern metaphysics consists in the process through which Being preserves the uncontested essential trait of being the condition of the possibility of beings; that is, in a modern sense, the possibility of what is represented; that is, of what stands over against us; that is, objects. Kant's metaphysics takes the decisive step in that process. His metaphysics is *the midpoint* within modern metaphysics, not only in terms of temporal reckoning but also in its essential history, in the way it takes up the beginning in Descartes, as altered in the dialogue with Leibniz. Kant's fundamental metaphysical position is expressed in the principle that Kant himself defined in the *Critique of Pure Reason* as the highest principle in his grounding of metaphysics (A 158, B 197). The principle states, "The conditions of the *possibility of experience* in general are at the same time conditions of the *possibility of the objects of experience.*"

Explicitly and definitively named here as the "conditions of possibility" are what Aristotle and Kant call *categories.* According to our earlier explanation of the term, what is meant by the categories are the definitions of the essence of beings as such; that is to say, beingness or Being—what Plato comprehends as "ideas." According to Kant, Being is the condition of the possibility of beings, is their beingness. Corresponding to the basic modern notion of representedness, beingness and Being mean objectiveness (objectivity). The highest basic principle of Kant's metaphysics says that the conditions of the possibility of representing what is represented are also—that is to say, are nothing else but—conditions of the possibility of what is represented. They constitute representedness. But this is the essence of objectivity, and the latter is the essence of Being. The basic principle says: Being is representedness. But representedness is presentedness-to, in such a way that the one representing can be sure of what is thus brought into place and brought to stand. Security is sought in *certitude.* Certitude defines the essence of *truth.* The ground of truth is representing; that is, "thinking" in the sense of *ego cogito;* that is, of *cogito me cogitare.* Truth as representedness of the object, objectivity, has its ground in subjectivity, in self-representing representation; but this is due to the fact that representing itself is the essence of Being.

Man *is,* however, in that he represents in this particular way; that is, as a creature of reason. Logic, as the unfolding of the essence of "Logos" in the sense of unifying representing, is the essence of beingness and the ground of truth as objectivity.

Kant does not simply repeat what Descartes had already thought before him. Kant is the first to think transcendentally, and he explicitly and consciously conceptualizes what Descartes posited as the beginning of inquiry against the horizon of the *ego cogito.* In Kant's interpretation of Being, the beingness of beings is for the first time expressly thought as a "condition of possibility," thus clearing the way for the development of value thinking in Nietzsche's metaphysics. Nevertheless, Kant does not yet think Being as value. But neither does he any longer think Being in Plato's sense, as *idea.*

Nietzsche defines the essence of value as the condition of the preservation and enhancement of will to power, and in such a way that such conditions are posited by will to power itself. Will to power is the fundamental character of beings as a whole, the "Being" of beings, and precisely in the broad sense which recognizes becoming too as Being, if indeed becoming "is not nothing."

Metaphysical thinking in values—that is to say, the interpretation of Being as a condition of possibility—is prepared in its essential features through various stages: through the beginning of metaphysics with Plato (*ousia* as *idea, idea* as *agathon*), through Descartes' transition (*idea* as *perceptio*), and through Kant (Being as the condition of the possibility of the objectivity of objects). Nonetheless, these remarks are not sufficient to make the metaphysical origin of value thinking wholly visible even in basic outline.

Of course, it has become clear to what extent Being was able to accede to the role of "making possible" and of "condition of possibility." But why and how do the "conditions of possibility" become values; how does beingness come to be a value? Why does everything that conditions and everything that makes possible (meaning, aim, purpose, unity, order, truth) slip into the character of value? This question seems to render itself superfluous as soon as we remember that Nietzsche interprets the essence of value as a *condition.* "Value" is then but another name for "condition of possibility," for *agathon.* But even as another name it still requires a justification for its emergence and for the preeminence it has everywhere in Nietzsche's thought. A name always hides within itself an interpretation. Nietzsche's concept of value certainly thinks the conditional, but not only the conditional, and no longer in the sense of the Platonic *agathon* and the Kantian "condition of possibility."

In "value," what is valued and evaluated is thought as such. Holding-something-for-true and taking and positing something as a "value" is estimating. But estimating also means assessing and comparing. We often think that "estimating" (for example, in estimating distances), as opposed to an exact account, is merely an approximate discernment and determination of a connection between things, relationships, or people. In truth, however, estimating underlies every "accounting" (in the narrow sense of a numerical e-"valuation").

The essential estimating is reckoning, whereby we grant the word the particular meaning that reveals a fundamental kind of behavior: reckoning as to reckon *on* something, to "count" on a man, to be certain of his allegiance and readiness; reckoning as to reckon *with* something, to take the force of its impact and its scope into consideration. Reckoning means positing that in accordance with which everything we reckon on and with is to play a role. Reckoning thus understood is a self-imposed positing of conditions in such a way that the conditions condition the Being of beings. The positing of conditions *is* as reckoning and certifies itself *as* reckoning in the midst of beings as a whole, and thus certifies itself and its relation *to* beings *from out of* beings. In that way, reckoning, when it is understood essentially, comes to be the representing and presenting-to of the condition of the possibility of beings; that is, of Being. Such essential "reckoning" first makes planning and reckoning in a purely "calculative" sense both possible and necessary. Essential reckoning is the basic character of estimating, through which everything evaluated and valued as conditioning has the character of "value."

But when does the representing of the Being of beings come to be an essential reckoning and estimating? When do "conditions" come to be what is evaluated and valued; that is, come to be values? Only when the representing of beings as such comes to be that representing which absolutely posits itself on itself and has to constitute of itself and for itself all the conditions of Being; only when the basic character of beings has become the sort of essence that itself demands reckoning and estimating as an essential requirement for the Being of beings. That happens when the basic character of beings is revealed as will to power. Will to power is the essence of willing. Nietzsche writes in 1884: "In every willing there is *estimating*" (XIII, note 395). Earlier we showed in terms of the fullness of the essence of will to power to what extent will to power is of itself a value estimating. Now, from the essence of estimating as absolute reckoning, its essential affinity to will to power has emerged.

27. The Projection of Being as Will to Power

How does the projection of Being as will to power come about? Granted that every projection of Being is cast in such a way that Being joins what essentially unfolds to its truth, then the response to the question we have raised is tantamount to the experience of the most concealed history of Being. We are ill-prepared for such an experience. The answer we are looking for can only be replaced by comments that are barely distinguishable from a historiological report of various interpretations of the Being of beings, while the nature and intent of these remarks is to carry out a historical meditation on the history of the truth of beings.

In the Platonic interpretation of the beingness of beings as *idea,* there is no hint of an experience of Being as "will to power." But even Descartes' grounding of metaphysics on representing as the *sub-iectum* merely seems to imply a revision of the Greek *idea* into the Latin *idea* as *perceptio,* and seems to think Being as representedness in which certitude becomes essential, although here too the character of will to power fails to appear. Kant's doctrine of the objectivity of objects unequivocally shows how the projection of beingness as representedness seeks to develop the essence of the latter and still knows nothing of a will to power. Transcendental subjectivity is the inner presupposition for the absolute subjectivity of Hegel's metaphysics, in which the "absolute idea" (the self-appearing of absolute representing) constitutes the essence of actuality.*

* In order to transpose the tone of the word *Wirklichkeit,* heretofore rendered as "reality," out of all empiricist and positivist registers, we will from now on render it as "actuality." The "action" of that word also rescues a bit of the related German words *Wirkung,* "effect" or "impact," and *Werk,* "work."

Does not Nietzschean "will to power" therefore descend on metaphysics without historical precedent as an arbitrary explanation of beings as a whole? But let us recall that Nietzsche himself explained Descartes' principle on the basis of the will to truth, and the will to truth as a kind of will to power. Consequently, Descartes' metaphysics is indeed a metaphysics of will to power, albeit an unwitting one. The question, however, does not aim to ask whether the will to certitude can be interpreted as will to power and thus be historically counted as a preliminary stage of the will to power. The question remains whether Being as representedness, according to its essential import, is a preliminary stage of the will to power, which, experienced as the basic character of beings, first permits certitude to be explained as a will to fixation, the latter to be explained as a form of will to power. "Idea," representedness, objectivity contain nothing of the will to power in themselves.

But is not representedness what it is in and through representing? Hasn't representing become visible as the fundamental essence of the *subjectivity* of the *subiectum?* Certainly, but in an essentially complete way only when we know to what extent subjectivity is not only the determining ground for beings as objectivity and objectiveness, but also at the same time the ground of the essence of beings in their actuality. Only when we consider beingness as actuality does the connection with effect and impact reveal itself; that is, the connection with the empowering of power as the essence of will to power. Consequently, an inner relationship obtains between beingness as subjectivity and beingness as will to power. We need only ponder the fact that the metaphysics of subjectivity has its decisive beginning in the metaphysics of Leibniz. Every being is *subiectum,* a monad. Every being is also an *obiectum,* an object determined by a *subiectum.* The beingness of beings becomes ambiguous through subjectivity. Being means objectivity and at the same time actuality; one stands for the other, and both belong together. The essence of actuality is effectiveness (*vis*); the essence of objectivity as representedness is visuality (*idea*). Leibniz brings the interpretation of *subiectum* (*substantia* as *monas*) in the sense of the *vis primitiva activa* (effectiveness) into contrapuntal relation with the medieval differentiation of *potentia* and *actus,* in such a way of course that *vis* is neither *potentia* nor *actus,* but is in an original way both at once—as the unity of *perceptio* and *appetitus.* The differentiation of *potentia* and *actus* points back to Aristotle's distinction between *dynamis* and *energeia.* Furthermore, Leibniz himself often explicitly indicates the connection between the *vis primitiva activa* and the "entelechy" of Aristotle.*

Thus it seems we have found the historical (or merely historiological?) thread along which we can pursue the historical provenance of the projection of beings as will to power. We have up to now comprehended metaphysics too exclusively as Platonism and have as a result undervalued the no less essential historical influence of Aristotle's metaphysics. Aristotle's basic metaphysical concept, *energeia,* "energy," points "energetically" enough toward the will to power. "Energy" pertains to power. But the question remains whether "energy" so understood touches even in the vaguest way on the essence of Aristotle's *energeia.* The question remains whether Leibniz' own reference to the connection between *vis* and *energeia* did not transform the essence of *energeia* in the direction of modern subjectivity, after Aristotelian *energeia* had already received its first reinterpretation through the medieval notion of *actus.* But what remains more essential than insight into these transformations and the "impact"—sustained by them—of Aristotelian thought on Western metaphysics is the fact that originally embraced in the essence of *energeia* is what later, as objectivity and actuality, separates and then comes together in an interplay, and is consolidated as the essential determinations of beingness in modern metaphysics. The essential historical connection between *energeia* and will to power is both more hidden and richer than it might appear from

* Twelve years before his lectures on nihilism, during the second "logic" course at Marburg (summer semester 1928), Heidegger had treated the question of Leibnizian *vis* in some detail. (As an exercise in interpretation of texts, this last Marburg lecture course is perhaps Heidegger's supreme effort of the 1920s.) The text of that course has been ably edited—as far as one can determine without access to the original notes—by Klaus Held as vol. 26 of the *Gesamtausgabe* (bibliographical information on p. 170 n.). On the monad as *vis primitiva,* see section 5a, esp. pp. 96–105; for Leibniz' explicit references to Aristotelian *entelecheia,* see pp. 104–05; and for *vis* as representational, *vor-stellend*—that is to say, for the relationship between *appetitus* and *perceptio,* which is so essential for Heidegger's interpretation—see section 5c, pp. 111–22.

the superficial correspondence of "energy" (force) and "power." We can now give only a rough indication of what is involved.

Through Leibniz all being becomes "subjectival"—that is, in itself eager to represent, and thus effective. Immediately and mediately (through Herder), Leibniz' metaphysics shaped German "humanism" (Goethe) and Idealism (Schelling and Hegel). Because Idealism above all grounded itself on transcendental subjectivity (Kant) and because at the same time it thought in a Leibnizian manner, the beingness of beings, through a peculiar melding and intensification in the direction of the absolute, was thought in Idealism as both objectivity and effectiveness. Effectiveness (actuality) is conceived as knowing will (or willful knowing); that is to say, as "reason" and "spirit." Schopenhauer's main work, *The World as Will and Representation,* with its altogether superficial and scanty analysis of Platonic and Kantian philosophy, gathers up in one all the basic directions of the Western interpretation of beings as a whole, although everything there is uprooted and cast down to a level of understanding befitting the positivism then on the rise. Schopenhauer's main work became for Nietzsche the proper "source" for the shape and direction of his thought. Nonetheless, Nietzsche did not take the projection of beings as "will" from Schopenhauer's "books." Schopenhauer could "captivate" the young Nietzsche only because the fundamental experiences of the awakening thinker found their first inevitable supports in such metaphysics.

Again, the basic experiences of the thinker never stem from his disposition or from his educational background. They take place in terms of Being's essentially occurring truth. To be transposed into the domain of truth constitutes what we usually know exclusively in a historical-biographical and anthropological-psychological way as the "existence" of a philosopher.

That the Being of beings becomes operative as will to power is not the result of the emergence of Nietzsche's metaphysics. Rather, Nietzsche's thought has to plunge into metaphysics because Being radiates its own essence as will to power; that is, as the sort of thing that in the history of the truth of beings must be grasped through the projection as will to power. The fundamental occurrence of that history is ultimately the transformation of beingness into subjectivity.

We are inclined to ask here whether absolute subjectivity, in the sense of limitless reckoning, is the ground for the interpretation of beingness as will to power. Or, on the contrary, is the projection of beingness as will to power the ground for the possibility of the dominance of the absolute subjectivity of the "body," through which the proper effects of actuality are first liberated? In truth, this either-or remains inadequate. Both are valid, yet neither is accurate, and even both together do not attain to the history of Being, which grants to the whole history of metaphysics what essentially unfolds as its proper historicity.

We would like to develop a sense for just this one thing: that Being itself essentially unfolds as will to power and therefore demands of thinking that it perfect itself in the direction of that unfolding as estimating; that is, that it absolutely reckon with, on, and in terms of conditions; that is, that it think in values.

But we must also keep something else in mind; namely, that Being as will to power arises from the determination of the essence of *idea* and therefore itself entails the differentiation of Being and beings, but in such a way that the differentiation, unexamined as such, forms the basic structure of metaphysics. Insofar as we do not trivialize metaphysics as a doctrine, we experience it as the articulation of the differentiation of Being and beings as "enjoined" by Being. But even where "Being" is interpreted in such a way that it rarifies into an empty but necessary abstraction, so that it then appears in Nietzsche (VIII, 78) as the "last wisp of evaporating reality" (that is to say, of the Platonic *ontōs on*), the differentiation of Being and beings reigns—not in the thought processes of the thinker, but in the essence of the history in which he himself is thinking and in which he is and has to be.*

---

* Cf. Heidegger's remarks during the summer semester of 1935 (in *Einführung in die Metaphysik,* p. 27; English translation, p. 29). In retrospect, Nietzsche's caustic reduction of Being to a "vapor and a fallacy" appears to have provoked, almost singlehandedly, Heidegger's ensuing lecture courses (1936–1940) on Nietzsche.

28. The Differentiation Between Being and beings, and the Nature of Man

We cannot withdraw from the differentiation of Being and beings, not even when we ostensibly refuse to think metaphysically. Everywhere we go we are continually moving on the path of the differentiation, a path that carries us from beings to Being and from Being to beings, in every comportment toward beings of whatever kind and rank, whatever certitude and accessibility they may have. Therein lies an essential insight into what Kant says about "metaphysics": "Thus in all men, as soon as their reason has become ripe for speculation, there has always existed and will always continue to exist some kind of metaphysics" (Introduction to the second edition of the *Critique of Pure Reason,* B 21). Kant is speaking about reason, about its ripening into "speculation"; that is, he is speaking about theoretical reason, representation, insofar as it undertakes to enjoin the beingness of all beings.

What Kant says here about metaphysics as a developed and self-developing "speculation" of reason, to wit, that it is a "natural disposition" (B 22), is wholly valid for that on which all metaphysics is grounded. That ground is the differentiation of Being and beings. Perhaps such differentiation is the proper core of the disposition of human nature toward metaphysics. But then the differentiation would actually be something "human"! Why shouldn't the differentiation be something "human"? That would provide the best and the ultimate explanation for the possibility and necessity of the demand voiced by Nietzsche—that philosophers finally act on the humanization of all things.

If the natural metaphysical disposition of man, the very core of that disposition, is the differentiation of Being and beings, in such a way that metaphysics arises from it, then by referring back to the differentiation we have reached the origin of metaphysics and at the same time attained a more original concept of metaphysics.

What we have just been examining in an indeterminate way, the relations of man with beings, is at bottom nothing other than the differentiation of Being and beings, which belongs to man's natural disposition. Only because man differentiates in such a way can he comport himself toward beings in the light of differentiated Being; that is, sustain relations with beings; which is to say, be metaphysically determined and defined by metaphysics.

However, *is* the differentiation of Being and beings the natural disposition—indeed the core of the natural disposition—of man? But what is man? In what does human "nature" consist? What does "nature" mean here, and what does "man" mean? Whence and in what way should human nature be defined? Doubtless, we must accomplish a delineation of the essence of man's nature if we wish to prove the disposition toward metaphysics in it, if we are going to identify the differentiation of Being and beings as the very core of that disposition.

But could we ever determine the essence of man (his nature) without heeding the differentiation of Being and beings? Does the differentiation occur only as a consequence of man's nature, or is man's nature and essence first and foremost determined on the basis of and out of the differentiation? In the second case, the differentiation would not be an "act" that man, already existing, also performs among others; rather, man could be man only insofar as he maintained himself in the differentiation, because he is sustained by it. Then the essence of man must have been built on a "differentiation." Is this not a fantastic thought? Is it utterly fantastic for the reason that the differentiation itself, essentially nebulous, is, as it were, a castle in the air?

All we know is that here we are approaching a domain, or perhaps only the frontier, of a decisive question which philosophy hitherto has shunned—that is to say, which it really could not even shun, because that would mean that it had already encountered the question of differentiation. We suspect, perhaps, that behind the confusion and noise broadcast by the "problem" of anthropomorphism looms the decisive question, which, like every question of its kind, conceals in itself a peculiar abundance of questions linked to it.

We ask the question once again within the limits of what is most germane to our task:

Is all metaphysics grounded in the differentiation of Being and beings?

What is that differentiation?

Is the differentiation grounded in the nature of man, or is the nature of man grounded in the differentiation?

Is even this either-or inadequate?

What does grounding mean here in each case?

Why are we thinking here in terms of grounds and asking about the "ground"?

Is not the groundable also an essential feature of Being? Thus, in all these formulations of the question, are we asking about man's relation to Being, over which no question can vault, but which nonetheless has not yet been questioned in any question? For we always find ourselves immediately forced to take man as a given, as a nature at hand on which we then impose the relation to Being. Corresponding to that is the inevitability of anthropomorphism, which even gets its metaphysical justification from the metaphysics of subjectivity. Doesn't the essence of metaphysics thereby become inviolable as the domain into which no philosophical inquiry may trespass? At best, metaphysics can relate itself to itself and thus for its part finally satisfy the essence of subjectivity.

Such meditation of metaphysics upon metaphysics would then be "metaphysics of metaphysics." In fact, such a thing is mentioned by the thinker who in the history of modern metaphysics occupies a position between Descartes and Nietzsche, a position that cannot be circumscribed in a few words.

Kant traces metaphysics as a "natural disposition" back to the "nature of man." As if the "nature of man" were unequivocally determined! As if the truth of that determination and the grounding of the truth were utterly unquestionable! We might of course now point out that Kant himself (see *Kant and the Problem of Metaphysics,* 4th ed., pp. 199 ff.) wishes to refer the basic questions of metaphysics and philosophy back to the question "What is man?" Through a properly conducted interpretation of Kantian philosophy, we might even show that Kant analyzed the "inner nature" of man and thereby made use of the differentiation of Being and beings, that he claimed something as the essence of human reason which points in the direction of the differentiation. For Kant proves how human understanding in advance, *a priori,* thinks in categories, and that through these an objectivity of objects and an "objective knowledge" are made possible.

And yet Kant does not ask what the reason is for our thinking in categories. He takes such thinking as a fact of human reason; that is to say, of human nature, which even for Kant is defined in the old traditional sense by the designation *Homo est animal rationale*—"Man is a rational animal."

But, since Descartes, reason has been conceived as *cogitatio.* Reason is the faculty of "principles," a faculty that represents in advance what defines everything representable in its representedness, to wit, the Being of beings. Reason would then be the faculty of the differentiation of Being and beings. And, because reason characterizes the essence of man, while according to modern thought man is the subject, the differentiation of Being and beings as well as the faculty for the differentiation is revealed as a property and perhaps the basic constituent of subjectivity. For the essence of that particular *subiectum* which is distinguished at the beginning of modern metaphysics is representation itself in its full essence: "reason" (*ratio*) is merely another name for *cogitatio.*

Even with these reflections we still have not made any progress. We have entered the realm of a question that is still undecided, indeed is yet to be asked, a question that, briefly put, asks: Is the differentiation of Being and beings grounded on the nature of man, so that his nature can be specified from the differentiation, or is the nature of man grounded on the differentiation? In the second instance, the differentiation itself would no longer be anything "human" and could not be subsumed under a "faculty of man" either in "potency" or in "act." That kind of arrangement became ever more current in modern thought, so that it finally proclaimed anthropomorphism or "biologism," or whatever other name this sort of thinking goes under, as absolute truth evident even to the most thoughtless.

How and in what respect we achieve a more original concept of metaphysics depends on our mastering the decisive question just referred to. Only now is it clear what such a concept of metaphysics is searching for: not for an improved or more "radical" concept, as if "radicalism" were always inherently more significant. Rather, we are seeking to advance into the ground of metaphysics because we wish to experience in it the differentiation of Being and beings, or more precisely, what the differentiation as such sustains in itself, namely, the relation of man to Being.

We therefore can ask the decisive question correctly only if we have first experienced in a more meaningful way what we have termed the "differentiation of Being and beings."

29. Being as the Void and as Abundance

We said that the differentiation was the path that at all times and places in every comportment and every attitude leads from beings to Being and from Being to beings. We formulate this in an image that prompts us to imagine that beings and Being are found to stand on opposite banks of a stream we cannot and perhaps never could identify. For where are we going to find a basis for this? Or, to stay with the image, could something that neither is a being nor belongs to Being somehow flow between beings and Being? But let us not permit the unreliability of "images" to keep us from the experience of what we call the *differentiation*. Above all, let us now consider more decisively what has engaged us in the foregoing deliberations ever since we began discussing "nihilism."

We speak about "Being," refer to "Being," hear the word, and repeat it again and again. It is almost like a passing remark. *Almost,* but not entirely. There always remains an aura of knowledge—even when we merely append to the echoing word a reminder that we are "thinking" something with it. Of course, what we understand by it is something altogether tenuous and vague, but in the next breath it leaps out at us as most familiar. "Being" [*das Sein*], viewed as a part of speech, is a substantive formed by making the verb *sein* into a noun, by placing *das* before it. The verb *sein* is the "infinitive" of "is," which is all too familiar to us. We do not need a lecture on nihilism and its frequent use of the noun *das Sein* in order to perceive at once that with every remark we utter we *still* more frequently and continuously, in every usage of the word "is," say *Sein.* "Is" drifts about as the most threadbare word in language, although it sustains all saying, and not only in the sense of spoken language. The "is" speaks even in every tacit comportment toward beings. Everywhere, even where we do not speak, we still comport ourselves toward beings as such and to the sort of thing that "is," that is in a particular way, that is not yet or is no longer, or that simply is not.

The uniformity of this used-up though often unused "is" conceals a rarely considered abundance behind the sameness of the sound and shape of the word.* We say, "This man is from Schwabenland"; "This book is yours"; "The enemy is in retreat"; "Red is portside"; "God is"; "There is a flood in China"; "The cup is silver"; "The earth is"; "The farmer is (as we say in dialect) afield"; "The potato bug is in the patch"; "The lecture is in Room 5"; "The dog is in the garden"; "This is a devil of a man"; "Above all peaks / is repose."

In each case, the "is" has a different meaning and range in what it says. "The man is from Schwabenland" means that he *comes from* there. "The book is yours" signifies: *belongs* to you. "The enemy is in retreat" says that he *has set out* in retreat. "Red is portside" means that portside is what the color *signifies*. "God is"; we experience Him as *really present*. "There is a flood in China"; it *prevails*. "The cup is of silver"; it *consists* of. "The farmer is afield"; he *has taken up his sojourn there*. "The potato bug is in the patch"; *has spread* there in its harmfulness. "The lecture is in Room 5"; *will take place*. "The dog is in the garden"; *is rooting about*. "This is a devil of a man"; he *behaves* like someone possessed by a demon. "Above all peaks / is repose"; repose *"is found"? "will take place"? "comes to rest"? "prevails"?* or *"lies"?* or *"holds sway"?* No paraphrase will work here. Nonetheless, the same "is" speaks here—simple, and at the same time irreplaceable, uttered in those few lines that Goethe wrote in pencil on the window-frame of a wooden hut on the Kickelhahn at Ilmenau (see the letter to Zelter, September 4, 1831).†

Yet it is remarkable that in explaining the familiar "is" we should waver and hesitate before this phrase of Goethe's, and finally give it up

---

* Many of the following examples—and the issue they are all meant to illustrate—derive from Heidegger's 1935 lecture course, "Introduction to Metaphysics." See *Einführung in die Metaphysik,* p. 68; English translation, pp. 74–75.

† Goethe's poem, written on the evening of September 6, 1780, and later designated as a second "Wanderer's Nocturne," reads as follows:

entirely and simply repeat the words once again. "Above all peaks / is repose." We attempt no explanation of the "is," not because it would be too complicated, difficult, or indeed hopeless to understand, but because the "is" is so simply spoken here, *still more* simply than every other kind of familiar "is" that is interspersed carelessly and constantly in our everyday speech. But what is simple in the "is" of Goethe's poem is far removed from a void indeterminacy that cannot be grasped. The simplicity of rare abundance speaks in the poem. The series of different statements in which we were able to interpret immediately each "is" from a particular point of view also testifies to this same abundance, although in a different way and only as a rough indication. The uniformity of "is" and "to be" thus proves to be a gross illusion that simply fastens on the identical sound and spelling of the word. Nor is it enough anymore to offer here the assurance that "is" belongs among the "multivalent" words; for it is not merely a question

---

Über allen Gipfeln
Ist Ruh,
In allen Wipfeln
Spürest du
Kaum einen Hauch;
Die Vögelein schweigen im Walde.
Warte nur, balde
Ruhest du auch.

In translation:

Above all peaks
Is repose,
In the treetops
You trace
Scarcely a breath;
The songbirds are silent in the wood.
Only wait, for soon
You too will repose.

See the commentary by Erich Trunz and Elizabeth M. Wilkinson in Goethe, *Gedichte* (Munich: C. H. Beck, 1974) pp. 533–34; the poem itself appears on p. 142.

Goethe's letter to Zelter of September 4, 1831, tells of his return that summer to the hut, where he found the inscription he had made a half-century earlier. "After so many years one beheld: the enduring, and the obliterated. What had gone well returned to cheer me, what had gone awry was forgotten, overcome." See *Goethes Briefe* (Hamburg: Chr. Wegner, 1967), IV, 442.

of varied meanings. An abundance in the sayability of Being is indicated that first makes possible what we, looking at it logically and grammatically, tend to account for in terms of "multivalence." What is under discussion here are not the words *is* and *to be,* but what they say, what comes to words in them: Being. Once more we stop at the same point in our meditation: "Being," indefinite and trivialized—and yet understandable and understood. We could put it to the test by taking a poll to establish what you listeners thought of each time the "is" was spoken; but these results would only confirm that in the "is" "Being" passes like a fleeting echo, while at the same time touching us in some respect, and saying something essential—perhaps what is most essential.

However, should we infer from the many meanings and many possible interpretations of the "is" an abundance of essence in Being? Does not the manifoldness of the "is" stem from the fact that in the statements just quoted various kinds of beings are contextually meant: the man, the book, the enemy, God, China, the cup, the earth, the farmer, the dog? Must we not rather conclude the opposite of all this: Because the "is" and "Being" are in themselves indeterminate and empty, they can lie ready for various kinds of filling? The putative manifoldness of definite meanings in the "is" therefore proves to be the opposite of what was supposed to be shown. Being must keep its meaning. If we restrict ourselves exclusively to the literal meaning of the words *is* and *to be,* then even this literal meaning must with all its utter vacuity and indeterminacy nonetheless have the kind of univocity that ing. If we restrict ourselves exclusively to the literal meaning of the words *is* and *to be,* then even this literal meaning must with all its utter vacuity and indeterminacy nonetheless have the kind of univocity that of itself permits a transformation into manifoldness. But the celebrated "universal" significance of "Being" is not the reified emptiness of a huge receptacle into which everything capable of transformation can be thrown. What misleads us in the direction of this notion is our long-accustomed way of thinking that thinks "Being" as the most universal determination of all, and that therefore can admit the manifold only as the sort of thing that fills the vast empty shell of the most universal concept.

Instead, we wish to concentrate on something else. We think "Being" and the "is" in a peculiar indeterminacy and *at the same time* experience them in a fullness. This Janus-head [*Doppelgesicht*] of "Being" might perhaps put us on the trail of Being's essence, and in any case prevent our employing abstraction, the simplest of all instruments of thought, to explain what is most essential in everything to be thought and experienced. But now we must also elucidate the duplicity of "Being" beyond a mere reference to it, without succumbing to the danger of substituting for abstraction an equally popular instrument of thought as a final answer, to wit, dialectic. Dialectic is always introduced the moment opposition is mentioned.

Being is what is emptiest and at the same time it is abundance, out of which all beings, known and experienced, or unknown and yet to be experienced, are endowed each with the essential form of its own *individual* Being.

Being is most universal, encountered in every being, and is therefore most common; it has lost every distinction, or never possessed any. At the same time, Being is the most singular, whose uniqueness cannot be attained by any being whatever. Over against every being that might stand out, there is always another just like it; that is, another being, no matter how varied their forms may be. But Being has no counterpart. What stands over against Being is the nothing, and perhaps even that is still in essence subject to Being and to Being alone.

Being is most intelligible, so that we pay no heed to the effortless way we maintain ourselves in the comprehension of it. The most intelligible is at the same time what is least comprehended and is apparently incomprehensible. On what basis would we comprehend it? What "is there" outside of it from which we could attribute a determination to it? The nothing is least of all suitable for a determining, because it "is" indeterminate, "is" indeterminateness itself. The most intelligible defies all intelligibility.

Being is most in use; it is what we call on in every action and from every standpoint. For we everywhere hold ourselves in being and comport ourselves toward beings. Being is used up and yet at the same time is unthought in its advent at every moment.

Being is what is most reliable; it never unsettles us with doubt. We occasionally wonder whether this or that being is or is not; we often consider whether a particular being is one way or another. Being, without which we can never wonder about beings in any respect whatsoever, offers us a reliance whose reliability cannot be surpassed anywhere. And yet Being offers us no ground and no basis—as beings do—to which we can turn, on which we can build, and to which we can cling. Being is the rejection [*Ab-sage*] of the role of such grounding; it renounces all grounding, is abyssal [*ab-gründig*].

Being is the most forgotten, so boundlessly forgotten that the very forgottenness is sucked into its own vortex. We all habitually hasten toward beings; scarcely anyone ponders Being. If he does, then the emptiness of what is most universal and intelligible absolves him from the commitment he had momentarily considered making. But what is most forgotten is at the same time most in remembering, which alone allows us to enter and inhabit the past, present, and future.

Being is the most said, not only because the "is" and all the forms of the verb "to be" are perhaps most often expressed, but because in *every* verb, even when its conjugated forms do not use the word "Being," Being is nonetheless said. Every verb, and not just every verb but also every substantive and adjective, all words and articulations of words, say Being. What is most said is at the same time the most reticent in the special sense that it keeps its essence silent, perhaps is reticence itself. No matter how loudly and how often we say "is" and name "Being," such saying and that name are perhaps only seemingly proper names for what is to be named and said. For every word as such is a word "of" Being, in fact a word *"of"* Being not only insofar as it talks "about" Being or "of" Being but a word "of" Being in the sense that Being expresses itself in each word and precisely in that way keeps its essence silent.

Being reveals itself to us in a variety of oppositions that cannot be coincidental, since even a mere listing of them points to their inner connection: Being is both utterly void and most abundant, most universal and most unique, most intelligible and most resistant to every concept, most in use and yet to come, most reliable and most abyssal, most forgotten and most remembering, most said and most reticent.

But are these, rightly considered, opposites in the essence of Being itself? Are they not opposites merely in the way *we* comport ourselves toward Being, in representing and understanding, in using and relying on, in retaining (forgetting) and saying? But even *if* they were opposites *only* in our relation to Being, we would still have attained what we were seeking: the determination of our relation to Being (not merely to beings).

That relation is revealed as discordant. The question still remains whether the discordancy of our relation to Being lies in us or in Being itself; the answer to that question may once again decide something important about the essence of the relation.

Still more pressing than the question of whether the opposites identified lie in the essence of Being itself, or whether they merely arise out of *our* discordant relation to Being, *or whether this relation of ours to Being in fact springs from Being itself,* since it abides by Being—more pressing than these indubitably decisive questions is the following: Viewed with respect to matters as they stand, *is* our relation to Being a discordant one? Do we comport ourselves toward Being so discordantly that the discord completely dominates *us;* that is to say, our comportment toward beings? We must answer in the negative. In our comportment, we merely stand on one side of the opposites: Being is for us the emptiest, most universal, most intelligible, most used, most reliable, most forgotten, most said. We scarcely even heed it, and therefore do not know it *as* an opposition to something else.

Being remains something neutral for us, and for that reason we scarcely pay attention to the differentiation of Being and beings, although we establish all our comportment toward beings on the basis of it. But it is not only we today who stand outside that still unexperienced discord of the relation to Being. Such "standing outside" and "not knowing" is characteristic of all metaphysics, since for metaphysics Being necessarily remains the most universal, the most intelligible. In the scope of Being metaphysics ponders only the multifaceted and multilayered universals of various realms of beings.

Throughout the whole history of metaphysics, from the time Plato interpreted the beingness of beings as *idea* up to the time Nietzsche defined Being as value, Being has been self-evidently well preserved as the *a priori* to which man as a rational creature comports himself.

Because the relation to Being has, as it were, dissolved in indifference, the *differentiation* of Being and beings also cannot become questionable for metaphysics.

By this state of affairs, we first come to know the metaphysical character of today's historical epoch. "Today," reckoned neither by the calendar nor in terms of world-historical occurrences, is determined by the period in the history of metaphysics that is most our own: it is the metaphysical determination of historical mankind in the age of Nietzsche's metaphysics.

Our epoch reveals a particularly casual matter-of-factness with respect to the truth of beings as a whole. Being is either explained in the conventional Christian theological explanation of the world, or else being as a whole—the world—is defined by an appeal to "ideas" and "values." "Ideas" reminds us of the beginning of Western metaphysics in Plato. "Values" intimates a reference to the end of metaphysics in Nietzsche. But "ideas" and "values" are not thought any further in their essence and in their essential provenance. The appeal to "ideas" and "values" and their positing constitute the most familiar and most intelligible framework for interpreting the world and for guiding one's life. Such indifference to Being in the midst of the greatest passion for beings testifies to the thoroughly *metaphysical* character of the age. The essential consequence of this situation is revealed in the fact that historical decisions are now consciously, willfully, and totally transferred from the separate areas of earlier cultural activities—politics, science, art, society—into the realm of *Weltanschauung*. *Weltanschauung* is that configuration of modern metaphysics which becomes inevitable when its fulfillment in the conditionless begins. The consequence is a peculiar uniformity of our heretofore multifarious Western European history, a uniformity that announces itself metaphysically in the coupling of "idea" and "value" as the standard paraphernalia for the interpretation of the world in terms of *Weltanschauung*.

Through the coupling of idea with value, the character of Being and its differentiation from beings vanishes from the essence of the Idea. That here and there in learned circles and within the scholarly tradition there is talk of Being, of "ontology" and metaphysics, is merely an echo in which there no longer resides any history-making force. The power of *Weltanschauung* has taken possession of the essence of metaphysics. That is to say, what is proper to all metaphysics, the fact that the differentiation of Being and beings which sustains metaphysics itself essentially and necessarily remains an unquestioned matter, a matter of indifference for it, this fact now comes to be what *distinguishes* metaphysics as *Weltanschauung.* This is the basis of the fact that complete, absolute, undisturbed, and undistracted dominion over beings can develop only with the beginning of the fulfillment of metaphysics.

The age of the fulfillment of metaphysics—which we descry when we think through the basic features of Nietzsche's metaphysics—prompts us to consider to what extent we first find ourselves in the history of Being. It also prompts us to consider—prior to our finding ourselves—the extent to which we must experience history as the release of Being into machination, a release that Being itself sends, so as to allow its truth to become essential for man out of man's belonging to it.*

* *Die Loslassung des Seins in die Machenschaft.* The "machination" meant here is not a conspiracy of Being, although the word does suggest the duplicity of the Janus-head. The "making," contriving, or planning referred to is that of reckoning and calculative thought in the age of "machine" technology. Heidegger concludes his lecture course on nihilism by invoking the possibility (fully discussed in "The Question Concerning Technology," 1953) that meditation on our technical doings—as a way of revealing beings—may compel a reflection on *alētheia* and on the history of Being.

Part Two

NIHILISM AS DETERMINED BY THE HISTORY OF BEING

Nietzsche's acknowledgment of the being as the most elemental factor (as will to power) does not conduct him to the thought of Being as such. Nor does he attain that thought by way of an interpretation of Being as a "necessary value." Nor does the thought of the "eternal return of the same" become the impetus to ponder eternity as a moment arising from the precipitance of luminous presencing, recurrence as the manner of such presencing, and both in accord with their essential provenance arising out of in-cipient "Time."

When Nietzsche clings to his acknowledgment of will to power in the sense of the "ultimate fact" as his fundamental philosophical insight, he acquiesces in the description of Being as one of those beings that are distinguished according to the genus "fact." Factuality as such is not pondered. Nietzsche's adherence to his fundamental insight is precisely what blocks him from the path that leads to thinking Being as such. The fundamental insight does not see the way.

In Nietzsche's thought, however, the question of Being itself cannot even be raised, because Nietzsche has already given an answer to the question of Being (in its sole known sense, as the Being of beings). "Being" is a value. "Being" means the being as such; that is, the permanent.

However extensively and from whatever point of view we prefer to interrogate Nietzsche, we do not find that his thought thinks Being from its truth as the essential occurrence of Being itself, in which Being is transformed and whereby it loses its name.

The meditation we have now engaged in gives rise to the general suspicion that we assume Nietzsche's thinking ought to think Being as such in its ground, that it neglects to do so and is therefore inadequate. We have nothing like that in mind. Rather, it is simply a matter of bringing ourselves from our thinking toward the question of the truth of Being into proximity to Nietzsche's metaphysics, in order to experience his thought on the basis of the supreme fidelity of his thinking. It is far from the intention of our effort to disseminate a perhaps more correct version of Nietzsche's philosophy. We are thinking his metaphysics solely in order to be able to inquire into what is worthy of question: *In Nietzsche's metaphysics, which for the first time experiences and thinks nihilism as such, is nihilism overcome or is it not?*

By asking whether or not it accomplishes the overcoming of nihilism, we are passing judgment on Nietzsche's metaphysics. However, we will let even this judgment go. We are simply asking, and addressing the question to ourselves, whether and how the proper essence of nihilism is revealed in Nietzsche's metaphysical experiencing and overcoming of nihilism. What we are asking is whether in the *metaphysical* concept of nihilism its essence can be experienced, whether its essence can be grasped at all, or whether that might not require a different rigor of saying.

In such questioning, we are of course supposing that the nothing exercises its essence in what we call *nihilism,* specifically in the sense that basically there "is" nothing to beings as such. We are in no way subjecting Nietzsche's thinking to an inappropriate or excessive claim. Insofar as Nietzsche experiences nihilism as the history of the devaluation of the highest values, and thinks of the overcoming of nihilism as a countermovement in the form of the revaluation of all previous values, and does so in terms of the expressly acknowledged principle of valuation, he is directly thinking *Being;* that is, beings as such; and in this way he understands nihilism mediately as a history in which something happens with beings as such.

Strictly speaking, it is not *we* who impute something to someone else; rather, we place *ourselves* under the claim of language. Language demands that in the word *nihilism* we think the *nihil,* the nothing, simultaneously with the thought that in beings as such something transpires. Language demands not only that we correctly comprehend mere words as lexical artifacts, but that we heed the matter expressed in and with the word. We submit ourselves to the claim of the name *nihilism* to think a history in which the being as such stands. In its own way, the name *nihilism* names the *Being* of beings.

Nietzsche's metaphysics is based on the explicitly implemented, fundamental insight that the being as such *is,* and that only the being that is acknowledged in this way grants thought a guarantee of its possibility as *being* thinking, no matter what it may be thinking about. Nietzsche's fundamental experience says that the being *is* a being as will to power in the mode of the eternal recurrence of the same. As a being in this form, it is *not* nothing. Consequently, nihilism, to the degree there is supposed to be nothing to beings as such, is excluded from the foundations of such metaphysics. Thus—it would seem—metaphysics has overcome nihilism.

Nietzsche acknowledges the being as such. Yet, in such an acknowledgement, does he also recognize the Being of beings, and indeed It itself, *Being,* specifically *as Being?* He does not. Being is determined as value and is consequently explained in terms of beings as a condition posited by the will to power, by the "being" as such. Being is not acknowledged as Being. Such "acknowledging" means allowing Being to reign in all its questionableness from the point of view of its essential provenance; it means persevering in the question of Being. But that means to reflect on the origin of presencing and permanence and thus to keep thinking open to the possibility that *"Being," on its way to the "as Being," might abandon its own essence in favor of a more primordial determination.* Any discussion of "Being itself" always remains interrogative.

For representing, which in value thinking aims at validity, Being is already outside the horizon of the *questionability* of the "as Being." There "is" nothing to Being as such: Being—a *nihil.* However, if we grant that beings are thanks to Being, and that Being never is thanks to beings; and if we also grant that Being cannot be nothing in the face of beings, then does not nihilism also, or perhaps first of all, put itself properly into play where not only is there nothing to beings but also nothing to Being? Indeed. Where there is simply nothing to beings, one might find nihilism, but one will not encounter its *essence,* which first appears where the *nihil* concerns Being itself.

The essence of nihilism is the history in which there is nothing to Being itself.

Our thinking, or better expressed, our reckoning and accounting according to the principle of noncontradition, can hardly wait to offer the observation that a history which is, but in which there is nothing to Being itself, presents us with an absolute absurdity. But perhaps Being itself does not trouble itself about the contradictions of our thought. If

Being itself had to be what it is by grace of a lack of contradiction in human thought, then it would be denied in its own proper essence.

Absurdity is impotent against Being itself, and therefore also against what happens to it in its destiny—that within metaphysics there is nothing to Being as such.

More essential than reckoning with absurdities is finding out to what extent there is nothing to Being itself in Nietzsche's metaphysics.

Therefore, we say that Nietzsche's metaphysics is nihilism proper. But does Nietzsche need us with our hindsight to calculate such a thing against his thinking? In describing the way Nietzsche himself sees the various forms and stages of nihilism,* we touched on the concluding sentence of note 14 (dated 1887) from *The Will to Power,* which runs: " 'Nihilism' as ideal of *the supreme powerfulness* of spirit, of superabundant life—partly destructive, partly ironic." However, the "recapitulation," which has been cited already, begins (WM, 617): "To *stamp* Becoming with the character of Being—that is the *supreme will to power.*"

Such thinking—that is, thinking *Becoming* as the *Being* of the totality of beings, thinking "will to power" in terms of the "eternal recurrence of the same"—is what the spirit of Nietzsche's metaphysics achieves as the ideal of its supreme powerfulness. It therefore corresponds to the supreme form of "nihilism." In that Nietzsche's metaphysics thinks a complete revaluation of all previous values, it completes the devaluation of the highest values hitherto. In this way, it belongs "destructively" within the course of the prior history of nihilism. But insofar as the revaluation is carried out expressly *in terms of the principle* of valuation, such nihilism pretends to be what it no longer is in *its own* sense: as "destructive," it is "ironic." Nietzsche understands his metaphysics as the most extreme nihilism; indeed, in such a way that it is no longer even a nihilism.

---

* The reference here is not to the lecture course on "European Nihilism" but is presumably to the essay "Nietzsche's Metaphysics," which also refers to WM, 14 and 617. (Cf. NII, 281–82, 288, and 327, included in Volume III of the present series.) The references below to "justification" and, indeed, to all five "major rubrics" of Nietzsche's metaphysics seem to refer to that essay.

We have said, however, that Nietzsche's metaphysics is nihilism proper. This implies not only that Nietzsche's nihilism does not overcome nihilism but also that it can never overcome it. For it is precisely in the positing of new values from the will to power, by which and through which Nietzsche believes he will overcome nihilism, that nihilism proper first proclaims that there is nothing to Being itself, which has now become a value. As a result, Nietzsche experiences the historical movement of nihilism as a history of the devaluation of the highest values hitherto. On the same basis, he represents overcoming as revaluation and carries it through, not only in a new valuation but also in such a way that he experiences will to power as the principle of the new—and ultimately of all—valuation. Value thinking is now elevated into a principle. Being itself, as a matter of principle, is not admitted as Being. According to its own principle, in this metaphysics there is *nothing* to Being. How can what is worthy of thought be given here with Being itself, namely, Being as—Being? How could an overcoming of nihilism occur here, or even make itself felt?

Consequently, Nietzsche's metaphysics is not an overcoming of nihilism. It is the ultimate entanglement in nihilism. Through value thinking in terms of will to power, it of course continues to acknowledge beings as such. But, by tying itself to an interpretation of Being as value, it simultaneously binds itself to the impossibility of even casting an inquiring glance at Being as Being. By means of the entanglement of nihilism in itself, nihilism first becomes thoroughly complete in what it is. Such utterly completed, perfect nihilism is the fulfillment of nihilism proper.

But if the essence of nihilism is the history in which there is nothing to Being itself, then neither can the essence of nihilism be experienced and thought as long as in thinking and for thinking there is indeed nothing to Being itself. Fulfilled nihilism definitively shuts itself off from the possibility of ever being able to think and to know the essence of nihilism. Is this not to say that the essence of nihilism remains closed to Nietzsche's thought? How dare we assert such a thing?

Nietzsche clearly asks, "What does nihilism mean?" and he answers succinctly, *"That the uppermost values devaluate themselves"* (WM, 2).

No less clearly and succinctly, however, the note shows that Nietzsche asks about what he experiences as nihilism in terms of an "interpretation," and that he interprets what is thus examined from the viewpoint of his value thinking. Consequently, Nietzsche's question about the meaning of nihilism is a question that for its part still thinks nihilistically. Even in his very manner of questioning, therefore, Nietzsche does not attain to the realm of what the question of the essence of nihilism seeks; that is, *whether* and *in what way* nihilism is a history that applies to Being itself.

However, insofar as for Nietzsche nihilism professes to be an occurrence of devaluation and decline, of enervation and death, Nietzsche's experience appears at least to confirm the negativity in nihilism. Instead of a "no" to beings as such, Nietzsche demands a "yes." He contemplates an overcoming of nihilism. But how is that possible as long as the essence of nihilism is not experienced?

Hence, *before* any overcoming, it is necessary to have the kind of confrontation with nihilism that will for the first time bring to light the essence of nihilism. If we grant that there is some way in which human thought is to participate in that confrontation with the essence of nihilism, which concerns Being itself, then such thinking must for its part first be stunned by the essence of nihilism. Therefore, with regard to the kind of metaphysics which first of all experiences and thinks nihilism as a general historical movement, but which at the same time for us begins to be the fulfillment of nihilism proper, we must ask in what the phenomenon of nihilism proper, and specifically its fulfillment, which is of immediate historical concern to us, has its ground.

Nietzsche's metaphysics is nihilistic insofar as it is value thinking, and insofar as the latter is grounded in will to power as the principle of all valuation. Nietzsche's metaphysics consequently becomes the fulfillment of nihilism proper, because it is the metaphysics of will to power. But, if that is so, then metaphysics as the metaphysics of will to power is indeed the ground of the *fulfillment* of nihilism proper, although it can in no way be the ground of proper nihilism *as such.* That ground, though still incomplete, must already reign in the *essence* of prior metaphysics, which is of course not the metaphysics of will to power, although it does experience beings as such and as a whole as *will.* Even if the essence of willing which is thought here is obscure in many respects, perhaps even necessarily obscure, we can see that, from the metaphysics of Schelling and Hegel, back beyond Kant and Leibniz to Descartes, the being as such is at bottom experienced as *will.*

Of course, that does not mean that the subjective experience of human will is transposed onto beings as a whole. Rather, it indicates the very reverse, that man first of all comes to know himself as a willing subject in an essential sense on the basis of a still unelucidated experience of beings as such in the sense of a willing that has yet to be thought. Insight into these connections is indispensable for an experience of the history of nihilism proper, an experience of its essential history. Those connections cannot be explained here, however. For the moment, that task is not a pressing one. What was said about nihilism proper in describing Nietzsche's metaphysics as a fulfillment of nihilism must have already awakened thoughtful readers to another supposition: that the ground of nihilism proper is neither the metaphysics of will to power nor the metaphysics of will, but simply metaphysics itself.

Metaphysics as metaphysics is nihilism proper. The essence of nihilism *is* historically as metaphysics, and the metaphysics of Plato is no less nihilistic than that of Nietzsche. In the former, the essence of nihilism is merely concealed; in the latter, it comes completely to appearance. Nonetheless, it never shows its true face, either on the basis of or within metaphysics.

These are disturbing statements. For metaphysics determines the history of the Western era. Western humankind, in all its relations with beings, and even to itself, is in every respect sustained and guided by metaphysics. In the equation of metaphysics and nihilism one does not know which is greater—the arbitrariness, or the degree of condemnation of our entire history heretofore.

But in the meantime we should also have noticed that our thinking has still scarcely responded to the essence of nihilism proper, let alone thought it adequately enough for us to reflect meditatively on the statements made about metaphysics and nihilism, so that afterward we might pass judgment on them. If metaphysics as such is nihilism proper, while the latter, in accord with its essence, is incapable of thinking its own essence, how could metaphysics itself ever encounter its own essence? Metaphysical representations of metaphysics necessarily lag behind that essence. The metaphysics of metaphysics never attains to its essence.

But what does *essence* mean here? We are not adopting the idea of "essentialities" from the word. In the name *essence* [*Wesen*] we perceive what occurs essentially [*das Wesende*]. What is "the essence" of metaphysics? How does it essentially unfold? How does the relationship to Being reign in it? That is the question. Our attempt to answer it in the radius of our meditation on Nietzsche's metaphysics is necessarily inadequate. Furthermore, insofar as our thinking proceeds from metaphysics, our attempt always remains tied to what is questionable. All the same, we must hazard a few steps. Let us concentrate on the question which Aristotle expressed as the enduring question for thought: What is the being?

Every question specifies as a question the breadth and nature of the answer it is looking for. At the same time, it circumscribes the range of possibilities for answering. In order to ponder the question of metaphysics adequately, we first of all need to consider it as a question, without considering the answers that have devolved on it in the course of the history of metaphysics.

In the question "What is the being?" we ask about the being as such. The being as a being *is* such thanks to Being. In the question "What is the being as such?" we are thinking of Being, and specifically of the Being of beings, that is to say, of what beings are. What they are—namely, the beings—is answered by their what-being, *to ti estin.* Plato defines the whatness of a being as *idea* (see *Plato's Doctrine of Truth*). The whatness of being, the *essentia* of *ens,* we also call "the essence." But that is no incidental and harmless identification. Rather, in it is hidden the fact that the Being of beings—that is to say, the way in which beings essentially occur—is thought in terms of whatness. "Essence" in the sense of *essentia* (whatness) is already a metaphysical interpretation of "essence," which asks about the "what" of beings as such. And, of course, "essence" here is always thought as the essence of beings. The Being of beings is examined *in terms of* beings as what is thought *toward* beings. Thought as what? As the *genos* and the *koinon,* as that from which every being in its being thus-and-so receives the common What.

Because the being is interrogated as such, it is also experienced with respect to the simple fact that it is. Therefore, a further question at once arises from the question of what the being as such is: Among all beings as beings, which one most nearly corresponds to what is defined as the What of the being? The being that corresponds to whatness, the *essentia* of beings as such, is what truly exists. In the question "What is the being?" the truly existing is thought at the same time with respect to *essentia* and *existentia.* In that way, the being is determined *as such;* that is, determined as to *what* it is and as to the fact *that* it is. *Essentia* and *existentia* of the *ens qua ens* answer the question "What is the being as such?" They define the being in its Being.

Accordingly, how does metaphysics comport itself to Being itself? Does metaphysics think Being itself? No, it never does. It thinks *the being* with a view to Being. Being is first and last what answers the question in which the being is always what is interrogated. What is interrogated is not Being as such. Hence, Being itself remains unthought in metaphysics, not just incidentally, but in accord with metaphysics' own inquiry. By thinking the being as such, the question *and* the answer necessarily think on the basis of Being; but they do not think about Being itself, precisely because in the most proper sense of the metaphysical question Being is thought as the being in its Being. Inasmuch as metaphysics thinks the being on the basis of Being, it does not think Being *as Being.*

To think on the basis of Being does not yet mean going back to Being, thoughtfully recalling it in its truth. Being remains unthought in the kind of thinking that, as metaphysical, passes for thinking pure and simple. That Being itself remains unthought in metaphysics as such is a remaining-unthought of a peculiar, distinctive, and unique kind.

The metaphysical question does not extend to Being itself. How could we expect it to ponder Being itself? However, dare we say that the question of metaphysics does not go far enough in its questioning, that it does not go far enough beyond beings? We leave that question open, simply because we have not yet decided whether or not metaphysics might in fact determine Being as such. We should not forget the characterization of Being which from the beginning of metaphysics and throughout its history is thought under the subsequent term *a priori.* The term says that Being is prior to beings. But in that way Being is thought precisely and solely on the basis of the being and for the being, whether metaphysics prefers to explain the *a priori* as materially prior, or as something precursory in the order of knowledge and of the conditions of the object.

As long as the Being of beings is thought as the *a priori,* that determination itself prevents any reflection on Being as Being from perhaps discovering how far Being as Being enters into the *a priori* relation to beings, whether that relation merely chances on and accompanies Being, or whether Being itself is the relation, and what Being and relation mean. That every metaphysics, even the reversal of Platonism, thinks the Being of beings as the *a priori,* merely certifies that metaphysics as such leaves Being unthought.

Of course, metaphysics acknowledges that beings are not without Being. But scarcely has it said so when it again transforms Being into a being, whether it be the supreme being in the sense of the first cause, whether it be the distinctive being in the sense of the subject of subjectivity, as the condition of the possibility of all objectivity, or whether, as a consequence of the coherence of both these fundamental conditions of Being in beings, it be the determination of the supreme being as the Absolute in the sense of unconditioned subjectivity.

The grounding of Being—which is barely remembered—in the utmost being among beings proceeds from the metaphysical question about the being as such. It discovers that beings are. The fact that Being essentially occurs brushes by it. But the latter experience indiscernibly attains the path of the metaphysical question which in Leibniz' subsequent formulation inquires, "Why are there beings at all, and why not rather nothing?"*

---

* Leibniz' formulation appears in section 7 of *The Principles of Nature and of Grace, Founded on Reason* (1714), in the translation of Robert Latta (revised by Philip P. Wiener) as follows:

7. Thus far we have spoken as simple *physicists:* now we must advance to *metaphysics,* making use of the *great principle,* little employed in general, which teaches

This question inquires into the first cause and highest existent ground of beings. It is the question of the *theion,* a question that had already arisen at the beginning of metaphysics in Plato and Aristotle; that is to say, arisen from the essence of metaphysics. Because metaphysics, thinking the being as such, is approached by Being but thinks it on the basis of and with reference to beings, metaphysics must therefore say (*legein*) the *theion* in the sense of the highest existent ground. Metaphysics is inherently theology. It is theology to the extent that it says the being as being, the *on hēi on.* Ontology is simultaneously and necessarily theology. In order to recognize the fundamentally onto-theological character of metaphysics,† we do not need to orient ourselves toward the purely scholastic concept of metaphysics. On the contrary, the scholastic concept is merely a doctrinal formulation of the essence of metaphysics thought metaphysically.

The names *ontology* and *theology* as they are used here do not possess the identical senses they have in the scholastic concept of meta-

---

that *nothing happens without a sufficient reason;* that is to say, that nothing happens without its being possible for him who should sufficiently understand things, to give a reason sufficient to determine why it is so and not otherwise. This principle laid down, the first question which should rightly be asked, will be, *Why is there something rather than nothing?* For nothing is simpler and easier than something. Further, suppose that things must exist, we must be able to give a reason *why they must exist so* and not otherwise.

Heidegger employs the first "Why?" question at crucial junctures in a number of his essays and lectures, for example, as the culmination of "What Is Metaphysics?" (1929; cf. also the 1949 "Introduction" to the inaugural lecture, *Wegmarken,* p. 210) and as the opening question of *Introduction to Metaphysics* (1935). I have altered the traditional English translation to capture the peculiar stress on the *potius quam,* or *plutôt que,* which Heidegger during his lectures on Leibniz at Marburg in 1928 found to be of the greatest importance. See *Metaphysische Anfangsgründe der Logik im Ausgang von Leibniz,* p. 141 and "Vom Wesen des Grundes," *Wegmarken,* pp. 65 and 68.

† Cf. Heidegger's 1957 lecture, "The Onto-Theo-Logical Constitution of Metaphysics," in Martin Heidegger, *Identität und Differenz* (Pfullingen: G. Neske, 1957), pp. 31–67; English translation by Joan Stambaugh in *Identity and Difference* (New York: Harper & Row, 1969), pp. 42–74. The Harper & Row edition also reprints the German text, pp. 107–43. In this lecture, Heidegger considers Hegel—especially the Hegel of *The Science of Logic*—as the apotheosis of ontotheology. In the antecedent Nietzsche lectures, the phrase is associated principally with Leibniz. Recall the delightful precursor of Heidegger's phrase in Voltaire's *Candide,* where it is averred of Pangloss that "he taught *la métaphysico-théologo-cosmolonigologie.*"

physics. Rather, "ontology" defines the being as such with respect to its *essentia,* and is found in psychology, cosmology, and theology. Yet "theology" too, rightly thought, reigns in both cosmology and psychology (or anthropology) as well as in *metaphysica generalis.*

As an *ontology,* even Nietzsche's metaphysics is *at the same time* theology, although it seems far removed from scholastic metaphysics. The ontology of beings as such thinks *essentia* as will to power. Such ontology thinks the *existentia* of beings as such and as a whole theologically as the eternal recurrence of the same. Such metaphysical theology is of course a negative theology of a peculiar kind. Its negativity is revealed in the expression "God is dead." That is an expression not of atheism but of ontotheology, in that metaphysics in which nihilism proper is fulfilled.

But if metaphysics as such does not think Being itself because it thinks Being in the sense of the being as such, ontology and theology, on the basis of their mutual dependence on each other, both must leave Being itself unthought. Theology derives the *essentia* of the being from ontology. Ontology, whether knowingly or not, transposes the being with respect to its *existentia,* that is, as what exists, into the first cause [*Grund*], which theology goes on to represent. The onto-theological essence of metaphysics thinks the being from the viewpoint of *essentia* and *existentia.* These determinations of the Being of beings are as it were thoughtfully intimated, but not thought in terms of Being itself, neither separately nor both together in their difference. That difference and everything it encompasses, as unthought, suddenly becomes determinative for metaphysical thinking—as though it had fallen out of the sky. Maybe it did. But then we would need to consider what that means with regard to Being itself.

The manifold yet scarcely explicated *coherence* of ontology and theology in the *essence* of metaphysics is enunciated with particular clarity where metaphysics, following the thrust of its own name, identifies the fundamental trait by which it knows the being as such. That is *transcendence.*

On the one hand, the word *transcendence* designates the transition of the being into what it is as a being in its whatness (its qualification). The surpassment to *essentia* is transcendence as the transcendental.

Kant, by critically limiting the being to an object of experience, equated the transcendental with the objectivity of the object. On the other hand, however, transcendence at the same time means the transcendent, which in the sense of the first existent cause of the being as existent surpasses the being, and in surmounting it looms over it in the perfect plenitude of what is essential. Ontology represents transcendence as the transcendental. Theology represents transcendence as the transcendent.

The unitary ambiguity named by transcendence and grounded in the—in terms of its provenance—obscure differentiation of *essentia* and *existentia* reflects the onto–theological essence of metaphysics. By virtue of its essence, metaphysics thinks the being by surpassing it transcendentally-transcendently, but only in order to represent the being itself; that is, to return to it again. Being is, as it were, skimmed over representationally in the transcendental-transcendent act of surpassing. The thinking that surpasses always passes over Being itself in thought, not as an oversight, but in such a way that it does not enter into Being as such, into what is questionable about its truth. Metaphysical thought does not enter into Being itself because it has *already thought* Being, namely as the being, insofar as the being is.

Being itself necessarily remains unthought in metaphysics. Metaphysics is a history in which there is essentially nothing to Being itself: *metaphysics as such is nihilism proper.*

The experience of the nihilistic essence of metaphysics that we have now indicated is still not sufficient for thinking the proper essence of metaphysics in an essentially correct way. This first of all requires that we experience the essence of metaphysics on the basis of Being itself. But, supposing that our thought is on the way toward this experience, approaching it from afar, then it must first of all have learned what it means to say that Being itself remains unthought in metaphysics. Perhaps that is all our thought has to learn in advance.

Being remains unthought in metaphysics because metaphysics thinks the being as such. What does it mean to say that the being as such is thought? It implies that the being itself comes to the fore. It stands in the light. The being is illumined, is itself unconcealed. The being stands in unconcealment. The latter is the essence of truth, which appears at the outset and then immediately disappears again.

In what truth does the being stand, if it is thought as the being in metaphysics? Obviously, metaphysics itself is the truth of the being as such. What is the essential mode of such unconcealment? Does metaphysics ever say anything about the essence of truth, in which and out of which it thinks the being, anything about the truth as which metaphysics itself essentially occurs? Never. Or are we talking this way, to all appearances presumptuously, merely because up to now we have searched in vain for what metaphysics says about the essence of the truth in which it stands? Have we been searching in vain merely because we have been asking inadequate questions?

If that is the case, then we must set things aright. The reference to Nietzsche's metaphysical concept of justification provisionally showed that Nietzsche was incapable of recognizing the justification thought by him either in the truth of its essence in general or as the essential character of the truth of his metaphysics. Is the reason for that incapacity the fact that his metaphysics is the metaphysics of will to power, or merely that it is metaphysics?

The reason is that metaphysics leaves Being itself unthought. By thinking the being as such it skims over Being in thought so as to pass it by in favor of *the being,* to which it returns and with which it remains. Thus metaphysics thinks the being as such; but it never ponders the *"as such" itself.* The "as such" implies that the being is unconcealed. The *hēi* in *on hēi on,* the *qua* in *ens qua ens,* the "as" in "the being as a being," *name unconcealment, which is unthought in its essence.* Language harbors such significant matters so inconspicuously in such simple words, if words they are. In its naming, the "as such" skims over the unconcealment of the being in its Being. But because Being itself remains unthought, the unconcealment of beings too remains unthought.

What if in both cases what is unthought were the selfsame? Then the unthought unconcealment of the being would be unthought Being itself. Then Being itself would unfold essentially as such unconcealment—as revealing.

Once again, and in an even more essential manner, what remains unthought in metaphysics, which is itself the truth of beings as such, has shown itself. It is finally time to ask how the "unthought" itself is to be thought. Along with this remaining-unthought, we are at the same time invoking the history in which there is nothing to Being itself. By contemplating the "unthought" in its essence, we come closer to the essence of nihilism proper.

If Being itself is unthought, that seems to be the fault of thinking, inasmuch as thinking is unconcerned with Being itself. Thinking omits something. Meanwhile, metaphysics thinks the Being of beings. It knows Being in terms of its own fundamental concepts *essentia* and *existentia.* But it knows Being only in order to recognize beings as such on the basis of it. In metaphysics, Being is neither bypassed nor overlooked. Nonetheless, the *metaphysical* view of Being does not allow for it as something explicitly thought; for that, Being as Being itself would have to be admitted by metaphysics as what metaphysics is to think. Being remains in the glare of concepts, indeed in the radiance of the absolute concept of speculative dialectics—and nonetheless remains *unthought.* Thus one might conclude that metaphysics repudiates Being as what is to be thought expressly.

Such a repudiation would, of course, presuppose that metaphysics had already somehow admitted Being itself into its domain as what is to be thought. Where is such admittance to be found within the history of metaphysics? Nowhere. Also absent, therefore, are any traces of a repudiation of Being as what is expressly to be thought.

Even where it does not *express* itself as ontotheology, metaphysics asserts and knows itself as a thinking that always and everywhere thinks "Being," although only in the sense of the being as such. Of course, metaphysics does not recognize this "although only." And it does not recognize it, not because it repudiates Being itself as to-be-thought, *but because Being itself stays away.* But if that is so, then the "unthought" does not stem from a thinking that neglects something.

How are we to understand the fact that Being itself stays away? Perhaps in the sense that Being halts somewhere, like a being, and, for whatever reasons, perhaps because it has lost its way, does not reach us? Except that in and for metaphysics Being stands in view, as the Being of beings.

In the meantime, it has become clearer that Being itself occurs essentially as the unconcealment in which the being comes to presence. Unconcealment itself, however, remains concealed as such. With reference to itself, unconcealment as such keeps away, keeps to itself. *The matter stands with the concealment of the essence of unconcealment. It stands with the concealment of Being as such. Being itself stays away.*

Thus matters stand with the concealment of Being in such a way that the concealment conceals itself in itself. The staying away of Being is Being itself *as this very default.** Being is not segregated somewhere off by itself, nor does it also keep away; rather, the default of Being as such is Being itself. In its default Being veils itself with itself. This veil that vanishes for itself, which is the way Being itself essentially occurs in default, is the nothing as Being itself.

Do we sense what occurs essentially in the nothing which is now to be thought? Do we dare think the possibility that the nothing is infinitely different from vacuous nullity? In the present case, the characterization of the essence of nihilism proper, in which there is nothing to Being itself, would have to contain something more than a merely negative conclusion.

Being remains unthought in metaphysics as such. This now suggests that Being itself stays away; as such default, Being itself essentially unfolds.

Insofar as the "un-" of unconcealment, with reference to itself, keeps away from unconcealment, staying with the concealment of Being, default evinces the character of *concealing.* In what sense must such concealing be thought? Is concealing simply a veiling or is it at the same time a storing away and preserving? The default "of" Being itself is such always in relation to beings. In its default is Being withheld from beings? Is the withholding in fact a refusal? We are only asking questions here, asking what we can surmise with respect to the default of Being itself. If we grant that Being itself *"is"* the *default,* then we will have to rely on Being, and on how Being strikes our thinking, to ascertain from it what features essentially occur in the default. For

* *Das Ausbleiben des Seins ist das Sein selbst* als dieses Ausbleiben. The jurisprudential term *default* will now help to translate *das Ausbleiben,* the "staying away" of Being, its *failure to appear* as such in the history of metaphysics.

the present, we will concentrate solely on what pertains to the default of Being itself. Nor are we hesitant to admit that the discussion of Being as just that—Being—still speaks an inadequate language, insofar as, in our perpetual references to Being itself, it is addressed with a name that continues to talk past Being as such.

In making this remark, we are voicing the assumption that Being—thought as such—can no longer be called "Being." Being as such is other than itself, so decisively other that it even "is" not. When put into words, all this sounds dialectical. In terms of the matter, it is otherwise.

Whether or not the concealing is a self-refusing preserving of Being itself, something like a self-withdrawal essentially occurs in it, and in such a way that it somehow remains in view, namely, as the Being of beings. The withdrawal, in which form Being itself occurs essentially, does not rob the being of Being. Nonetheless the being, precisely and only when it is a being, stands in the withdrawal of Being itself. We might say that the being is abandoned by Being itself. The abandonment by Being applies to beings as a whole, not only that being which takes the shape of man, who represents beings as such, a representing in which Being itself withdraws from him in its truth.

Being itself withdraws. The withdrawal happens. The abandonment by Being of the being as such takes place. When does it happen? Now? Only yesterday? Or a long time ago? How long has it been? Since when? Since the being came into the unconcealed as the being itself. Metaphysics has prevailed ever since this unconcealment occurred; for metaphysics is the history of the unconcealment of the being as such. Since that history came to be, there has historically been a withdrawal of Being itself; there has been an abandonment by Being of beings as such; there has been a history in which there is nothing to Being itself. Consequently, and from that time on, Being itself has remained unthought.

Since that time, however, nihilism proper has also been essentially unfolding, covertly, as accords with its essence. Let us now consider the name *nihilism* insofar as it names the *nihil.* We think the nothing as it applies to Being itself. We think the "applying" itself as what is historical. We think the historical as what happens in the history of

Being itself, whereby what occurs essentially in such historicity is likewise determined by Being itself.

*The essence of nihilism proper is Being itself in default of its unconcealment, which is as its own "It," and which determines its "is" in staying away.**

Perhaps now it may be clear to us, at least in a few respects, that the remaining-unthought of Being as such, which we mentioned earlier, derives from the default of Being itself, a default that Being itself "is." Nevertheless, we would be overstating the case if we went on to put forth the proposition that remaining-unthought lies in Being itself and not in thinking. Does thinking therefore belong *with* the default of Being? Depending on the way it is thought, an affirmation of this question can hit upon something essential. However, it can also miss it. In the same way the proposition which asserts that remaining-unthought lies in Being itself can say too much and yet express what is alone essential.

Thinking does not belong with the default of Being as such in the sense that it observes the default, as though Being itself were one thing off by itself somewhere and thinking another that, founded on itself, either troubles itself or not about Being in its unconcealment as such. Thinking is not an independent activity over against Being, certainly not in such a way that, as the representational activity of the subject, it would already sustain Being as what is most universally represented by it and in it.

Apart from the fact that this description mistakes the simple appearance and proper intent of thinking as such, locating Being in the representing subject's domain of disposition would not allow us to see or

* Heidegger's use of the *Es,* "It," here and below foreshadows the theme of *Ereignis,* the propriative event, by which there is / it gives (*Es gibt*) Time and Being. Crucially important is the matrix of the thought of *Ereignis* in the history of nihilism: throughout the history of metaphysics, for which Being amounts to nothing, the unconcealment of Being remains *itself* withdrawn in concealment. For precisely that reason, the "itself" and "It" resist all depiction. Heidegger's capitalization of the latter is not meant to refer to a supreme being, or to a being of any kind. Prophylactic against all reification of the It are Heidegger's remarks on the finitude of *Ereignis* during his Todtnauberg Seminar on "Time and Being." See *Zur Sache des Denkens* (Tübingen: M. Niemeyer, 1969), pp. 53 and 58. Cf. Volume I of this series (*The Will to Power as Art*), p. 156 n.

understand whether and how Being as such in its unconcealment withdraws from thinking *along with* unconcealment as long as, and to the extent that, thinking already represents the being as such, that is, its Being. On the contrary, thinking belongs to Being itself, insofar as thinking, true to its essence, maintains access to something that never comes to Being as such from just anywhere, but approaches *from* Being itself, indeed as It itself, and "is" Being itself *withal.* What is that?

What we are asking about here, and what we must experience in its simplicity, we already identified without noticing it when we proceeded to describe the default "of" Being as a feature of Being itself. We said that Being itself is not something that keeps itself isolated somewhere. From what could Being separate itself in any case? Not from the being, which dwells in Being, although Being persists in a difference with respect to beings. Not from Being, which Being itself "is" as Being itself. Rather, in staying away, there comes to be a relation to something like a place, away from which the staying away remains what it is: the default of unconcealment as such. That place is the shelter in which the default of unconcealment essentially persists. But if it is precisely concealment that remains in the staying away of unconcealment as such, then the staying of concealment also retains its essential relation to the same place.

The staying away of unconcealment as such and the staying of concealment essentially occur in a shelter which is the very abode for the proper essence of both. But the staying away of unconcealment and the staying of concealment do not subsequently search about for an abode; rather, the abode occurs essentially with them as the advent that Being itself is. The advent is in itself the advent of their abode. The locale of the place of Being as such is Being itself.

That locale, however, is the essence of man. It is not man for himself as subject, insofar as he merely busies himself with his human affairs, considering himself as one being among others, and always, when he is explicitly concerned with Being, immediately explaining it solely from the viewpoint of beings as such. But to the extent that man already comports himself to Being even when he knows it exclusively in terms of beings, he is comporting himself to Being. Man stands in the relationship of Being itself to him, to man, to the extent that as man he comports himself to beings as such. *Being bestows itself by betaking itself into its unconcealment—and only in this way is It Being —along with the locale of its advent as the abode of its default.* This "where," as the "there" of the shelter, belongs to Being itself, "is" Being itself and is therefore called *being-there* [*Da-sein*].

"The *Dasein* in man" is the essence that belongs to Being itself. Man belongs to that essence in such a way that he has to be such Being. *Da-sein* applies to man. As his essence, it is in each case his, what he belongs to, but not what he himself makes and controls as his artifact. Man becomes essential by expressly entering into his essence. He stands in the unconcealment of beings as the concealed locale within which Being essentially occurs in its truth. He stands in this locale, which means that he is ecstative in it, because he is as he is always and everywhere on the basis of the relationship of Being itself to his essence; that is, to the locale of Being itself.

As the relation to Being, whether it is to the being as such or to Being itself, ecstative inherence in the openness of the locale of Being is the essence of thinking. The essence of thinking experienced in this way, that is, experienced on the basis of Being, is not defined by being set off against willing and feeling. Therefore, it should not be proclaimed purely theoretical as opposed to practical activity and thus restricted in its essential importance for the essence of man.

If in our meditation on the essence of nihilism we have been talking about the unthought, it is always the unthought of a thinking that is determined by the essence of Being. Thinking is taken as the activity of the intellect. The issue for the intellect is understanding. The essence of thinking is the understanding of Being in the possibilities of its development, which are conferred by the essence of Being.

From the abode of its advent—It being this abode—Being itself applies to man along with his essence. As the one approached by Being, man is the one who thinks. The "whether it be this, whether it be that," in which the essential possibility of being one way or the other is revealed for thinking, stands in a *certain* way in *man's* thinking; but it rests on Being itself, which can itself withdraw as such and *does withdraw* by *showing* itself in beings as such. But because it concerns the essence of man, even that possibility of thinking is in some sense founded on his essence, which as the locale of Being in turn rests on Being itself.

In that way man, as the one who thinks, can relate himself to beings as such. Thinking therefore brings Being in the form of a being as such to language. Such thinking is metaphysical. It does not repudiate Being itself, but neither does it keep to the default of Being as such. Of itself, thinking does not correspond to the withdrawal of Being.

However, the twofold omission of repudiation and correspondence is not nothing. Rather, it happens not only that Being as such stays away, but that its default is thoughtlessly misplaced and suppressed by thinking. The more exclusively metaphysics gains control of the being as such and secures itself in and by the being as the truth "of Being," the more decisively has it already dispensed with Being as such. Being is the condition of beings, posited by the being as such, and as this condition is one value among others.

The default of Being itself is expressly, if unknowingly, misplaced in its default by the nature of metaphysical thinking, as thinking in values, whereby the very misplacing does not know itself as such. The nothing of Being itself is sealed in the interpretation of Being as value. It belongs to this sealing that it understand itself as the new "yes" to beings as such in the sense of the will to power, that it understand itself as the overcoming of nihilism.

Thought in terms of the *essence* of nihilism, Nietzsche's overcoming is merely the *fulfillment* of nihilism. In it the full essence of nihilism is enunciated for us more clearly than in any other fundamental position of metaphysics. What is authentically its own is the default of Being itself. But insofar as the default occurs in metaphysics, such authenticity is not admitted *as* the authenticity of nihilism.* Rather, the default as such is precisely what is omitted in metaphysical thought, and in such a way that metaphysics omits even the omission as its own act. The default is covertly left to itself by means of the

*"Authenticity" here translates *das Eigentliche.* Heidegger's prior references to *der eigentliche Nihilismus* have been rendered as "nihilism proper." It is still the issue of what is *proper* to nihilism as such that Heidegger explores here, even if the requirements of English compel a return to the problematic renderings "authenticity" and (for *das Uneigentliche*) "inauthenticity."

omission. Precisely in the way it takes place, the authenticity of nihilism *is not* something authentic. To what extent? Nihilism takes place as metaphysics in its own inauthenticity. However, such inauthenticity is not a lack of authenticity but its fulfillment, because it is the default of Being itself and because it devolves upon Being to see that the default remains entirely itself. The authenticity of nihilism historically takes the form of inauthenticity, which accomplishes the omission of the default by omitting this very omission. What with its unqualified affirmation of beings as such, it does not and cannot get involved with whatever might concern Being itself. The full essence of nihilism is the original unity of its authenticity and inauthenticity.

If therefore nihilism is experienced and brought to concepts within metaphysics, metaphysical thought can treat only the inauthenticity of nihilism, and that only in such a way that the inauthenticity *is not experienced as such* but is explained according to the procedures of metaphysics. The omission of the default of Being as such appears in the shape of an explanation of Being as value. Reduced to a value, Being is derived from the being as a condition for it as such.

Nihilism—that there is nothing to Being itself—always means precisely this for metaphysical thought: there is nothing to the being as such. *The very path into the experience of the essence of nihilism is therefore barred to metaphysics.* Insofar as metaphysics in every case decides for either the affirmation or the negation of the being as such, and sees both its beginning and its end in the corresponding elucidation of the being from its existing ground, it has unwittingly failed to notice that Being itself stays away *in the very priority of the question about the being as such.* In staying away, Being abandons the thinking of metaphysics to its own nature, which is precisely to omit the default as such and not to involve itself in the omission. Insofar as such thought, which has become historical as metaphysics, belongs in its essence to Being itself, insofar as it thinks on the basis of the unconcealment of the being as such, the inauthenticity of nihilism is also determined by Being itself.

Inauthentic nihilism is inauthenticity in the essence of nihilism, precisely insofar as nihilism fulfills authenticity. A difference unfolds in the essential unity of nihilism. The inauthenticity of nihilism is not eliminated from its essence. That indicates that nonessence belongs to essence. One might think that the relationship between the authenticity and inauthenticity of nihilism is a particular instance of a universally valid connection between essence and nonessence, so that the former can serve as an example of the latter. But the statement "Nonessence belongs to essence" is by no means a formal, universal assertion of ontology concerning an essence which is represented metaphysically as "essentiality" and appears definitively as *"idea."* In the word (*verbum*) "essence," taken as a verb, the statement thinks Being itself in the way in which it is, a default as such that dwells in an omission and thus is preserved. However, the omission itself occurs essentially in accord with the concealment of the unconcealment of Being in what is withdrawn. Thus thinking, which as metaphysical represents the being as such by way of the omission, is as unlikely to pay attention to the omission as it is incapable of experiencing the abandonment of beings as such by Being itself.

If we think the essence of nihilism in the way we have attempted, then we think it from Being itself as the history of Being, which Being itself "is" as Being. However, the essence of nihilism in the history of Being still does not reveal those features that usually describe what one means by the familiar term *nihilism:* something that disparages and destroys, a decline and downfall. The essence of nihilism contains nothing negative in the form of a destructive element that has its seat in human sentiments and circulates abroad in human activities. The essence of nihilism is not at all the affair of man, but a matter of Being itself, and thereby of course also a matter of the *essence* of man, and only in *that* sequence at the same time a human concern. And presumably not merely one among others.

Though what has been identified as negative within the proximate phenomenon of nihilism in its usual sense does not belong to the essence of nihilism, that in no way implies that the actuality of destructive phenomena should be overlooked, denied, or explained away as irrelevant. Rather, it becomes necessary to ask about the source of these destructive phenomena in their essence, not merely about causal relations concerning their effects.

But how will we even pose the decisive question if we have not first pondered the essence of nihilism and at the same time brought ourselves to ask whether the staying away of the question concerning the essence of nihilism does not partly occasion the dominance of those phenomena? Is it the case that the dominance of destructive nihilism and of our not asking, not being able to ask, about the essence of nihilism ultimately derive from a common root?

If that were so, then there would be little to be gained by maintaining that if the essence of nihilism does not consist in what is negative, then it is automatically something positive. For the positive shares a domain with its opposite. Ascent versus decline, waxing versus waning, exaltation versus degradation, construction versus destruction, all play their roles as counterphenomena in the realm of beings. The essence of nihilism, however, applies to Being itself, or, more appropriately expressed, Being applies to the essence of nihilism, since Being itself has brought it to pass in history that there is nothing to Being itself.

We could now, especially if we have adequately thought through the foregoing discussion of nihilism, profess that the negative phenomena referred to do not immediately pertain to the essence of nihilism, since they do not reach that far. Nevertheless, we continue to insist that something "negative" must reign in the essence of nihilism. Otherwise how could this name, which we would like to take seriously in its naming, still have anything to say? The preceding determination of the essence of nihilism has laid all the stress on the difference between authenticity and inauthenticity in nihilism. The "in-" of inauthenticity brings the negative to the fore.

Certainly it does. But what does "the negative" mean? Are we not appealing to a notion that is indeed familiar, but also a mere commonplace? Does one believe that inauthenticity in nihilism is bad, even malignant, in contrast to authenticity as good and just? Or does one take authentic nihilism to be bad, malignant, and inauthentic nihilism, if not as good, then at least as nonmalignant?

Even discounting their rashness, these opinions would be equally erroneous. Both judge authenticity and inauthenticity in the essence of nihilism superficially. Furthermore, they use standards of judgment whose appropriateness must first be decided. This much ought to have become clear by now: with the essential question we have posed we are moving in the realm of Being itself, which we can no longer explain and judge from any other standpoint, granted that the way of thinking we have attempted is at all adequate. If the "in-" in the essence of nihilism does come forward, then it also lets itself be thought only from the *unity* of that essence. The unity reveals a difference which the "in-" accentuates. But whether the "in-" and the "not" have their essence in the difference, or whether the negative in the "in-" is simply ascribed to the difference, and only as a consequence of a negation, still remains concealed.

But what is it in the essential unity of nihilism that provides an occasion and a footing for such negation? The question cannot be answered immediately. We therefore content ourselves with the insight that something differentiated reigns in the essence of nihilism, something differentiated that applies to Being itself. The "in-" does not merely or primarily rest on a negation and its negativity. But if the basic feature of what is negative in the sense of something destructive is entirely absent from the essence of nihilism, then the intention to overcome nihilism immediately as something that is supposedly purely destructive appears in a strange light. Still more curious, of course, would be the notion that a thinking that refuses the immediate overcoming of a nihilism which is thought essentially must therefore affirm nihilism in the ordinary sense.

What does "overcoming" mean? To overcome signifies: to bring something under oneself, and at the same time to put what is thus placed under oneself behind one as something that will henceforth have no determining power. Even if overcoming does not aim at sheer removal, it remains an attack against something.

To *want* to overcome nihilism—which is now thought in its essence—and to *overcome* it would mean that man of himself advance against Being itself in its default. But who or what would be powerful enough to attack Being itself, no matter from what perspective or with what intent, and to bring it under the sway of man? An overcoming of Being itself not only can never be accomplished—the very attempt would revert to a desire to unhinge the essence of man. The hinge of that essence consists in the fact that Being itself, in whatever way, even as staying away, lays claim to the essence of man. That essence is the abode which Being itself provides for itself, so that it might proceed to such an abode as the advent of unconcealment.

To want to overcome Being itself would mean unhinging the essence of man. One could understand the impossibility of such a plan as if it were an absurd gesture of thought, which as such thinks *on the basis* of Being while wanting to launch an attack *against* Being; as if such a plan were any more absurd (provided there are degrees here) than that effort of thought which, in thinking—which is surely in being—tries to deny beings as such. But what is at stake here is not merely whether thinking, taken for itself, contradicts itself in its own activity and so lacks any basic rules for itself, thereby falling into absurdity. Quite often human thought is entangled in contradiction and nonetheless remains on a path where it meets with success.

It is not merely or primarily that in advancing against Being itself thinking falls into what is logically impossible, but that with such an attack on Being it rises to renounce Being itself, and pursues the surrender of man's essential possibility. That pursuit, despite its absurdity and logical impossibility, could be fatefully realized.

Nor is the essential matter the fact that in the attempt to advance against the default of Being as such, and thus against Being itself, we are not abiding by the rules of thought; it is rather that Being itself is not admitted as Being; that, on the contrary, it is omitted. In such omission, however, we recognize the essential feature of nihilism. To want to assail the default of Being itself directly would mean not heeding Being itself as Being. The overcoming of nihilism willed in such a way would simply be a more dismal relapse into the inauthenticity of its essence, which distorts all authenticity. But how would it be if the overcoming did not directly assail the default of Being itself and stopped trying to measure up to Being itself, while advancing upon the omission of the default? The omission, in the form of metaphysics, is the work of human thought. Would it not be possible for thought to advance upon its own failure, namely, the failure to think Being itself in its unconcealment?

The necessity of such an effort can scarcely be contested, but such a necessity must first be experienced. That of course implies that man experience the omission as such; that is, the inauthenticity in the essence of nihilism. But how can he do so without first being struck by what is authentic—by the default of Being in its unconcealment?

Meanwhile, Being does not merely keep to itself in its unconcealment, as though to reserve this for itself; rather, in accord with the essential relationship of Being itself to the essence of man, Being at the same time also determines the fact that its omission takes place in and through human thought. Even an overcoming of the omission could occur only mediately from man's point of view; that is, in such a way that Being itself first of all would immediately prompt the essence of man to experience the *default* of Being's unconcealment as such for the first time *as an advent* of Being itself, and to ponder what is thus experienced.

If we heed the essence of nihilism as an essence of the history of Being itself, then the plan to overcome nihilism becomes superfluous, if by overcoming we mean that man independently subject that history to himself and yoke it to his pure willing. Such overcoming of nihilism is also fallacious in believing that human thought should advance upon the default.

Instead of such overcoming, only one thing is necessary, namely, that thinking, encouraged by Being itself, simply think to encounter Being in its default as such. Such thinking to encounter rests primarily on the recognition *that Being itself withdraws, but that as this withdrawal Being is precisely the relationship that claims the essence of man, as the abode of its (Being's) advent.* The unconcealment of the being as such is bestowed along with that abode.

Thinking to encounter does not omit the default of Being. But neither does it attempt to gain control of the default and to brush it aside. Thinking to encounter follows Being in its withdrawal, follows it in the sense that it lets Being itself go, while for its own part it stays behind. Then where does thinking linger? No longer where it lingered as the prior, omitting thought of metaphysics. Thinking stays behind by first taking the decisive *step back,* back from the omission—but back to where? Where else than to the realm that for a long time has been granted to thinking by Being itself—granted, to be sure, in the veiled figure of the *essence* of man.

Instead of rushing precipitously into a hastily planned overcoming of nihilism, thinking, troubled by the essence of nihilism, lingers a while in the advent of the default, awaiting its advent in order to learn how to ponder the default of Being in what it would be in itself. In the default as such, the unconcealment of Being conceals itself as the essential occurrence of Being itself. But insofar as Being is the unconcealment of beings as such, Being has nonetheless already addressed itself to the essence of man. Being has already spoken out for and insinuated itself in the essence of man insofar as it has withheld and saved itself in the unconcealment of its essence.

Addressing in this way, while withholding itself in default, *Being is the promise of itself.* To think to encounter Being itself in its default means to become aware of the promise, as which promise Being itself "is." It is, however, in staying away; that is to say, insofar as there is nothing to it. This history—that is, the essence of nihilism—is the destiny of Being itself. Thought in its essence and authenticity, nihilism is the promise of Being in its unconcealment in such a way that it conceals itself precisely as the promise, and in staying away simultaneously provides the occasion for its own omission.

In what does the essence of nihilism consist if such authenticity is at the same time thought with regard to inauthenticity? The inauthenticity in the essence of nihilism is the history of omission; that is, of the concealing of the promise. Granted, however, that Being itself saves itself in its default, then the history of the omission of the default is precisely the preservation of that self-saving of Being itself.

What is essential to the inauthenticity of nihilism is not something base or deficient. The essential occurrence of the nonessence in essence is nothing negative. The history of the omission of the default of Being itself is the history of the preservation of the promise—in the sense that such self-preservation is concealed in what it is. It remains concealed because it is occasioned by the self-concealing withdrawal of Being itself and in that way is imbued by Being with its preserving essence.

That which according to its essence preservingly conceals, and thus remains concealed in its essence and entirely hidden, though nonetheless it somehow appears, is in itself what we call *the mystery.* In the inauthenticity of the essence of nihilism, the mystery of the promise occurs, in which form Being is Itself, in that it saves itself as such. The history of the secret, the mystery itself in its history, is the essence of the history of the omission of the default of Being. The omission of Being itself in the thought of beings as such is the history of the unconcealment of beings as such. That history is metaphysics.

The essence of metaphysics consists in the fact that it is the history of the secret of the promise of Being itself. The essence of metaphysics, which is thought on the basis of Being itself in its history, is the essential factor in the nonessence of nihilism that pertains to the unity of the essence of nihilism. As in the case of the essence of nihilism, therefore, the essence of metaphysics may not be assessed either positively or negatively. But if the plan for an immediate overcoming of nihilism hurries on by its essence, then the intention to overcome metaphysics is also null and void, unless the talk of overcoming metaphysics embraces a meaning that intends neither to disparage nor to eliminate metaphysics.

Metaphysics first attains its essence when it is thought in the way we have attempted to think it, in terms of the history of Being. Its essence is withdrawn from metaphysics itself, and is withdrawn in accord with metaphysics' own essence. Every metaphysical concept of metaphysics assists in barring metaphysics from its own essential provenance. Thought in terms of the history of Being, "the overcoming of metaphysics" always means simply surrendering the metaphysical interpretation of metaphysics. Thinking abandons the pure "metaphysics of metaphysics" by taking the step back, back from the omission of Being in its default. In the step *back,* thinking has already set out on the path of thinking to *encounter* Being itself in its self-withdrawal. That self-withdrawal, as the self-withdrawal of Being, still remains a mode of Being—an advent. By thinking to encounter Being itself, thinking no longer omits Being, but admits it: admits it *into* the originary, revealing unconcealment of Being, which is Being itself.

A little while ago we stated that Being itself remains unthought in metaphysics. In the meantime, we have more clearly illustrated what happens in such remaining-unthought and what takes place as remaining-unthought itself: it is the history of Being itself in its default. Metaphysics belongs within that history. In its essence, metaphysics first approaches thinking from its provenance in the history of Being. Metaphysics is the inauthenticity in the essence of nihilism, and takes place in an essential unity with the authenticity of nihilism.

Until now, the dissonance of something negative—in the sense of destructive—has sounded in the name *nihilism.* Until now, metaphysics has been taken as the supreme region in which the most profound matters are thought. Presumably, the dissonance in the name *nihilism* and the prestige of metaphysics are both genuine, and in that way necessary, semblances. The illusion is inevitable. Metaphysical thought cannot overcome it.

Is it also indomitable for the thinking that thinks the history of Being? The apparent dissonance in the name *nihilism* could indicate a more profound accord that would be determined not from metaphysical heights but from a different domain. The essence of metaphysics reaches deeper than metaphysics itself, indeed reaches into a depth that belongs to a different realm, so that the depth no longer corresponds to a height.

According to its essence, nihilism is the history of the promise, in which Being itself saves itself in a mystery which is itself historical and which preserves the unconcealment of Being from that history in the form of metaphysics. The whole of the essence of nihilism, to the extent that—as the history of Being—it bestows itself as an abode for the essence of man, grants thinking everything that is to be thought. Consequently, what is given to thinking as to be thought we call *the enigma.*

Being, the promise of its unconcealment as the history of the secret, is itself the enigma. Being is that which of its essence gives only that essence to be thought. It, Being, *gives food for thought,* and indeed not just sometimes or in a particular respect, but always and from every point of view, because essentially the fact that It, Being, hands thinking over to its essence—this is a mark of Being itself. Being itself is the enigma. This does not mean (provided such a comparison is fitting here) that Being is the irrational, from which everything rational rebounds, so as to tumble into incapacity for thought. Rather, Being, as what gives food for thought—that is, gives what is to be thought—is also the unique matter which of itself and for itself raises the claim of being what is to be thought; it "is" as this very claim. In the face of Being itself, the unworthy game of hide and seek which is supposed to be played between the irrational and the rational is exposed in all its mindlessness.*

Nevertheless, is not the essence of nihilism in the history of Being the mere product of an enthusiastic thinking into which a romantic philosophy flees, escaping from true reality? What does the essence of nihilism thus thought signify as opposed to the reality—which alone is effective—of actual nihilism, which sows confusion and strife everywhere, which instigates crime and drives us to despair? What is the nothing of Being which we have considered in the face of the actual an-nihil-ation [*Ver-nichts-ung*] of all beings, whose violence, encroaching from all sides, makes almost every act of resistance futile?

We hardly need to illustrate in detail the spreading violence of actual nihilism, which we all personally experience to a sufficient degree, even without an ivory-tower definition of its essence. Furthermore, Nietzsche's experience, in spite of the one-sidedness of his interpretation, deals with "actual" nihilism so forcefully that by comparison our attempt at determining the essence of nihilism appears insubstantial, not to say utterly useless. When every divine, human, material, and natural thing is threatened in its existence, who would want to trouble himself about something like the omission of the default of Being itself, even granting that such a thing takes place and is not merely the subterfuge of a desperate abstraction?

If only a connection between actual nihilism, or even the nihilism experienced by Nietzsche, and the essence of nihilism as thought here were at least perceptible. Then we would remove from the essence of nihilism the undeniable impression of complete unreality, which seems to be even greater than the admittedly enigmatic nature of this essence.

The question remains, in fact emerges for the first time, whether the

* The above paragraph sets the tone for Heidegger's 1951–52 lecture course "What Calls for Thinking?" In the *Spiegel* interview of September 23, 1966, Heidegger complained that in Germany the resulting publication was the least read of all his books; in a conversation with J. Glenn Gray he noted that it was a book he himself had to re-read, since "it contained almost all of my ideas."

"essence" of Being comes from beings, whether the being, as actual, in all its concatenations, is capable of determining actuality, Being, or whether the effectuality that stems from Being itself calls forth everything actual.

Does what Nietzsche experiences and thinks, namely, the history of the devaluation of the highest values, stand for itself? Does not the essence of nihilism in the history of Being essentially unfold within that history? That Nietzsche's metaphysics interprets Being as a value is the effectual, actual omission of the default of Being itself in its unconcealment. What comes to language in the interpretation of Being as value is the eventuating inauthenticity in the essence of nihilism, an inauthenticity that does not know itself and nonetheless only *is* in essential unity with the authenticity of nihilism. If Nietzsche really experienced a history of the devaluation of the highest values, then what is experienced in that way, together with the experience itself, is the *actual* omission of the default of Being in its unconcealment.

The omission *is* as actual history and takes place as that history within the essential unity of the inauthenticity and authenticity of nihilism. That history is nothing alongside "essence." It is the essence itself, and this alone.

Nietzsche appends to his interpretation of nihilism (*"that the uppermost values devaluate themselves"*) an explanation: "The aim is lacking; the 'why?' receives no answer" (WM, 2).

Let us consider the question the "why?" raises here more precisely with regard to what it interrogates and what it asks for. It interrogates beings as such and as a whole, asking them why they are in being. As a metaphysical question, it asks about the being that might be a ground for what is and for the way in which it is. Why does the question about the highest values contain the question about what is supreme? Is it only the *answer* to the question that is lacking? Or is the question itself defective as the question which it is? It is defective as a question because in asking about the existent ground of beings it fails to ask about Being itself and its truth. The question has already failed *as a question* —not simply because it lacks an answer. The inadequate question is no mere mistake, as though some flaw or other had slipped past it. The question misplaces itself. It places itself in a region without prospect, against whose horizon all merely possible answers are bound to fall short.

But as Nietzsche confirms, the fact that the answer to the question "why?" really is lacking, and that where it is still given it remains ineffective from the point of view of being as a whole, the fact that all this is so, and the way in which it is so, implies something else. The question governs all questioning even when it remains without an answer. The exclusive, actual dominance of the question, however, is nothing other than the actual omission of the default of Being itself. Considered from such a viewpoint, is the essence of nihilism something abstract? Or is the essential unfolding of the history of Being itself *the* occurrence on the basis of which all history now takes place? That historiography, even one with the prestige and scope of Jacob Burckhardt's, knows nothing and can know nothing at all of this—is this proof enough that the essence of nihilism "is" *not?*

If Nietzsche's metaphysics interprets Being as a pure value in terms of beings and in accord with the sense of will to power; if Nietzsche in fact thinks the will to power as the principle of a new valuation and understands and wills the latter as the overcoming of nihilism; then metaphysics' utmost entanglement in the inauthenticity of nihilism comes to language in the desire to overcome. It does so in such a way that the entanglement closes itself off from its own essence and thus, under the guise of an overcoming of nihilism, transposes nihilism into the effectuality of its deracinated nonessence.

The putative overcoming of nihilism first establishes the dominion of an absolute omission of the default of Being itself in favor of the being in the form of valuative will to power. Through its withdrawal, which nonetheless remains a relationship to beings, in which form "Being" appears, Being itself releases itself into will to power. As will to power, the being seems to reign above and over all Being. In such reigning and radiating of Being, which is concealed with respect to its truth, the default of Being occurs essentially in such a way that it permits the most extreme omission of itself. It thus aids and abets the advance of the purely actual—of those popularly acclaimed realities—which prides itself on being what is, while at the same time presuming itself to be the measure for deciding that only what is effectual—what is palpable and makes an impression, what is experienced and its expression, what is useful and its success—should pass as being.

In the most extreme form of the inauthenticity of nihilism, which apparently comes to appear of itself, the essential unity of nihilism in the history of Being essentially unfolds. *Granted that the unconditioned appearance of the will to power in the whole of beings is not nothing, is the essence of nihilism in the history of Being, an essence that reigns concealed in this appearance, merely a product of thought or even something utterly fantastic?*

Does not the fantasy—if we are going to talk about it at all—consist more in our indulging the habit of accepting any isolated set of negatively interpreted appearances as results of a nihilism which we do not experience in its essence, taking these appearances as what alone is actual, and throwing to the winds what occurs essentially in the actual, as though it were nothing at all? What if this truly fantastic notion, full of good faith and desirous of order, were one of a kind with nihilism, which it imagines it has not been touched by, or has been absolved from?

The essence of nihilism in the history of Being is not something produced in thought, nor does it hover rootlessly above actual nihilism. Rather, what one takes to be "the real" is something that comes to be only on the basis of the essential history of Being itself.

Of course, the difference between inauthenticity and authenticity which reigns in the essential unity of nihilism could diverge into the most extreme disjunction of inauthentic from authentic. Then, in keeping with its own essence, the essential unity of nihilism would have to conceal itself in what is most extreme. It would have to disappear, as though it were nothing at all, in the unconcealment of the being as such, which everywhere passes for Being itself. It would then have to appear as if in truth there were nothing to Being itself, provided that such a thought could still occur at all.

If he were to consider what has been said up to now, who would not suppose Being itself capable of such a possibility? Who, if he thinks, could escape being affected by the most extreme withdrawal of Being, sensing that in the withdrawal there is an exaction by Being—*Being itself as such exaction*—which applies to man in his essence? That essence is nothing human. It is the abode of the advent of Being, which as advent grants itself an abode and proceeds to it, so that precisely as a result *"There is / It gives Being."* * The essence of nihilism in the history of Being takes place as the history of the secret. The essence of metaphysics proceeds as the mystery.

The essence of nihilism is an enigma for thinking. This has been admitted. However, the admission does not belatedly and of itself yield something that it was previously able to enjoin for itself. The admission merely places itself in insistence; that is, into the tarrying inherence in the midst of the self-veiled truth of Being. Only through such insistence is man capable of maintaining his essence as the one who, in his essence, thinks.

When thinking dispatches itself into thought, it stands already in the admission of the enigma of the history of Being. At the moment thinking thinks, Being has already been intended for it. *The mode of this primordial summoning is the default of the unconcealment of Being in the unconcealed being as such.*

For a long time, thinking did not heed this. That prevented it from discerning that the phenomena of nihilism in the ordinary sense are unchained by the release of Being. Such release surrenders the default of the unconcealment of Being to an omission through metaphysics, which at the same time and in a concealed fashion prevents the advent of self-concealing Being. Insofar as nihilistic phenomena emerge from the release of Being, they are evoked by the predominance of the being itself, and they in turn effect the disjunction of the being from Being itself.

In the occurrence of the default of Being itself, man is thrown into the release of the being by the self-withdrawing truth of Being. Representing Being in the sense of the being as such, he lapses into beings, with the result that by submitting to beings he sets himself up as the

---

* *So dass* "Es"—*demzufolge und nur so*—"das Sein gibt." The translation tries to capture both the idiomatic and the literal senses of the German *Es gibt*—"there is," "it gives." Note that Heidegger's formulation of the *Es gibt* throughout these pages differs from his later interpretation of *Ereignis*. The present formulation tends to equate the "It" with Being, whereas Heidegger's final efforts leave the "It" of the granting unnamed. Yet these pages too voice the suspicion that the word *Being* names the enigma inadequately, and that the word may therefore have to be surrendered.

being who in the midst of beings representationally and productively seizes upon them as the objective. In the midst of beings, man freely posits his own essence as certainty for and against the being. He seeks to accomplish this surety in the being through a complete ordering of all beings, in the sense of a systematic securing of stockpiles, by means of which his establishment in the stability of certainty is to be completed.

The objectification of all being as such, on the basis of man's insurrection on behalf of the exclusive self-willing of his will, is the essence of that process in the history of Being by which man sets forth his essence in subjectivity. In accord with subjectivity, man installs both himself and what he represents as world into the subject-object relation, which is sustained by subjectivity. *All transcendence, whether it be ontological or theological, is represented relative to the subject-object relation.* Through the insurrection into subjectivity even theological transcendence and thus the supreme being of beings—one calls it, indicatively enough, "Being"—shifts into a kind of objectivity, specifically, the objectivity of the subjectivity of moral-practical faith. It makes no difference in the essence of this fundamental metaphysical position concerning the human essence whether man takes that transcendence seriously as "providence" for his religious subjectivity or takes it merely as a pretext for the willing of his self-seeking subjectivity.

There is no reason for astonishment over the fact that both these opinions about providence, opinions which when viewed individually are opposites, should prevail at the same time alongside each other, for both stem from the same root of the metaphysics of subjectivity. As metaphysics, they leave Being itself unthought in its truth from the outset. As the metaphysics of subjectivity, however, they make Being in the sense of the being as such into the objectivity of representing and pro-posing. The pro-posing of Being as a value posited by the will to power is merely the final step of modern metaphysics, in which Being comes to appearance as will to power.

But the history of metaphysics, as the history of the unconcealment of the being as such, is the history of Being itself. The modern metaphysics of subjectivity is the granted closure of Being itself, which in the default of its truth causes the omission of that default.* The essence of man, however, which in a covert way is the abode of Being itself in its advent, an abode that belongs to Being itself, becomes more and more omitted the more essentially the advent is preserved in the form of the withdrawal of Being. Man becomes uncertain when confronting his own essence, which lingers with Being itself in the withdrawal, without being able to discover the source and essence of his uncertainty. Instead, he seeks primal truth and permanence in self-certainty. He therefore strives for self-assurance, which he himself provides in the midst of beings, which are always surveyed with regard to what they can offer by way of new and continuous possibilities of surety. What becomes evident thereby is that, of all beings, man is transposed into uncertainty in a special way. This allows us to assume that man, particularly in his relation to his own essence, is at stake. With that, the possibility glimmers that all being as such could occur essentially as a game in which everything is at stake, and that being itself is such "world-play."

In the years he was working toward his planned *magnum opus,* Nietzsche summarized the fundamental thoughts of his metaphysics in the following poem. It belongs in the sequence of "Songs of the Outlaw Prince," which was published in the second edition (1887) of the book *The Gay Science* as an "Appendix" (V, 349)†:

---

* In the expression "the granted closure of Being itself," *die Zulassung des Seins selbst,* we find the paradox of the oblivion of Being stated most pointedly. *Zu-lassen* means "to leave closed"; *Zulassen* means "to grant entry," "admit." Being remains closed to the metaphysics of subjectivity, and yet is somehow granted—as closure, default, omission.

† The poem appears in CM, vol. V, Division 2, p. 323, as follows:

An Goethe

Das Unvergängliche
Ist nur dein Gleichnis!
Gott der Verfängliche
Ist Dichter-Erschleichnis . . .

Welt-Rad, das rollende,
Streift Ziel auf Ziel:
Not—nennt's der Grollende,
Der Narr nennt's—Spiel . . .

To Goethe

The Ever-enduring
Is but your conceit!
And God, the alluring,
A poet's retreat.

World-wheel, spinning by,
Skims goals on its way:
Calamity! is rancor's cry;
The jester calls it Play!

World-play, the ruling,
Mixes "Seems" with "To Be":
Eternally, such fooling
Mixes *us* in—the melee!

Let the following remarks suffice in place of the detailed interpretation of the poem that belongs here but that would repeat much of what was said earlier. The last stanza enables us to see that "world-play" as "the ruling" thinks on the basis of will to power. The latter posits "Being" as the condition of its securing of permanence. The will to power posits "Being" at the same time in unity with "semblance" (art) as the condition of its own enhancement. Both Being and semblance are mixed with each other. The blending, however, the way in which will to power *is,* the poem calls "eternal fooling," and the "world-

---

Welt-Spiel, das herrische,
Mischt Sein und Schein:—
Das Ewig-Närrische
Mischt *uns*—hinein! . . .

Nietzsche's poem, especially its concluding stanza, holds a special place in Heidegger's esteem. The sole extant typescript of the essay "Nietzsche's Metaphysics" (1940; see Volume III of this series) shows a second title page with the words, "Nietzsche's Metaphysics, Interpreted on the Basis of the Lines. . . ." (Heidegger then reprints the concluding stanza of "To Goethe.") A handwritten note at the top of this sheet refers to "the winter semester of 1938–39," indicating perhaps—although this is uncertain—a three-hour "exercise" with the title "Toward an Interpretation of Nietzsche's Second *Untimely Meditation,* 'On the Use and Disadvantage of History for Life.' " Strangely, the typescript of "Nietzsche's Metaphysics" makes no mention of the stanza in question. It may well be that the materials on which Heidegger based his seminar on "world-play" are lost—unless these few lines of the "nihilism" essay rescue their substance.

wheel, spinning by." It is the eternal recurrence of the same, which posits no indestructible aims, but merely "skims goals on its way."

Insofar as man is, he is a configuration of will to power. He is mixed by the blending power of the world-wheel "into" the whole of becoming-being.

In the metaphysical domain of the thought of will to power, as the eternal recurrence of the same, all that is left to express the determination of the relationship of man to "Being" is the following possibility:

Eternally such fooling
Mixes *us* in—the melee!

Nietzsche's metaphysics thinks the playful character of world-play in the only way it can think it: out of the unity of will to power and eternal recurrence of the same. Without a perspective on this unity, all talk about world-play remains vacuous. But for Nietzsche these are thoughtful words; as such, they belong to the language of his metaphysics.

The unity of will to power and eternal recurrence of the same rests on the coherence of *essentia* and *existentia,* whose differentiation remains obscure with respect to its essential provenance.

The unity of will to power and eternal recurrence signify that the will to power is in truth the will-to-will, a determination in which the metaphysics of subjecticity* attains the peak of its development, its fulfillment. The metaphysical concept of "world-play" identifies the affinity in the history of Being between what Goethe experienced as "nature" and Heraclitus as *kosmos* (see Fragment 30).†

* *Subiectität.* At this point, Heidegger inserts a reference to his essay "Metaphysics as History of Being" (1941). See Martin Heidegger, *The End of Philosophy,* tr. Joan Stambaugh (New York: Harper & Row, 1973), pp. 46–49, and NII, 450 ff.

† Fragment 30 reads, "This cosmos, the same for all, was created neither by god nor man, but always was, is, and shall be ever-living fire, kindling in measures, dwindling in measures." Heidegger refers to it in his essay "Aletheia," *Early Greek Thinking,* pp. 115 and 117, and it is one of the mainstays of Eugen Fink's "cosmological" interpretation of Heraclitus. See Martin Heidegger and Eugen Fink, *Heraclitus Seminar 1966/67,* tr. Charles Seibert (University, Ala.: University of Alabama Press, 1979), sections 2, 5, and 6. Cf. John Sallis and Kenneth Maly, eds., *Heraclitean Fragments: A Companion Volume to the Heidegger/Fink Seminar on Heraclitus,* published by the University of Alabama Press in 1980, p. 8 and throughout. Curiously, Heidegger does not here refer

In the sometimes visible, sometimes undescried reigning of world-play, thought metaphysically, the being at times reveals itself as the will-to-will as such, and at times conceals itself again. Everywhere, the being as such has brought itself into an unconcealment that lets it appear as what posits itself on itself and brings itself before itself. That is the fundamental trait of subjecticity. The being as subjecticity omits the truth of Being itself in a decisive way, insofar as subjecticity, out of its own desire for surety, posits the truth of beings as certitude. Subjecticity is not a human product: rather, man secures himself as the being who is in accord with beings as such, insofar as he wills himself as the I-and-we subject, represents himself to himself, and so presents himself to himself.

That the being as such is in the mode of subjecticity and that man searches high and low in the midst of beings, seeking means of securing his certainty, in all cases merely testifies that in the history of its default Being keeps to itself with its unconcealment. *Being itself occurs essentially as such keeping to itself.* The essence of Being itself does not take place behind or beyond beings, but—provided the notion of such a relationship is permissible here—*before* the being as such. Therefore, even the presumed actuality of nihilism in the ordinary sense falls behind its essence. That our thinking, which for centuries has been accustomed to metaphysics, still does not perceive this is no proof for the opposite conclusion. In fact, we ought to ask here in a general way whether proofs of thought, of whatever kind they may be, are what is essential—or whether what is essential are hints of Being.

But how can we be certain of these hints? Even this question, which sounds so serious and poised, arises from a claim that still belongs to the realm of the metaphysics of subjecticity. This does not mean that it may be disregarded. Rather, it is necessary to ask whether the call for criteria of certitude has considered and pondered everything that belongs within the radius of what must be heard.

The essential unfolding of nihilism is the default of Being as such. In staying away, it promises itself in its unconcealment. The default

---

to Fragment 52, "Aion is a child at play, playing at draughts; dominion is the child's." See Martin Heidegger, *Nietzsche, vol. II: The Eternal Recurrence of the Same,* section 11 (NI, 333–34); *Holzwege,* p. 258; and *Der Satz vom Grund* (Pfullingen: G. Neske, 1957), pp. 187–88.

abandons itself to the omission of Being itself in the secret of history. As history, metaphysics keeps the truth of Being concealed in the unconcealment of the being as such. As the promise of its truth, Being keeps to itself with its own essence. The admission of the omission of the default takes place on the basis of its keeping to itself. From the respective distance of the withdrawal, which conceals itself in any given phase of metaphysics, such keeping to itself determines each epoch of the history of Being as the *epochē* of Being itself.

But when Being itself withdraws into its remotest withholding, the being as such arises, released as the exclusive standard for "Being," into the totality of its dominion. Beings as such appear as will to power, whereby Being as will fulfills its subjecticity. The metaphysics of subjectivity omits Being itself so decisively that it remains concealed in value thinking and can barely allow value thinking to be known as or to pass for metaphysics at all. While metaphysics plunges into the vortex of its omission, the latter, unrecognizable as such, is established for the truth of beings in the form of the securing of permanence; it completes the closing off of the truth of beings as such from the truth of Being. But, in accord with the prevailing blindness of metaphysics to itself, the closing off appears as a liberation from all metaphysics (see *Twilight of the Idols,* "How the 'True World' Finally Became a Fable"; VIII, 82 f.).*

In this way, the inauthenticity in nihilism reaches absolute predominance, behind which the authenticity—and along with authenticity and its relation to inauthenticity the *essence* of nihilism—remains submerged in the inaccessible and unthinkable. In our epoch of the history of Being, only the consequences of the predominance of the inauthenticity in nihilism take effect, although never *as* consequences, but simply as nihilism itself. Nihilism therefore reveals only destructive features. These are experienced, furthered, or resisted in the light of metaphysics.

Antimetaphysics and the reversal of metaphysics, but also the defense of previous metaphysics: these constitute the sole occupation of the long-eventuating omission of the default of Being itself.

The struggle over nihilism, for it and against it, is engaged on a field

* See the first volume of this series, *The Will to Power as Art,* section 24.

staked out by the predominance of the nonessence of nihilism. Nothing will be decided by this struggle. It will merely seal the predominance of the inauthentic in nihilism. Even where it believes itself to be standing on the opposite side, the struggle is everywhere and at bottom nihilistic—in the usual destructive sense of the word.

The will to overcome nihilism mistakes itself because it bars itself from the revelation of the *essence* of nihilism as the history of the default of Being, bars itself without being able to recognize its own deed. The mistaking of the essential impossibility of overcoming metaphysics within metaphysics, or even through the reversal of metaphysics, could go so far that one might take the denial of that possibility as an affirmation of nihilism, or even as a complacent observation of the course of nihilistic decadence that will not lend a hand to stop it.

Because the default of Being is the history of Being and thus is authentically existing history, the being as such, especially in the epoch of the dominance of the nonessence of nihilism, lapses into the unhistorical. The sign of this lapse is the emergence of the historical sciences, which advance a claim to be the definitive representation of history. They take history to be of the past, and explain it in its emergence as a causally demonstrable continuum of effects. The past, objectified by recounting and explaining, appears against the horizon of that present which in each case performs the objectification; at its culmination, the present explains itself as the product of the past occurrence itself. One believes one knows what facts and factuality are, and what sorts of beings take the form of the past, because through historical research objectification is always bringing forward some kind of factual material, and it knows how to put it in a frame of reference that is topical and, above all, "relevant" to the present.

Our historical situation is being analyzed everywhere. It is the point of departure and the goal for the mastery of beings, in the sense of securing man's standpoint and status within them. Historical research consciously or unconsciously stands in service to the will of human cultures to establish themselves among beings according to a comprehensible order. The will to nihilism as normally understood, and to its campaign, as well as the will to an overcoming of nihilism, become operative in the historiological reckoning of historiologically analyzed spirit and of world-historical situations.

Sometimes historical research also asks what history is, but always merely as an "also," and therefore belatedly and by the way, always as if historiological representations of history could furnish a determination of the essence of history by making sufficiently broad generalizations. When philosophy takes up the inquiry, however, and attempts to set forth an ontology of the happening of history, it persists in the metaphysical interpretation of beings as such.

History as Being—indeed, as coming from the essence of Being itself—remains unthought. Every historiological meditation of man on his condition is therefore metaphysical, and thus pertains to the essential omission of the default of Being. It is necessary to contemplate the metaphysical character of history as a discipline if we are going to measure the impact of historiological thought, which at times considers itself authorized to enlighten, if not to rescue man, who is at stake in the age of the self-fulfilling nonessence of nihilism.

Meanwhile, following the claims and demands of the age, the effective completion of academic history has advanced from being a scientific discipline to journalism. If it is understood correctly, and not in a disparaging way, "journalism" identifies the metaphysical securing and establishment of the everydayness of our dawning age, everydayness in the form of solid historical research; that is to say, research that works as hastily and reliably as possible, through which everyone is provided with the ever-useful objectivities of the day. At the same time, it reflects the self-completing objectification of beings as a whole.

The epoch of the unconditioned and complete objectification of everything that is begins with the self-fulfilling metaphysics of subjectivity, which corresponds to the most extreme withdrawal of the truth of Being, because it obscures the withdrawal until it is unrecognizable. In that objectification, man himself and every aspect of human culture is transformed into a stockpile which, psychologically reckoned, is incorporated into the working process of the will-to-will, even if some people view that process as free, while others interpret it as purely mechanical. Both mistake the covert essence in the history of Being, that is, the nihilistic essence, which when expressed in the language of metaphysics is always something "spiritual." Even the fact that in the process of the absolute objectification of beings as such mankind has become a "human resource," ranked behind natural resources and raw materials, does not betray a supposedly materialistic preference for matter and energy over the human spirit. It is grounded in the unconditioned character of objectification itself, which must bring every stockpile, no matter what its nature, into its own possession and must secure this possession.

The absolute objectification of the being as such results from the self-fulfilling dominion of subjectivity. This occurs essentially as the most extreme release of the being as such into the omission of Being itself; in that way Being refuses its default to the extreme and as such refusal dispatches Being in the form of beings as such—dispatches it as the destiny of the complete concealment of Being in the midst of the thoroughgoing securing of beings.

History, concealed in its historicity, is still interpreted historiologically—that is always to say, metaphysically—albeit from different if not indeed necessarily opposing standpoints. The positing of aims in all ordering, the assessment of the value of the human, establishes for itself a public according to the positings of value thinking, and procures for that public its legitimacy.

Just as the unconcealment of the being, the truth of the being, has come to be a value, so has the kind of unconcealment known as publicity become—in the essential sequence of this interpretation of the essence of truth—a necessary value for securing the permanence of the will to power. In each case publicity yields metaphysical or, what is the same thing here, antimetaphysical explanations of what is to be considered being and what nonbeing. But the being, thus objectified, is nonetheless not what *is.*

What is, is what takes place. What takes place has already taken place. That does not mean that it is past. What has already taken place is only what has gathered itself into the essence of Being, into the having-occurred-essentially [*das Ge-Wesen*], from which and as which the advent of Being itself is—even if in the form of the self-withdrawal that stays away. The advent holds the being as such in its unconcealment and leaves unconcealment to the being as the unthought Being of beings. What happens is the history of Being, Being as the history of default. The latter pertains to the essence of man, specifically insofar as man in our time has neither recognized nor acted on the admission that his essence has been withheld from him. The default of Being comes toward the essence of man in such a way that in his relationship to Being man unwittingly turns away from it, understanding Being solely in terms of beings, wanting to have every question regarding "Being" understood in that way.

Had the admission of man into his essence in the history of Being already taken place, he surely would have been able to experience the essence of nihilism. Such an experience would have induced him to consider that what is commonly known as nihilism is what it is on the basis of the completed dominion of the nonessence of its essence. That nihilism does not allow itself to be overcome is implicit in the essential provenance of nihilism in the metaphysical sense. It does not allow itself to be overcome, not because it is insuperable, but because all wanting-to-overcome is inappropriate to its essence.

The historical relation of man to the essence of nihilism can only consist in his thoughtfully undertaking to think to encounter the default of Being itself. Such thinking of the history of Being brings man face to face with the essence of nihilism; in contrast, all wanting-to-overcome puts nihilism behind us, but only in such a way that in the still-dominant horizon of metaphysically determined experience nihilism rises up around us unperceived, ever more terrible in its power, beguiling our thoughts.

Thinking in terms of the history of Being lets Being arrive in the essential space of man. Because the essential domain is an abode with which Being as such provides itself, thinking in terms of the history of Being lets Being occur essentially as Being itself. Thinking takes a step back from metaphysical representing. Being lightens as the advent of the keeping-to-itself of the refusal of its unconcealment. What is identified with "lighting," "arriving," "keeping to itself," "refusal," "revealing," and "concealing" is one and the same essential occurrence, namely, Being.

Nevertheless, the name *Being* at the same time loses its naming power in the step back, because it always unwittingly says "presence and permanence," determinations to which the *essentially occurring* character of Being can never be attached as a mere addendum. On the other hand, the attempt to think Being as Being with regard to the tradition must go to utmost extremes in order to experience whether and why Being no longer allows itself to be defined as—"Being." That limitation does not extinguish thinking, but transforms it into that essence which is already predetermined by the withholding of the truth of Being.

When metaphysical thinking takes the step back, it dispatches itself to liberate man's essential space. But such liberation is occasioned by Being in order that we think to encounter the advent of its default. The step back does not cast metaphysics aside. Rather, now for the first time thinking has the essence of metaphysics before it and around it in the radius of its experiences of the being as such. The provenance of metaphysics in the history of Being remains what is to be thought. In this way the essence of metaphysics is preserved as the secret of the history of Being.

The default of Being is its withdrawal, its keeping to itself with its unconcealment, which it promises in its refusing, self-concealing. Thus Being essentially occurs as promise in the withdrawal. But that is a relating: in it Being itself lets its abode come to it, that is, draws it forth. As such relating, Being never, even in the default of its unconcealment, relents from unconcealment, which in keeping to itself is released solely as the unconcealment of the being as such. As the advent that never abandons its abode, Being is the unrelenting. In this way, it is compelling. Being occurs essentially in this way to the extent that as the advent of unconcealment it requires unconcealment, not as something alien, but as Being. Being needs an abode. Requiring an abode, Being lays claim to it.

Being is compelling in a twofold, harmonious sense: it is unrelenting and needful in relating to an abode that essentially occurs as the essence to which man belongs, man being the one who is needed. What is doubly compelling is, and is called, the need. In the advent of the default of its unconcealment, Being itself is need.*

* Being "needs" (*braucht*) an abode, and thus "uses" (also: *braucht*) man. But when Being advenes in default of unconcealment, it can only be "needy," its history a

But need veils itself by staying away. At the same time the default is hidden by the omission of the truth of Being in the history of metaphysics. Within the unconcealment of the being as such, which the history of metaphysics determines as the fundamental occurrence, the need of Being does not come to the fore. The being *is*, and gives rise to the illusion that Being is without need.

But the needlessness that establishes itself as the dominion of metaphysics brings Being itself to the utmost limit of its need. Need is not merely what compels in the sense of the unyielding claim that occupies an abode by using it as the unconcealment of the advent; that is, by letting it unfold essentially as the truth of Being. The relentlessness of its usage extends so far in the default of its unconcealment that the abode of Being—that is, the essence of man—is omitted; man is threatened with the annihilation of his essence, and Being itself is endangered in its usage of its abode. By extending so far into default, Being consigns itself to the danger that the need, in which form it compellingly unfolds, never becomes for historical man the need that it is. At its outermost limit, the need of Being comes to be the need of needlessness. The predominance of the still-veiled needlessness of Being, which in its truth is the doubly compelling need of an unrelenting usage of the abode, is nothing other than the absolute preeminence of the fully developed nonessence in the essence of nihilism.

As the veiled and extreme need of Being, however, needlessness reigns precisely in the age of the darkening of beings, our age of confusion, of violence and despair in human culture, of disruption and impotence of willing. Both openly and tacitly, boundless suffering and measureless sorrow proclaim the condition of our world a needful one. All the same, at the basis of its history it is needless. Yet in the history of Being this is its supreme and at the same time most concealed need. It is the need of Being itself.

But how can the need as such expressly involve man—and involve him specifically in his essential distance from himself? What can man

"calamity" (*die Not*). "Need" is thus twofold, referring to the "destitute time" in which we live but also to the "usage" of Being as such in every epoch. Heidegger discusses this difficult matter further in "The Anaximander Fragment," *Early Greek Thinking,* pp. 52–59.

do, if in truth the need is a need of Being itself? The need of Being itself, which the essence of nihilism embodies historically and which—perhaps—will bring its authenticity to advent, is patently not a need in the sense that man might meet it by controlling and restraining it. How should he meet it if he does not even know it? And would not restraint be a relation that is altogether contrary to the essence of such need?

To correspond to the need of needlessness can only mean above all else to assist in experiencing needlessness for the first time as the essential occurrence of need itself. That would require that we point toward the need-less quality of need, which in turn requires that we experience the omission of the default of Being itself. In what is thus experienced, it is appropriate to think the essence of nihilism as the history of Being itself. But that means to think to encounter the advent of the self-withdrawal of Being in relation to its abode; that is to say, the advent of the essence of historical man.

But what vista opens up here? To think to encounter the extreme need of Being suggests that we broach the extreme threat to man; that is, the danger that threatens to annihilate his *essence.* It means thinking what is dangerous. Then the path of contemplation would be fortunate in having arrived at that "dangerous thinking" which the human world, already sufficiently confused, still condemns as irresponsible and groundless. The glorification of danger and the misuse of force—do they not reciprocally enhance each other?

Nietzsche's oft-repeated phrase about "living dangerously" belongs to the realm of the metaphysics of will to power; it calls for an active nihilism, which is now to be thought as the absolute dominion of the nonessence of nihilism. But danger as the risk of the uncontrolled implementation of force, and danger as the threat of the annihilation of man's essence, although they both derive from the default of Being itself, are not identical. Yet neglecting to think about the omission of the need of Being itself, an omission that takes place as metaphysics, is blindness in the face of needlessness as the essential need of man. Such blindness comes from unconfessed anxiety in the face of the anxiety that experiences with trepidation the default of Being itself.

When it is viewed with respect to the duration of the history of

Being, it may well be that blindness in the face of the extreme need of Being, in the form of the needlessness that prevails in the midst of crowds of beings, is still more hazardous than the crass adventures of a merely brutal will to violence. The greater danger consists in optimism, which recognizes only pessimism as its opponent. But both are value assessments in relation to beings and among beings. Both move in the realm of metaphysical thinking and institute the omission of the default of Being. They increase needlessness, and, without being able to meditate on it, merely see to it that needlessness is not and cannot be experienced *as need.*

The need of Being consists in the fact that it is doubly compelling, but that in its default it is accompanied by the danger of the annihilation of man's essence, insofar as Being occasions the omission of its own default. Need-lessness signifies that the need, which Being itself essentially unfolds as, remains veiled—a destiny that endangers need by elevating it to the utmost extremity and perfecting it as the need of needlessness.

However, if historical man were capable of thinking needlessness as the need of Being itself, then he could presumably discover what *is* in the history of Being.* In the era of the fulfilled nonessence of nihilism, man might then for the first time learn that what "is," *is*—in the sense of an "is" determined by the truth of Being. For he would already have thought on the basis of Being itself. Man would discover what emerges from needlessness as need in terms of the history of Being, what in that way has already arrived in its provenance but comes to presence in a concealed advent; that is, from the viewpoint of metaphysical experience, comes to absence. Metaphysically considered, absence means the exact opposite of presencing as Being: nonbeing in the sense of vacuous nothingness. What is it that emerges from the need of needlessness into the unthought of Being itself—that is to say, amid beings as such—in such a way that it passes for nothingness?

* The use of the verb *is* in this and the following sentence points forward to Heidegger's lecture series to the Bremen Club in 1949 entitled *Einsicht in das, was Ist,* "Insight into What Is." The four lectures were "The Thing," "The Enframing" (later entitled "The Question Concerning Technology"), "The Danger," and "The Turning."

The default of the unconcealment of Being as such releases the evanescence of all that is hale in beings. The evanescence of the hale takes the openness of the holy with it and closes it off. The closure of the holy eclipses every illumination of the divine. The deepening dark entrenches and conceals the lack of God. The obscure lack lets all beings stand in the unfamiliar, even though the being, as what is objectified in limitless objectification, seems to be a secure possession and is everywhere well-known. The unfamiliarity of beings as such brings to light the homelessness of historical man within beings as a whole. The "where" of a dwelling in the midst of beings as such seems obliterated, because Being itself, as the essential occurring of every abode, fails to appear.

The partly conceded, partly denied homelessness of man with regard to his *essence* is replaced by the organized global conquest of the earth, and the thrust into outer space. Homeless man—thanks to the success of his management and ordering of ever greater numbers of his kind—lets himself be driven into flight in the face of his own essence, only to represent this flight to himself as a homecoming to the true humanity of *homo humanus,* and to make humanity part of his own enterprise. The pressure of the actual and effectual increases. Needlessness in relation to Being is entrenched in and through the increased demand for beings. The more the being requires beings, the less it craves the being as such; even less is it inclined to heed Being itself. The destitution of beings with respect to the unconcealment of Being is complete.

The epoch of the concealment of Being in the unconcealment of the being in the form of will to power is the age of the accomplished destitution of the being as such. However, this age first begins to establish the dominion of the nonessence of nihilism in its completeness. The historical course of our era entertains the illusion that man, having become free for his humanity, has freely taken the universe into his power and disposition. The right way seems to have been found. All that is needed is to proceed rightly and thus to establish the dominion of justification as the supreme representative of the will-to-will.

The essence of the destitution of this era in the history of Being consists in the need of needlessness. Because it is more essential, and older, the destiny of Being is less familiar than the lack of God. As such a destiny, the truth of Being refuses itself in the midst of the throng of beings and nothing but beings. What is unfamiliar in our absent-present need closes itself off thanks to the fact that everything actual, the being itself which concerns the man of our era and carries him along with it, is thoroughly familiar to him; but precisely on that account, not only is man unacquainted with the truth of Being, but wherever "Being" crops up he proclaims it the specter of sheer abstraction, thus mistakes it and repudiates it as vacuous nothingness. By surrendering all remembrance, instead of ceaselessly recollecting the essential historical fullness of the *words* "Being" and "to be," he hears mere *terms,* whose empty reverberations he rightly finds irritating.

The unfamiliarity of the need of needlessness does close itself off; it does extend its misconstrued reign in the omission of Being itself. But the unfamiliarity of the need derives from what is simple. Such simplicity bodies forth in the stillness of Being's default, which *remains* still. However, man in the age of fulfilled metaphysics hardly encounters in thought what is simple. To the extent that he is able to think Being as such, he immediately encumbers it with the freight of a metaphysical concept, whether he takes the latter seriously as the labor of a limited comprehension, or frivolously as the mere sport of a futile grappling. In any case, metaphysical knowledge, whether as a positive investment or a negative withdrawal, is enriched only by the labors of scientific knowledge.

But thinking, which encounters in inquiry the default of Being, neither is grounded on science nor can it ever find its way by setting itself off against science. Whenever it *is,* thinking rests in the occasioning of, and is as an occasion from, Being itself, insofar as it involves itself in the unconcealment of Being.

To the extent that a thinking of Being, according to its own essence in the history of Being, can experience what remains for it to experience only in the need of needlessness; that is, can experience need itself as the destiny of the default of Being in its truth; to that extent it necessarily dispatches itself—still under the dominance of metaphysics, and within its unlimited sphere of control—with those first steps that lead it toward the drawing pull of Being on the essence of man, a drawing in the form of withdrawal.

Thinking of Being is so decisively caught up in the metaphysical thought of the being as such that it can only grope its way with the help of a staff borrowed from metaphysics. Metaphysics helps and hinders at the same time. It makes the passage more difficult, not because it is metaphysics, but because it maintains its own essence in what is unthinkable. The essence of metaphysics, however, the fact that in concealing it shelters the unconcealment of Being and thus is the *secret* of the history of Being, first of all permits the experience of thinking the history of Being passage into the free region. The truth of Being itself essentially occurs as the free region.

If needlessness is the most extreme need and *is* precisely as if it were not, then in order for the need to be compelling in the realm of man's essence, man's capacities must first be directed toward the needlessness. To experience needlessness as such is a necessity. Granted, however, that it is the need of Being as such, and granted that Being as such is entrusted preeminently and only to thinking, then the matter of Being—that in its unconcealment it is the Being of beings—passes over to thinking. For thinking, Being itself in its unconcealment and thus unconcealment itself must become questionable; but this is to happen in the age of metaphysics, through which Being is devalued into a value. Yet the worth of Being, as Being, does not consist in being a value, even the supreme value. Being essentially occurs in that it—the freedom of the free region itself—liberates all beings to themselves. It remains what is to be thought by thinking. But the fact that the being *is* as if Being "were" *not* unrelenting in its usage of the abode, as if it "were" *not* the compelling need of truth itself—this fact constitutes the dominion of needlessness entrenched in metaphysics as fulfilled.

ANALYSIS AND GLOSSARY

Analysis

By DAVID FARRELL KRELL

At the outset, three extracts to broach the themes of will to power, nihilism, and the nothing.

First, Ulysses to the Greek princes on the plains of Troy:

> Take but degree away, untune that string,
> And, hark, what discord follows! each thing meets
> In mere oppugnancy: the bounded waters
> Should lift their bosoms higher than the shores,
> And make a sop of all this solid globe:
> Strength should be lord of imbecility,
> And the rude son should strike his father dead:
> Force should be right; or, rather, right and wrong,—
> Between whose endless jar justice resides,—
> Should lose their names, and so should justice too.
> Then everything includes itself in power,
> Power into will, will into appetite;
> And appetite, an universal wolf,
> So doubly seconded with will and power,
> Must make perforce an universal prey,
> And last eat up himself.
>
> SHAKESPEARE, *Troilus and Cressida,* I, iii

Second, Hyperion to Bellarmine:

O you hapless creatures, who feel it, but who do not like to speak of what defines man; you who are transfixed by the nothing that governs us; you who thoroughly comprehend that we are born for nothing, that we love a nothing, believe in the nothing, toil away for nothing, in order gradually to pass over into the nothing;—what can I do to prevent your collapsing when you contemplate it in earnest? . . . O, I can fall on my knees, wring my hands, and plead (with whom I know not) that there be other thoughts. But I cannot suppress the crying truth. Have I not convinced myself twice over? When I gaze into life, what is the end of it all? Nothing. When my spirit ascends, what is the highest height of all? Nothing.

HÖLDERLIN, *Hyperion,* I, 1

Third, the merciless Melville, raising the curtain on a shivering author and delivering himself of "some philosophical remarks":

Some hours pass. Let us peep over the shoulder of Pierre, and see what it is he is writing there, in that most melancholy closet. . . . "A deep-down, unutterable mournfulness is in me. Now I drop all humorous or indifferent disguises, and all philosophical pretensions. . . . Away, ye chattering apes of a sophomorean Spinoza and Plato, who once didst all but delude me that the night was day, and pain only a tickle. Explain this darkness, exorcise this devil, ye cannot. Tell me not, thou inconceivable coxcomb of a Goethe, that the universe cannot spare thee and thy immortality, so long as—like a hired waiter—thou makest thyself 'generally useful.' . . .

"Cast thy eye in there on Vivia; tell me why those four limbs should be clapped in a dismal jail . . . and himself the voluntary jailor! Is this the end of philosophy? . . .

"I hate the world, and could trample all lungs of mankind as grapes, and heel them out of their breath, to think of the woe and the cant,—to think of the Truth and the Lie! . . ."

From these random slips, it would seem, that Pierre is quite conscious of much that is so anomalously hard and bitter in his lot, of much that is so black and terrific in his soul. Yet that knowing his fatal condition does not one whit enable him to change or better his condition. Conclusive proof that he has no power over his condition. For in tremendous extremities human souls are like drowning men; well enough they know they are in peril; well enough they know the causes of that peril; nevertheless, the sea is the sea, and these drowning men do drown.

HERMAN MELVILLE, *Pierre, Or, The Ambiguities,* XXII, iii

I. THE STRUCTURE AND MOVEMENT OF THE LECTURE COURSE AND ESSAY

Heidegger's 1940 lecture course, "Nietzsche: *The Will to Power* (*European Nihilism*)," comprises twenty-nine unnumbered sections.[1] Although no other divisions appear, this course too (see Volume I in this series) may be seen as unfolding in three stages. The first stage (sections 1–9) offers an account of nihilism, will to power, and valuation in Nietzsche's thought; the second (sections 10–20) interprets valuation and the metaphysics of will to power in terms of the modern metaphysics of subjectivity; the third (sections 21–29) postulates the end of such metaphysics—although not the cessation of nihilism—and calls for an inquiry into the history of Being. Here too, as in Volume I, the first and last sections of the central part serve as hinges for the triptych, so that my Analysis will have to pay special heed to them: section 10, "Valuation and Will to Power," and section 20, "The Inner Connection Between the Basic Positions of Descartes and Nietzsche." Yet even these cursory delineations of the structure of Heidegger's lecture course on nihilism betray the movement of that course. Beginning with a criticism of Nietzsche's valuative thought as the culmination of Western metaphysics since Plato, and advancing through a detailed account of the "modernity" of such thought—that is to say, its Cartesian heritage—Heidegger's lectures conclude with an effort to redefine in a nonvaluative mode of thought the relationship of Being and Man in the epoch of metaphysics' fulfillment, the epoch of nihilism.

Heidegger begins (in section 1) by distinguishing Nietzsche's understanding of nihilism in terms of the collapse of all transcendent values from other, more "symptomatic" uses of the word and by defining Nietzsche's understanding of the being in terms of will to power. The latter is acknowledged as the source of all valuation. But because power is essentially enhancement, any revaluation of values must itself revert to perpetual becoming, hence to eternal recurrence. Finally, the affirmation of eternal recurrence, Nietzsche's principal thought, demands

[1] Throughout the English translation numbers have been added to facilitate reference.

a new type of humanity, namely, Overman. These five expressions (nihilism, revaluation of all values, will to power, eternal recurrence of the same, and Overman) yield five complementary perspectives on Nietzsche's metaphysics.

At the very outset Heidegger proposes his thesis that Nietzsche's "classical" nihilism itself precludes the possibility of a thoughtful encounter with the *nihil,* described as "the veil that conceals the truth of the Being of beings." Heidegger now (section 2) raises the question of valuative thought and the "validity" of values in terms of the question of their Being; he asserts that nihilism has to do, not primarily with the collapse of "values," but with the fact that all being is experienced as *being nothing* (section 3). Heidegger ventures the assertion that the essence of nihilism consists in *not* taking the question of the *nihil* seriously, and that in this respect the history of nihilism is coterminous with the history of metaphysics. The latter, up to and including Nietzsche, unfolds as the nonessence of Being.

In a lengthy note (WM, 12), Nietzsche defines nihilism as the collapse of "cosmological" values such as purpose, unity, truth, and Being. Nietzsche reckons the impact of that collapse "psychologically" in terms of the inapplicability of the "categories of reason" to the world (sections 4–6). Although the three forms of nihilism defined by Nietzsche cannot be aligned with particular historical epochs, Nietzsche's own position in the history of nihilism may be defined (section 7) as an *active,* transitional position. Its activity (section 8) consists in actively knowing—that is, reckoning—the source of all valuation as will to power. Section 9 summarizes the foregoing in two statements:

> First, nihilism, as Nietzsche thinks it, is the history of the devaluation of the highest values hitherto, as the transition to the revaluation of all prior values, a revaluation that comes to pass in the discovery of a principle for a new valuation, a principle Nietzsche recognizes as the will to power. Second, Nietzsche conceives of the essence of nihilism solely on the basis of valuative thought, and in that form alone does it become an object of his critique and his attempt at an overcoming. But because the valuation has its principle in the will to power, overcoming nihilism by fulfilling it in its classical form develops into an interpretation of being as a whole as will to power. The new valuation is a metaphysics of will to power.

Now the long middle section of the course commences, seeking in the history of metaphysics the origin of the convergence of will to power and valuative thought. In section 10, Heidegger asks, "What occurs essentially and reigns in Western metaphysics, that it should finally come to be a metaphysics of will to power?" The principal clue to an answer is the role of valuative thought in modern metaphysics, value thinking being the essence and fulfillment of the metaphysics of subjectivity. As conditions of will to power, values must assure not only the stability and continuance, but also the enhancement, of will to power. Values, whose validity can be ascertained only by a calculative thinking, revert to "viewpoints" and "perspectives," terms that have been current in the history of metaphysics since Leibniz. Values are "conditioned conditions"; valuation and will to power are the same. Only in that sense can values "condition" will to power, since the latter constitutes the basic trait of beings. At the end of section 10, Heidegger restates the questions that will dominate the central portion of his course: "Why does the thought of will to power become dominant *along with* valuative thought in metaphysics? How and why does metaphysics become a metaphysics of the will to power?"

That Nietzsche calls the highest values "categories of reason" testifies to his remaining within the orbit of modern metaphysics (section 11), although he thinks "category" differently from the way Hegel, Kant, and certainly Aristotle do. But Heidegger now makes the important concession that he himself cannot overcome the limitation of his own point of view in the history of Being in order to ascertain precisely where Nietzsche stands. For Nietzsche's interpretation of metaphysics on the basis of a genealogy of *morals* (section 12) is something altogether unique in the history of philosophy. Although it does arise from the tradition that asserts the anthropomorphic origins of metaphysics, a tradition that extends from Protagoras through Descartes (section 13), Nietzsche's "humanization" of metaphysics and morals is sufficiently radical to constitute the end of the tradition. For Protagoras and the Greeks in general, man is a restricted radius of measured unconcealment of beings (section 14); for Descartes, man is the *subiectum* proper; that is, the ground of the representation of beings in terms of truth as certitude (sections 15–18). Released from the Greeks' limited radius, modern man is leashed to the task of his own liberation and self-determination. On the quest of security in certitude, he pursues the goal of power, power to unconditioned dominion over the earth. As the philosopher of power, Nietzsche fails to recognize the dependence of his interpretation of beings as will to power on Descartes' own fundamental position (section 19): Nietzsche too interprets Being as representedness. This failure derives from a "self-mistaking" that is essential to the completion of metaphysics: "Thinking in values conceals the collapse of the essence of Being and truth." Placing the body in the position of consciousness as methodologically primary alters nothing in that "self-mistaking."

Section 20, "The Inner Connection between the Fundamental Positions of Descartes and Nietzsche," summarizes the middle section of the course and introduces the third cluster of themes—Being, truth, and the ontological difference in the history of metaphysics. The paradoxical thesis of the central portion of Heidegger's course is that although Nietzsche misapprehends the essential inner connection between his metaphysics of will to power and Descartes' metaphysics of subjectivity, Nietzsche's metaphysics "fashions for itself an essentially correct insight into the essence of metaphysics." Referring to the four criteria that ascertain the character of a fundamental metaphysical position (see section 14), namely, the understanding of *man,* the projection of *beings* upon *Being,* the understanding of *truth,* and the *measure* for the truth of beings, Heidegger now compares Nietzsche's and Descartes' positions. First, Descartes posits *man* as the representing subject, while for Nietzsche the body's "drives" and "affects" are decisive. Second, with regard to beings in their *Being* (or beingness), Descartes insists on their representedness (*Vorgestelltheit*), while Nietzsche stresses the inadequacy of all representation of becoming. Even so, however, Nietzsche's emphasis on perspectival will to power reverts to the understanding of Being as representedness. Third, *truth* for Descartes is certitude of representation, whereas for Nietzsche it is taking-for-true; that is, a futile permanentization. Nonetheless, an understanding of truth as representation seems to underlie Nietzsche's critique of Descartes. Fourth, Descartes removes the limits from the Greek understanding of man as *measure,* making the representing subject the absolute ground of certitude; Nietzsche rejects man as epistemological measure, but only to affirm the Overman as will to power which is absolutely empowered to assume lordship over the earth. Heidegger emphasizes that the differences between Descartes' and Nietzsche's positions—for they are not identical—cannot be reduced to a straightforward alteration in man's conception of himself; the innermost history of metaphysics is rather "a history of the truth of Being." The following thesis brings section 20 to a close and introduces the final third of the lecture course: "As the fulfillment of modern metaphysics, Nietzsche's metaphysics is at the same time the fulfillment of Western metaphysics in general and is thus—in a correctly understood sense—the end of metaphysics as such."

Heidegger insists (section 21) that the role of the human being as subject is not a subjective decision on man's part; it results from the understanding of Being as representedness and of truth as certitude. That understanding has man in its grip and has become man's stranglehold on the world. Whereas Hegel's thought may be described as a metaphysics of absolute subjectivity which in one sense constitutes the end of metaphysics, Nietzsche's is a metaphysics of the absolute dominion of will to power, constituting the "full ending" (*Vollendung*) of metaphysics (section 22). The metaphysics of Hegel celebrates rationality; that of Nietzsche bestiality. Both together exhaust the traditional sense of humanity. But the phrase "end of metaphysics" means that the essential possibilities of metaphysics too are exhausted. "At the end of metaphysics stands the statement *Homo est brutum bestiale.*" But that end is just beginning.

Heidegger can claim no "bird's-eye view" of our present age, but he nonetheless calls for a "decision." The standpoint for such a decision is recognition of the way European nihilism essentially unfolds in and as the history of Being. The four guidelines mentioned earlier (sections 14 and 20) express in their unity that essential unfolding. They exhibit as their unifying ground the ontological difference, here (section 23) defined as the distinction between man's relationship to Being and his sundry relations with beings. Heidegger calls the differentiation between Being and beings the "settlement." The principal proviso of that settlement in the history of metaphysics is the *a priori* character of

Being (section 24), seen from the point of view and for the sake of beings. The *a priori* is defined early on as the Idea of the Good, the earliest prototype of Nietzsche's value thinking, although not its replica (section 25). "Idea" is interpreted as the "condition" of beings with a view to their visuality, to human seeing and knowing, hence, in the modern age, to *perceptio.* "Idea" must be reckoned with as a condition of the representedness (Being) of objects. But ideas as conditions can only become *values:* thus the movement from Plato, through Descartes, Leibniz, Kant, and Hegel, to Nietzsche (section 26). Being as *idea* can be projected, can essentially unfold, only as will to power (section 27). Yet the very possibility of "idea," "condition," and "value" lies in the differentiation between Being and beings (section 28), for that differentiation constitutes the metaphysical in man. The nature of man is grounded in the differentiation—as our language suggests when it (section 29) employs the "is" of Being so abundantly that even in the age of *Weltanschauung* nothing appears beyond its scope. But the scope of "Being," Janus-headed, duplicitous, vacuous yet rich in possibility, becomes the crucial mystery for the epoch of nihilism.

Heidegger's essay or brief treatise, "Nihilism as Determined by the History of Being," maps more thoroughly than any other text in the *Nietzsche* volumes Heidegger's path of thought toward the "Letter on Humanism" (see Heidegger's "Foreword to All Volumes" in Volume I of this series). The central theme of that "Letter"—namely, the relationship of Being and human being—along with a host of related themes such as nihilism, valuative thought, ontotheology, the history of Being as abandonment and withdrawal, Da-sein as the abode of Being's advent, and the essence of Da-sein as meditative thinking, receive detailed treatment here. Roughly speaking, the movement of Heidegger's essay is *from* Nietzsche's valuative thought *to* the thought that encounters Being in withdrawal *via* the "step back" out of metaphysics into the history of Being.

Heidegger begins with the complaint that neither the metaphysics of will to power nor the thought of eternal recurrence develop adequately the question of Being and Time. But he immediately concedes the irrelevance of such a complaint, and, responding to the fidelity of

Nietzche's own thinking, asks whether in Nietzsche's metaphysics nihilism as such is overcome. Prior to that, of course, he must ask how nihilism is experienced there. Because Nietzsche's metaphysics insists that the being *is* (as) will to power in the mode of eternal recurrence, nihilism *appears* to be overcome there: in Nietzsche's metaphysics there is ultimately no room for the nothing. But acknowledgment of beings does not think Being; it misses the *essence* of nihilism. "The essence of nihilism is the history in which there is nothing to Being itself." Nietzsche's metaphysics is nihilism proper, for it insists that Being is a "value," hence, ironically, that there is "nothing to it." It is thus the fulfillment of the metaphysics that began with Plato.

The "essence" or "essential unfolding" of nihilism as metaphysics takes center stage in Heidegger's inquiry. Metaphysics establishes essences in terms of "whatness," and thus interprets beings in terms of other beings and their beingness, never raising the question of Being *as* Being. Metaphysics is onto-theology. Nietzsche's thought too is onto-theological, although as fulfilled nihilism it is "negative" onto-theology, neither transcendental nor transcendent in character. Like all prior metaphysics, Nietzsche's metaphysics neglects to think *unconcealment* as the truth of Being. Being remains in default. The history of Being comes to nothing. The emphasis falls equally on all these terms: Being *remains* in default; history *comes* to nothing. Heidegger recognizes that the word *Sein* itself misses what is to be thought here. He therefore attempts to think the default of Being as such with the help of a metaphorics of sojourn: "advent," "locale," "abode," "shelter." All these are names for *Da-sein,* ecstative inherence in openness, the essence of which is to think Being. The relation of Being to Man is thus the crucial problem.

In Heidegger's discussion of that problem, the terms "authenticity" and "inauthenticity," nihilism "proper" and nihilism *manqué,* "essence" and "nonessence" are thoroughly relativized, because the omission of the default of Being (in metaphysical thought) is the *Gift* of duplicitous Being itself. Thus "the full essence of nihilism is the original unity of its authenticity and inauthenticity." The full essence of nihilism in the history of Being therefore may not be identified with "destructive nihilism," but is itself something essentially differentiated.

That difference cannot be expunged. But human thought can advance toward the omission of the default of Being, provided it has experienced the necessity of such an advance, as "promise," "mystery," and "enigma," by thinking to encounter it. Thinking encounters the withdrawal of Being but does not pursue it; it remains behind, takes the "step back," descends to a depth "which no longer corresponds to a height." It eschews all forms of objectification, especially those endemic to the historical disciplines, and all willfulness, including the will to overcome nihilism. The withdrawal of Being assumes a particularly striking form with the insight that in the step back "Being" loses its power to name, "because it always unwittingly says 'presence and permanence,' determinations to which the *essentially occurring* character of Being can never be attached as a mere addendum." Thus, in the end as at the beginning, the thinker of Becoming penetrates to the thinker of Being. The Heidegger-Nietzsche confrontation culminates in a shared recognition of *need* and *danger* in the present historical age.

II. CONTEXTS

It is with trepidation that I write anything at all about the contexts of nihilism, for they are invariably intricate and highly explosive. Whatever the context in question, nihilism remains bewildering and hazardous. It has therefore been a painful embarrassment for me to read a number of contemporary monographs and essays on nihilism by professional philosophers for whom the matter is ultimately quite simple. Such essays boil down to the remonstrance, "If you people would only put away such dangerous and destructive writers as Nietzsche and Heidegger, and go back to the truly inspirational philosophers of our tradition, embracing the timeless wisdom of their texts (as elucidated in my own modest commentaries), all of this nihilism business would vanish like a bad dream." What is painful is not the condemnation of "dangerous" thinkers but the adulation of "safe" ones. To proclaim any Socrates "safe" is to outdo Alcibiades in violence; it is to proffer the deadliest of draughts. What is embarrassing is the assumption that by doing what they have been taught to do in graduate schools philosophers are redeeming the world. Against such pomposity and covert violence the following lines from Yeats's "Nineteen Hundred and Nineteen" are effective—and they introduce the most troubling of contexts.

> Now days are dragon-ridden, the nightmare
> Rides upon sleep: a drunken soldiery
> Can leave the mother, murdered at her door,
> To crawl in her own blood, and go scot-free;
> The night can sweat with terror as before
> We pieced our thoughts into philosophy,
> And planned to bring the world under a rule,
> Who are but weasels fighting in a hole.

In the *Spiegel* interview of September 23, 1966, Heidegger himself invokes the most distressing context. There he twice identifies his Nietzsche lectures of the late 1930s and early 1940s as one of the principal sites of his confrontation (*Auseinandersetzung*) with National Socialism.[2] The context is grievously distressing for at least two reasons: first, the unspeakable consequences of Nazism, what has come to be called "the holocaust"; second, the way the retrospective illusion causes us to jumble the multiple facets of German fascism—the racism and anti-Semitism, the relentless propaganda, the mass enthusiasm masking mass despondency, industrial and military mobilization, chauvinism and xenophobia, police terror and the death camps—into a nightmarish composite portrait we call *nihilism.* Our initial question, formulated with little thought and a great deal of passion, is

[2] *Der Spiegel,* 1976, *30* (23), 204. An English translation of the interview by Maria P. Alter and John D. Caputo appears in *Philosophy Today,* 1976, *20* (4–4), 267–84. The *Spiegel* interview is an important document because it is one of the rare places where Heidegger speaks of his political engagement in the 1930s. Yet Heidegger is less than candid about many matters; for example, his and Frau Heidegger's relations with the Jaspers and Husserl households. Heidegger's defensive attitude throughout the interview precludes genuine self-criticism, so that the piece often seems self-serving when what is called for is profound forthrightness. Unfortunately, the documents that would shed most light on Heidegger's political blunder—namely, his extensive correspondence with figures such as Jaspers, Karl Löwith, and Hannah Arendt—will not be made available to scholars for some time.

"How could Heidegger have been mixed up in all of this—or in *any* of it?"

Such a question cannot be answered to the satisfaction of passion, and perhaps even less to the satisfaction of thought. For one thing, we lack an adequate notion of National Socialism, one that can differentiate among the various years, places, and circumstances of the movement. Otto Pöggeler writes,

> It is altogether inappropriate to treat National Socialism as an indissoluble, homogeneous unit, and then to take it as a mere instance of European fascism and a countermovement to Communism. National Socialism, with its insistent grasp after world rule and its attempt to annihilate European Jewry, is utterly unique. But neither can the later totalitarian system simply be equated with the early "resurgence" of those desperate persons who responded to the movement, or with the elements that crystallized about such resurgence.[3]

Yet it is important to reiterate the particular attraction National Socialism exercised on Heidegger, an attraction, it is true, that began to wither soon after he had taken up his duties as rector of the University of Freiburg.[4] That attraction may be glimpsed in what Ernst Bertram and Karl Jaspers—who went opposite ways in the 1930s—say concerning the fate of Germany in the twentieth century. In his influential work, *Nietzsche: Attempt at a Mythology,* Bertram includes a chapter entitled "German Becoming."[5] There he elaborates on the tradition that begins with Luther and continues through Lessing, Herder, Goethe, Schiller, Novalis, Hölderlin, Jean Paul, Hebbel, Stifter, and Nietzsche, a tradition in which poets and educators in the

---

[3] Otto Pöggeler, "Heideggers Begegnung mit Hölderlin," in *Man and World,* 1977, *10* (1), 25. Pierre Trotignon, *Heidegger: Sa vie, son oeuvre* (Paris: Presses Universitaires de France, 1965), p. 3, quotes Helvétius as saying, "L'aurore de la tyrannie n'annonce jamais les meurtres."

[4] I presuppose that the reader is familiar with the chronology of Heidegger's political engagement, although the extent and character of his involvement is disputed everywhere and on all points. For a brief account, see my "General Introduction" to Martin Heidegger, *Basic Writings* (New York: Harper & Row, 1977), pp. 27–28. In addition to the sources cited there, see the fine critical account by Karsten Harries, "Heidegger as a Political Thinker," in M. Murray, ed., *Heidegger and Modern Philosophy,* (New Haven, Conn.: Yale University Press, 1978), pp. 304–28.

[5] Ernst Bertram, *Nietzsche: Versuch einer Mythologie* (Berlin: Georg Bondi, 1918).

German lands prod the nation *to become* what it must be, to develop through *Erziehung* and *Bildung* a German "essence." For, politically and historically speaking, the German "essence" is precisely a lack of Being. Hence the almost desperate clinging to Becoming, the hope in transition and transformation, the longing after something ill-defined and ever unattained.[6] In the eighth chapter of his *Philosophical Autobiography,* Karl Jaspers recounts the crisis of German "Becoming" in the current century. In the course of his reflections he comments on the frenzied search for a German "essence":

> Other nations accuse us of unending reflection on what it means to be German, of wanting so badly to *be* German; they insist that we turn what is natural into something artificial and forced. . . . But for Germans the question is . . . unfortunately unavoidable.[7]

---

[6] Cf. Heidegger's remarks in *The Will to Power as Art,* the first volume of this translation, pp. 103–4, which pertain to the task of German "Becoming." Heidegger is discussing Hölderlin's conceptual pair "holy pathos" and "*Junonian sobriety* of representational skill," related to Nietzsche's later distinction between the "Dionysian" and "Apollonian," respectively:

> The opposition is not to be understood as an indifferent historical finding. Rather, it becomes manifest to direct meditation on the destiny and determination of the German people. . . . It is enough if we gather from the reference that the variously named conflict of the Dionysian and the Apollonian, of holy passion and sober representation, is a hidden stylistic law of the historical determination of the German people, and that one day we must find ourselves ready and able to give it shape. . . . By recognizing this antagonism Hölderlin and Nietzsche early on placed a question mark after the task of the German people to find their essence historically. Will we understand this cipher? One thing is certain: history will wreak vengeance on us if we do not.

Cf. *Der Spiegel,* p. 214; English translation, p. 281. While it is tempting to regard the German fascination with Becoming as *sui generis,* as something specifically German, and while that fascination (visible in Heidegger's words here) does display traits found nowhere else, we would do well to reflect on parallel situations in nineteenth- and twentieth-century Eurasia and America; for example, in the ideologies of Pan-Slavism, of the "glory" of the French nation, or of the divinely sanctioned "manifest destiny" of the United States to extend its frontiers endlessly. We can no longer be confident that American faith in the New Frontier or the politicized nostalgia for the Old Frontier will have less devastating consequences for world history than the earlier German faith in Becoming. And there seems to be no one to inscribe a question mark between such nostalgia and the gathering vengeance.

[7] Karl Jaspers, *Philosophische Autobiographie,* new, expanded edition (Munich: R. Piper, 1977), pp. 76 ff.

Hardly an explanation—more a confession of impotence in the face of a long and tyrannical tradition. Indeed, Jaspers displays a helpless fascination for "grand politics" in his 1936 *Nietzsche*;[8] and even in his autobiography he celebrates "the grand politics of the philosophers" extending from "Plato and Kant, and on to Hegel and Kierkegaard and Nietzsche." "A philosophy shows what it is," he concludes, "in its political manifestation."[9] But now to the crisis.

With the outbreak of World War I, the Germans, perhaps more acutely than other European peoples, sensed that they had been caught up in, or "thrown into," a turbulent stream of "relentless, uncomprehended" events. The initial problem for reconstruction after the war was therefore how to achieve some modicum of comprehension concerning what had happened. Because of Versailles, of course, that comprehension tended to be defensive or, through overcompensation, offensive, self-inflating, and self-assertive. Jaspers credits Max Weber's "national thinking" with whatever political insight he (Jaspers) attained. Weber had insisted that Germany was to fulfill a special mission in Europe: Germany would rescue the liberal tradition in Western political thought from the Soviet "lash" and from Anglo-Saxon "conventionalism." Russian Bolshevism was feared as the more formidable enemy—its victory in Germany would spell the virtual end of European liberalism. Germany would therefore have to confront "its momentous world-historical task" (Jaspers), the task of salvaging the threatened "between."[10] It would have to assume leadership in *der grossen Politik,* understood not in terms of Ludendorff's militarism but as a diplomacy based on a volatile mixture of shrewdness and liberal principles—precisely the kind of diplomacy practiced by "Paul Arnheim" (i.e., Walther Rathenau) in *The Man Without Qualities,* Robert Musil's brilliant portrayal of prewar Austria-Hungary. Yet one remark by Jaspers is revealing, even devastating in the present context:

---

[8] Karl Jaspers, *Nietzsche: Einführung in das Verständnis seines Philosophierens* (Berlin: W. de Gruyter, 1936), Book II, ch. 4.

[9] K. Jaspers, *Philosophische Autobiographie,* p. 85.

[10] Cf. Martin Heidegger, *Einführung in die Metaphysik* (Tübingen: M. Niemeyer, 1953), pp. 28–29; English translation by Ralph Manheim, *An Introduction to Metaphysics* (Garden City, N.Y.: Anchor-Doubleday, 1961), pp. 31–32.

he confesses that he felt unequal to Weber's political mission and that he never discussed politics during the Weimar years, feeling that he had no right to do so—because he had not been a soldier![11] So much for a *grosse Politik* not disfigured by militarism.

The contrast between Weber's *nationales Denken* and the realities of Weimar Germany was no less devastating. In the everyday life of the Republic, amid the newspapers scattered on the breakfast table, such thinking could only express its contempt for the tepid liberalism, contentious socialism, and reactionary conservatism of the day.[12] Heidegger took part in the impatient search for something *authentic* in public life. He yearned for a "fundamental change," *Aufbruch* or *risorgimento,* that would totally recast the social, political, and academic order in Germany. Pöggeler, alluding to an analysis by Ernst Bloch, expresses the attraction of National Socialism for young intellectuals such as Heidegger in the following way:

> In the early years National Socialism had its positive aspect—which attracted many—in the fact that during a period that witnessed the destruction of every tradition that had once granted meaning—destruction by the new forces of the world economy and technology, destruction by the hectic promotions of the new mass media—and during a period that witnessed the uprooting of the old peasant and bourgeois classes of society, it promised to rescue and even to renew a sense of "homeland."[13]

In addition to Heidegger's participation in the general disaffection with Weimar political life, a disaffection the Nazis knew well how to cultivate and manipulate, one must also stress his hopes for university reform. At the outset of his discussion with *Spiegel* editors Rudolf Augstein and Georg Wolff, Heidegger mentions his conversations with a Freiburg colleague in 1932–33 concerning the "hopeless" situation of university students at that time; this is perhaps another way of saying what Heidegger had insisted in his inaugural lecture at Freiburg in 1929, "What Is Metaphysics?" There he bemoaned the fragmentation of the various faculties which represented disciplines that had lost all

[11] Jaspers, *Philosophische Autobiographie,* p. 71.

[12] See Otto Pöggeler, *Philosophie und Politik bei Heidegger* (Freiburg and Munich: K. Alber, 1972), p. 109.

[13] Pöggeler, "Begegnung," p. 25.

connection to their "essential ground," to wit, philosophy. The amorphous and utterly contingent configurations of *Wissenschaft* had to disturb a man who at least to some extent still thought of himself as a proponent of scientifically rigorous phenomenology; the fragmentation of the faculties and the absence of common goals, methods, and intentions in the university had to trouble an admirer of Wilhelm von Humboldt's university reforms. (Precisely what sorts of faculty reforms Heidegger had in mind, precisely what proposals he laid before Rust, the *Reichsminister* of Culture, in November 1933, we are not told.) At all events, in order to prevent the accession of a mere functionary of the Culture Ministry to the rectorship—that is to say, in order to preserve whatever autonomy and even "self-assertion" the university could aspire to—Heidegger gave way to the importunities of his younger colleagues and accepted the nomination to the rectorship.[14]

Heidegger's involvement in National Socialism in 1933–34 thus stemmed from two related sets of motives: first, a genuine hope that the promised "resurgence" would grant the nation a new sense of direction and the university a possibility for academic reform; second, the fear that if he did not accept the rectorship the university would lose whatever autonomy it still possessed. Heidegger's private ambitions surely colored both sets of motives, but the strength and quality of those ambitions is hard to judge. In any case, when Heidegger assumed the post it became clear to him that he would not be able to succeed in any of his plans "without compromises."[15] While resisting the most abusive actions of the students' branch of the *Sturmabteilung,* Heidegger spoke out vigorously in support of the *Führer* and his aggressive policies. Those dreary documents collected so assiduously by Guido Schneeberger record a different "voice"; in fact, in them the voice of

[14] Heidegger several times mentions his "younger colleagues" during the *Spiegel* interview, and this seems to be important. Himself a product of the provinces, with none of the advantages of family connections and social status to aid his rise in the academic world, Heidegger could hardly have been immune to the allure of academic prestige and power; as rector, Heidegger placed as many of those younger, more sympathetic colleagues in positions of power, such as deanships, as he could, and even opened various faculty meetings to student representatives, all to the chagrin of the older, more established professors.

[15] *Der Spiegel,* p. 198.

Martin Heidegger recedes, drowned in a crescendo of "the They." Ironically, the notion of *das Man* is often criticized for its imputed "elitist" and "protofascist" asocial tendencies; the rehabilitation of the notion may be furthered when we realize that Heidegger himself was fully capable of subsumption under it. For a time.

As rector, then as professor of philosophy, Heidegger soon sensed that National Socialism had perverted the drive to resurgence by making so atavistic, cynical, and demagogic a notion as race the center of its ideology. In his 1934–35 lecture course on Hölderlin he inveighed against such crass "biologism," attacking one of Rosenberg's ideological prototypes in supremely sardonic style:

> Herr Kolbenheyer, who is a writer, says that poetry "is a biologically necessary function of the *Volk*." We do not need a great deal of intelligence to discern that the same is true of digestion. Digestion too is an essential biological function of a people—especially of a healthy people.[16]

But to what extent do the Nietzsche lectures themselves represent a confrontation with National Socialism? Heidegger's resistance to "biologism" is of course visible throughout, as is his rejection of the "official" Nietzsche, the monumentalized Nietzsche promulgated by Frau Förster and embraced by the Nazi leadership.[17]

One of the most influential perpetrators of the "official" Nietzsche was Alfred Baeumler, professor of philosophy in Berlin from 1933 to 1945 (note the place and dates, which tell it all), author of *Nietzsche,*

[16] Quoted by Pöggeler in "Begegnung," p. 24; cf. pp. 44–45. The "writer" Heidegger here derides is Erwin Guido Kolbenheyer, author of several novels and of *The Philosophy of the Lodge* (*Bauhütte*), the latter published in 1925. Kolbenheyer developed a brand of "metabiology" that lent itself easily to the *völkisch*-racist ideology of National Socialism. Heidegger labels him a *Schriftsteller* in order to scorn his pretensions to "metaphysics." The quoted passage now appears in Martin Heidegger, *Hölderlins Hymnen 'Germanien' und 'Der Rhein'* (Frankfurt am Main: V. Klostermann, 1980), p. 27.

[17] Walter Kaufmann has told the grim tale of the "Nietzsche legend" so well in the Prologue and the tenth chapter of his *Nietzsche: Philosopher, Psychologist, Antichrist* (Princeton, N.J.: Princeton University Press, 1950), pp. 3 ff. and 252 ff., that there is no need to recapitulate it here. I will restrict my discussion to matters directly pertinent to Heidegger's *Nietzsche*.

Philosopher and Politician.[18] At the outset of his first lecture course on Nietzsche,[19] Heidegger vigorously criticized Baeumler's adoption and political adaptation of "will to power" and his scornful rejection of "eternal recurrence." Heidegger insisted that these two teachings did not contradict one another, as Baeumler had claimed. He then added,

> But even if we concede that here we have a contradiction which cannot be transcended and which compels us to decide in favor of either will to power or eternal recurrence, why does Baeumler then decide *against* Nietzsche's most difficult thought, the peak of his meditation, and *for* will to power? The answer is simple: Baeumler's reflections on the relationship between the two doctrines do not press toward the realm of actual inquiry from either side. Rather, the doctrine of eternal recurrence, where he fears "Egypticism," militates against his conception of will to power, which, in spite of the talk about metaphysics, Baeumler does not grasp metaphysically but interprets politically.[20]

Baeumler's conception of politics is perhaps best betrayed by his affirmation of Nietzsche's ostensible world view—namely, "heroic realism"—and of the pseudo-Heraclitean world of Becoming, "of struggle and victory."[21] Baeumler devotes his energies in the second half of his book to an explanation of why Nietzsche merely *seems* to be anti-German—Nietzsche, who says in a hundred different ways, "The man is blond and stupid: he must be German." Baeumler's reassuring discovery is that Nietzsche is anti-German only because Roman-Christian-Mediterranean elements have infiltrated *Deutschtum,* and that Nietzsche wishes to revert to "Germanic undercurrents" and strictly "Nordic elements" in founding a new German state.[22] The great transformation in Nietzsche, from philosopher to politician, occurs when in the autumn of 1888 he alters the title of his projected major work from *The Will to Power* to *The Revaluation of All*

---

[18] Alfred Baeumler, *Nietzsche der Philosoph und Politiker* (Leipzig: P. Reclam, 1931).

[19] See Volume I of this translation, pp. 22–23.

[20] Ibid., p. 22.

[21] Baeumler, *Nietzsche,* p. 15.

[22] Ibid., pp. 88 ff.

Values.[23] Presumably from 1888 on Nietzsche dedicates himself to his political mission. Germany is to become Europe's "leader," and not in any "idealistic" sense. "He does not wish to make Germany into a nation of thinkers and poets again; he does not speak of a kingdom of the German Spirit or of the Christmas tree of the German Soul. . . . He wants to guide the Germans *zur grossen Politik.*"[24]

By now, of course, the grand style of art and "grand politics" have parted company irrevocably: not *Dichten* and *Denken,* which he reduces to Christmas-tree tinsel, but another vision dances in Baeumler's head. He capitulates to that vision three years later in an article entitled "Nietzsche and National Socialism."[25] There he identifies Nietzsche and Hitler as opponents of democratic-parliamentarian bourgeois society and government: "If we transpose Hitler's position with respect to the Weimar Republic to a lonely thinker of the nineteenth century, then we have Nietzsche." —It is pointless and unpleasant to go on, but let me at least reprint Baeumler's grandiloquent peroration:

> When we see German youth today marching under the symbol of the swastika, we recall Nietzsche's *Thoughts Out of Season,* in which our youth is summoned for the first time. It is our greatest hope that the state stands open to our youth. And when we greet them with the call *"Heil Hitler!"* we greet at the same time Friedrich Nietzsche.

One reader of Baeumler's *Nietzsche, Philosopher and Politician,* who had borrowed the copy deposited in Freiburg's university library some time before I did, could not resist jotting down on the title page the lament of Ophelia, "O, what a noble mind is here o'erthrown!" He or she was not referring to Baeumler's mind.

[23] Ibid., p. 153. See also Baeumler's ordering of the *Nachlass,* entitled *Die Unschuld des Werdens,* 2 vols., 2nd ed. (Stuttgart: A. Kröner, 1978), II, 313. In his Introduction to the volumes (I, xvii–xviii) Baeumler calls the Nietzsche of "revaluation" a "destroyer in the grandest style," "brandishing his sword" and dying a heroic death. Heidegger's rejection of Baeumler's political interpretation may also be mirrored in Heidegger's critique of the project of revaluation and of value thinking as such: surely Baeumler shows how low the project of revaluation can go.

[24] Baeumler, *Nietzsche,* p. 166.

[25] In the *Nationalsozialistische Monatshefte,* edited by Alfred Rosenberg, 1934, 5(49), 289–98. The following two quotations appear on pp. 290 and 298.

I reprint so much of Baeumler's blasphemy and bavardage, not to distract the reader from Heidegger's own involvement in National Socialism, or to minimize it, but to make clear the context in which Heidegger had to address the students attending his Nietzsche lectures. What they heard from Heidegger was something different—it was in fact totally *out of context.*

Related to the most troubling context, yet coming closer to the matter of Heidegger's own career of thought, is Hannah Arendt's thesis that the *Nietzsche* volumes reflect a "reversal" in Heidegger's thought that took place between 1936 and 1940.[26] Professor Arendt surrenders to the temptation "to date the 'reversal' as a concrete autobiographical event precisely between Volume I and Volume II."[27] But she is unable or unwilling to specify such an event: the "catastrophic defeat" of Nazi Germany in 1945, mirrored according to Arendt in "The Anaximander Fragment," may not be confused with this earlier unspecified event. Presumably, that earlier event would have to do with Heidegger's growing disaffection from National Socialism, even though Heidegger himself insists that the disaffection had burgeoned by 1934, two years before the first Nietzsche lecture.

Whatever the ostensible "event" that would insert itself as a wedge between the *Nietzsche* volumes, and however futile speculations about it must be, the reason behind Arendt's "temptation" merits critical discussion. Her own reason, "put bluntly," is that "the first volume explicates Nietzsche by going along with him, while the second is written in a subdued but unmistakably polemical tone."[28] To be sure, one senses a difference between the lectures and the treatises in

[26] Hannah Arendt, *The Life of the Mind,* 2 vols. (New York: Harcourt Brace Jovanovich, 1977–1978), II, 172 ff. It would be churlish of me not to admit that in what follows I have singled out what appears to be one of the weaker and ultimately less interesting theses in Arendt's section on Heidegger and the "will-not-to-will." There are astonishing lapses there, such as the initial claim that "Nietzsche's name is nowhere mentioned in *Being and Time.*" (For a list of the references, see my Analysis to Volume I of this series, p. 247.) Yet there are gems as well, such as Arendt's reading of "The Anaximander Fragment." The lapses are signs of haste, testimony perhaps of the death that was too impatient; the gems are testimony to her intelligence and incredible vitality.

[27] Ibid., pp. 172–73.

[28] Ibid., p. 173.

Heidegger's *Nietzsche,* although the division into lectures and treatises does not in any case coincide with the division between Volume I and Volume II; and it is true that the lectures engage themselves with Nietzsche's texts intimately and at great length, whereas the treatises tend to formulate, foreshorten, differentiate, and delimit positions. But whether the *polemos* ever becomes a *polemic* is doubtful. Surely in the lecture on "European Nihilism," contained in the *second* volume of the German edition, Heidegger "goes along" with Nietzsche as far as he ever goes in previous lecture courses; and surely the very first lecture course, "Will to Power as Art," contains some of Heidegger's keenest criticisms of Nietzsche.

Nevertheless, what Hannah Arendt is trying to indicate is what both she and J. L. Mehta, along with many others, call a "change of mood" in Heidegger's writings during the 1930s. Mehta describes the mood of *Being and Time* and other "early" writings in terms of a "Promethean, aggressive attitude, in which man thinks of himself as destined to take truth and reality by storm, as it were."[29] Among the key words for the Promethean attitude would be *Wissenschaft,* "science," as the destiny of Dasein in the Western world, and particularly in the "between" of Germany; *Selbstbehauptung,* "self-assertion," both of the university and of the man who wills to know; *Wesenswille,* the will to assert the essence of one's self and one's nation; and *Entscheidung,* a resolute decision-making in service to that essence. Among these key words, *Selbstbehauptung* and *Wille* do play a role in the first volume of Heidegger's *Nietzsche* that they no longer play in the second. In the first volume of the English translation (sections 7–10), Heidegger discusses the will at great length. There, as Arendt notes, will is

[29] J. L. Mehta, *The Philosophy of Martin Heidegger* (New York: Harper & Row Torchbooks, 1971), pp. 110–11. I refer to this edition throughout, but readers should be aware of the larger volume, *Martin Heidegger: The Way and the Vision* (Honolulu: University of Hawaii Press, 1976), one of the very best books on Heidegger available. Mehta quickly qualifies the remark I have cited here by noting the essential role of *Seinlassen,* "letting-be," in Heidegger's "early" work as well. He observes correctly that the essay "On the Essence of Truth" is devoted entirely to the notion of "letting." Mehta therefore resists the reductive tendency of his own thesis, which would divide Heidegger's thought into two sequences, one marked by *Angst,* the other graced by *Gelassenheit.*

identified with the authentic self of Dasein, with steadfast resoluteness, and even with "care," the essence of finite transcendence as such.[30] As for the term *Selbstbehauptung,* Heidegger writes in that same volume,

> Life not only exhibits the drive to maintain itself, as Darwin thinks, but also is self-assertion. The will to maintain merely clings to what is already at hand, stubbornly insists upon it, loses itself in it, and so becomes blind to its proper essence. Self-assertion, which wants to be ahead of things, to stay on top of things, is always a going back into its essence, into the origin. *Self-assertion is original assertion of essence.*[31]

Professor Arendt is right about the fact that the detailed descriptions of the act of willing and of self-assertion in *Nietzsche I* are absent from the later treatises in *Nietzsche II.*[32] Indeed, there are other subtle differences she does not mention. For example, Heidegger's 1936–37 discussion of "the event of nihilism" invokes *die grosse Politik.*[33] Here Heidegger refers to those forces that grant the "historical existence of peoples" their coherence and power, forces that "sustain and propel preparation of the new realm, the advance into it, and the cultivation of what unfolds within it, forces which induce it to undertake bold deeds." By 1940 the German nation had amply demonstrated the quality of its bold deeds. While the second volume of *Nietzsche* is not devoid of political references, the public realm invoked there is dark indeed, and there is no talk of grand politics.[34]

---

[30] Arendt, p. 176.

[31] Volume I of this series, pp. 60–61. These words are highly reminiscent of Heidegger's *Rektoratsrede,* "The Self-Assertion of the German University," which is dominated by the terms *Selbstbehauptung* and *Wille* (usually in the verbal form *wollen*). See Martin Heidegger, *Die Selbstbehauptung der deutschen Universität* (Breslau: W. G. Korn, 1933), throughout.

[32] Note that in the lecture course contained in the present volume (p. 33), Heidegger does *not* identify with the human being's "self-assertion" in the midst of beings. *Selbstbehauptung* is here equated with the valuative thought against which Heidegger inveighs.

[33] See Volume I of this series, pp. 157–58, for this and the following quotation.

[34] This difference is also reflected in the fact that although "deeds which found the state" are elevated to the rank of works of art in the 1935 lectures "On the Origin of the Work of Art," the postwar lecture "The Question Concerning Technology," which contraposes art to technology, leaves "the state" utterly out of account. See Martin Heidegger, *Der Ursprung des Kunstwerkes* (Stuttgart: P. Reclam, 1960), pp. 68–69;

Yet to style the Heidegger of *Nietzsche I* as "Promethean" and the Heidegger of *Nietzsche II* as the meek prophet of "releasement" and "tranquil detachment" is far too crude a reduction. The very designation "Promethean" is misleading in the extreme. Both Mehta and Arendt use the word to portray a heaven-storming, aggressively self-assertive Heidegger; yet the passage in the *Rektoratsrede* to which they appeal displays a Prometheus who has "failed" to master his fate. *Technē d'anankēs asthenestera makroi,* "But knowledge is far less powerful than necessity."[35] Both Prometheus and Nietzsche are cited in the rectoral address as witnesses of man's helplessness in the midst of beings, his utter subjection to what is uncertain, concealed, and questionable. As such, they are figures that tend to restrain the generally will-full exhortations of the *Rektoratsrede.* However, it remains true that the later treatises on Nietzsche often turn their back on the richness of Nietzsche's central thought, the eternal recurrence of the same, and treat will to power as a metaphysical construct or "a will to rule and dominate rather than as an expression of the life instinct."[36] Will to power there becomes indistinguishable from the "essentially destructive" will-to-will and the accomplished subjectivism and nihilism of planetary technology. Heidegger's developing insight into the metaphysico-technological matrix of the will-to-will and his struggle to escape that matrix and to advance the thought of letting-be surely can be witnessed in the years 1936 to 1946; surely, the political debacle and national disaster can only have spoken for such a move. The desperately somber tone of the second part of the present volume, the essay composed in 1944–46—so much darker than the tone of the first part written in 1940—testifies to the impact of political catastrophe

English translation by Albert Hofstadter in *Poetry, Language, Thought* (New York: Harper & Row, 1971), p. 62. Cf. the whole of "Die Frage nach der Technik" in Martin Heidegger, *Vorträge und Aufsätze* (Pfullingen: G. Neske, 1954); English translation by William Lovitt, *The Question Concerning Technology* (New York: Harper & Row, 1977), also contained in *Basic Writings,* pp. 283–317.

[35] Mehta's reference (p. 112) is more cautious: following Walter Schulz, he refers to the figure of Prometheus as an incarnation of "heroic nihilism," representing "the self-assertion of Dasein in its impotence and finitude." See Heidegger, *Selbstbehauptung,* pp. 8–9; on Nietzsche, cf. p. 12.

[36] Arendt, p. 177, for this and the following.

on thinking. Yet it is crucial to recognize that the origins of Heidegger's insight, struggle, and advance go far back; they resist easy "dating" and all biographical reductionism. Professor Mehta is therefore wise to ascribe any "reversal" or shift in mood—which in any case he dates circa 1935—not to a shattering personal experience but to Heidegger's "study of Nietzsche."[37]

Not that the study of Nietzsche stands in isolation. Interwoven with it are a number of involvements that effect the altered *Stimmung* of Heidegger's thought: the critique of *Wissenschaft* and of the subjectivist philosophy of modernity, a critique that does not leave Heidegger's own project of fundamental ontology unscathed; the turn to Schelling, whom ten years earlier in a fit of phenomenological pique Heidegger had derided as a "mere *littérateur*";[38] the overpowering attraction to Hölderlin, for whom poetizing was anything but willful self-assertion; and the expanding influence of arts and letters in general on a man who once had styled himself an "ahistorical mathematician."[39] These preoccupations, along with Heidegger's prolonged confrontation with Nietzsche, are the quieter but more decisive events of the 1930s, these the more fertile contexts.

III. QUESTIONS

If in Heidegger's view Nietzsche's metaphysics of will to power and valuative thought prevent him from encountering the *nihil* as such, what kind of thinking does Heidegger propose for such an encounter? What role does the nothing play in Heidegger's own texts before and after the Nietzsche lectures? If those lectures derive from "the one experience out of which *Being and Time* is thought,"[40] and yet if they spurn "fundamental ontology" in order to promote inquiry into the history of Being, how are we to conceive of *the* "fundamental

[37] Mehta, p. 112.

[38] See Jaspers, *Philosophische Autobiographie,* p. 96.

[39] See Martin Heidegger, *Frühe Schriften* (Frankfurt am Main: V. Klostermann, 1972), p. 3.

[40] Martin Heidegger, "Nietzsches Wort 'Gott ist tot,'" in *Holzwege* (Frankfurt am Main: V. Klostermann, 1950), p. 195; English translation by William Lovitt, *Question,* p. 56.

experience" of Heidegger's thought? What does that experience have to do with the nothing?

It would be misleading to single out this or that "place" in *Being and Time* as the locus of the problem of the *nihil.* It would be no exaggeration to say that the nothing plays a principal role in virtually every phase of the analysis of Dasein, whether under the aspect of worldhood or selfhood, and at virtually every critical juncture of Heidegger's methodical inquiry into the meaning of Being. Readers will recall, for instance, the negativity implied in the reduction of *Zuhandenheit* to *Vorhandenheit,* being "on hand" to sheer being "at hand": Heidegger uses such words as *loss, disturbance,* and *breach* to describe that transition. But two sections of *Being and Time* (section 40, "The Fundamental Mood of Anxiety as an Exceptional Disclosure of Dasein," and section 58, "Understanding the Call, and Guilt") do thematize the problem. In section 40, Heidegger describes the everyday drift of Dasein as a flight "in the face of itself," a flight that allows Dasein to get "behind" itself, as it were, and so attain awareness of its existence. That in the face of which Dasein wishes to flee, that before which it experiences anxiety, is its being in the world as such. Anxiety is not fear of this or that being which may be on or at hand; intramundane entities are not "relevant" to the experience of anxiety. What threatens in anxiety cannot be located: it is nowhere, and it is nothing. "It was really nothing," we say, and on occasion we mean it. The no-thing that is no-where indicates that region in which beings—ourselves and others—can be disclosed. Such disclosure is the primal event of world, and of our being in the world. That *in the face of which* we are anxious is the world as such; that *about which* we are anxious is the possibility of our being there at all.[41] Why should the possibility of my

[41] The most important structural device in section 40 is Heidegger's alternation of *Angst-vor* and *Angst-um,* the first expressing the moment of world as a relational totality, the second the moment of Dasein as the capacity to be, possibility-being, or being *in* a world. The convergence of these two moments is one of the most dramatic and methodologically decisive junctures in *Being and Time.* For the very core of being-in is *disclosure,* and the phenomenon of anxiety, as disclosive, proves to be decisive for the analysis of Dasein as both disclosed and disclosing. Heidegger italicizes the following words: *"The existential selfsameness of the disclosing with what is disclosed, in such a way that in the latter world is disclosed as world, and being-in as individualized, pure, and*

being in the world make me anxious? Because I am not the *ground* of my own capacity to be there; because it is eminently possible that I *not* be there. In the second division of *Being and Time* (section 62; SZ, 308) Heidegger writes,

> The indefiniteness of death is disclosed originally in anxiety. . . . Anxiety clears away every obfuscation of the fact that Dasein has been abandoned to itself. The nothing with which anxiety brings us face to face unveils the nullity that defines Dasein in its very *ground,* unveils that ground itself as thrownness into death.

The uncanny circle of anxiety, the nothing, death, disclosure, and nullity-as-ground constitutes the core of the second division of *Being and Time,* "Dasein and Temporality." Although much of the language employed there is fatal to Heidegger's efforts—"the call," "conscience," "guilt," and "resoluteness" all allowing existential analysis to slip back into the categories of Christian theology and moral philosophy—Heidegger continued to probe the nexus of *ground* and *nullity* during all the later phases of his career.[42]

Section 58 of *Being and Time* takes up the problem of ground *as* nullity. While trying to subordinate to existential analysis the juridical and moral interpretations of guilt as an apparent "lack" or "deficiency" in the Being of Dasein, Heidegger defines the character of such negativity in the following way: to be Dasein is "to be the ground of a Being which is determined by a not," "to be the ground of a nullity." The "not" nestles in all the existential structures of Dasein and in all the dimensions of care: as thrown, Dasein has *not* brought it on itself to exist; as projecting itself into this or that possibility, Dasein chooses this but *not* that; as falling or drifting through its quotidian routine, Dasein for the most part is *not* attuned to its own capacity to be, a capacity that in any case has *not* been granted it as its own. Nullity permeates care, which may be defined as "the (nugatory) being a ground of a nullity" (SZ, 285). That paradoxical formula results from

---

thrown capacity-to-be, makes it clear that with the phenomenon of anxiety an exceptional mood has become thematic for our interpretation." See Martin Heidegger, *Sein und Zeit,* 12th ed. (Tübingen: M. Niemeyer, 1972), p. 188. Cited in the text as SZ, 188.

[42] For a basic bibliography of that nexus in the "later phases," see p. 284, footnotes 56–57.

the paradox of existence: "The self, which as such is to establish the ground of itself, can *never* master that ground; and yet by existing it is to take upon itself its being a ground" (SZ, 284). In spite of Heidegger's later disavowals, we know where Jean-Paul Sartre unearthed his striking formulations of *mauvaise-foi,* the being that "must be what it is not and not be what it is," or of *la réalité humaine,* which "rises in being as perpetually haunted by a totality which it is without being able to be it."[43] Heidegger himself does not flit from one dramatic description to the next, however, but immediately invokes the problem of the "ontological sense of nullity," which, he admits, "remains obscure":

> True, ontology and logic have exacted a great deal from the not and have thereby made its possibilities visible in piecemeal fashion, without unveiling the not itself ontologically. Ontology came across the not and made use of it. But is it so obvious that every not signifies a *negativum* in the sense of a lack? Is its positivity exhausted in the fact that it constitutes "passing over" something? Why does all dialectic take refuge in negation, without grounding something like negation *itself* dialectically, indeed, without being able to pinpoint negation *as a problem?* Has the *ontological origin* of nullity ever been declared a problem at all? Or, *prior to that,* has anyone ever sought *the condition* on the basis of which the problem of the not and its nullity, the very possibility of that nullity, might be posed? And where else are such conditions to be found *if not in the thematic clarification of the meaning of Being in general?*[44]

---

[43] Jean-Paul Sartre, *Being and Nothingness,* tr. Hazel Barnes (New York: Philosophical Library, 1956), pp. 67, 90.

[44] SZ, 285–86. In his doctoral dissertation, "The Doctrine of Judgment in Psychologism" (University of Freiburg, 1914; now in *Frühe Schriften*), Heidegger had already recognized the troublesome nature of the negative in logic: if judgment is a relation—namely, a relation of validity (*Gelten*)—negative judgments appear to truncate the relation, cancel validity, and destroy judgment as such. The young Heidegger tries to solve the dilemma by removing the negative from the copula to the predicate (instead of "The book is not yellow," one might say "Not-being-yellow is true of the book"). Unsatisfied with such logistical legerdemain, which only postpones the problem, Heidegger asks, "Can we penetrate still further into the essence of negation?" Negation must be allowed to affect the copula, to separate subject and predicate, even if such separation—which seems to presuppose a relationship of some kind—remains mysterious. Heidegger's acceptance here of the Lotzean theory of four distinct modes of actuality, of which *Geltung* is one, prevents him from pushing on to the existential-ontological problem of negation. Decisive advances will occur during the Marburg years both prior to *Being and*

After the publication of *Being and Time* in the spring of 1927, Heidegger devoted his attention to the related problems of the not (*das Nicht*), negation (*die Verneinung*), nullity (*die Nichtigkeit*), and the nothing (*das Nichts*). All these converged in the crucial problem of ground (*der Grund*). At the same time, Heidegger's thinking underwent what he himself called "a meta-ontological turn."[45] His project of "fundamental ontology" would now have to seek its own fundament or ground in the history of metaphysics, which inquired not only into human Being or Dasein but also into, and beyond, beings as a whole (*das Seiende im Ganzen*). In his lecture courses at Marburg during the summer semesters of 1927 and 1928—which I cannot discuss here at length[46] —Heidegger focused not only on the experience of anxiety as an opening onto the groundlessness of Dasein but also on the nothing itself as the source of "the ontological difference." The nothing was, after all, the "not" of "things"; that is, of beings as a whole. Heidegger even spoke of the world as a *nihil originarium*. The nothing would be the common *ground* of the radical finitude of man, of Being, and even of Time itself. But what could "ground" mean for a philosophy that experienced keenly its own radical finitude? That question reverberates through all three principal texts from this period (*Kant and the Problem of Metaphysics,* "On the Essence of Ground," and "What Is Metaphysics?"). Although each of these merits discussion here, I will for reasons of economy consider only the last mentioned: Heidegger's inaugural lecture at the University of Freiburg in 1929, *Was ist Metaphysik?*[47]

Time (see Martin Heidegger, *Logik: Die Frage nach der Wahrheit* [Frankfurt am Main: V. Klostermann, 1976], section 12, esp. p. 141) and immediately following it (see Martin Heidegger, *Die Grundprobleme der Phänomenologie* [Frankfurt am Main: V. Klostermann, 1975], section 16d, esp. p. 283.

[45] See Martin Heidegger, *Metaphysische Anfangsgründe der Logik im Ausgang von Leibniz* (Frankfurt am Main: V. Klostermann, 1978), esp. pp. 196–202.

[46] For a detailed treatment of this period of Heidegger's career, see D. F. Krell, "From *Fundamental-* to *Frontalontologie:* A Discussion of Heidegger's Marburg Lectures of 1925–26, 1927, and 1928," in *Research in Phenomenology,* 1980, *10,* 208–34.

[47] The inaugural lecture (cf. footnote 50) has provoked a flurry of irate responses. Apart from the two best-known replies—Günther Grass's parody at the close of *The Dog Years* and Rudolf Carnap's scornful reduction of it in "Overcoming Metaphysics Through Logical Analysis of Language," tr. Arthur Pap, in A. J. Ayer, ed. *Logical*

In his inaugural lecture Heidegger carefully balances the existential-ontological and meta-ontological aspects of the question of the nothing. Anxiety, along with other moods, reveals the nothing; but the nothing points toward beings as a whole. It does so not merely as the complete "negation" of beings in ensemble but as "nihilation" (*das Nichten, die Nichtung*). The latter is not annihilation of beings, however, but an indication of their slipping away from Dasein. Paradoxically, such slippage attunes Dasein to beings as a whole in the region of openness. Openness is the work of nihilation: only when the quotidian flight toward beings is suspended, only when beings as a whole withdraw in such a way that they draw attention to their departure, can the Being of beings, the bare "is-ness" of things, assert itself. Although the phenomenon of anxiety still retains its privileged position with respect to nihilation, the withdrawal of beings as a whole may also be sensed in other exceptional moods such as profound boredom or intense joy. (Rilke, we recall from Volume I of this series, pp. 116–17, identifies joy in beauty as terror before what we but barely endure.) In section 26 of "Song of Myself," Walt Whitman invokes an experience of nihilation that combines an astonishing variety of moods:

The orchestra whirls me wider than Uranus flies,
It wrenches such ardors from me I did not know I possess'd them,
It sails me, I dab with bare feet, they are lick'd by the indolent waves,
I am cut by bitter and angry hail, I lose my breath,

Positivism (New York: Free Press, 1959, pp. 60–81) —and apart from the vast expository literature on Heidegger, one might also note the protracted (but singularly unhelpful) "Discussion" in the *Zeitschrift für philosophische Forschung,* 1949–1951, *4–6.* The best indication of the helplessness of most commentators is Gertrud Kahl-Furthmann, *Das Problem des Nicht,* 2nd ed. (Meisenheim am Glan: A Hain, [1934] 1968). This is a broadbased account of "the not" in Western logic and metaphysics from Parmenides to Heidegger. Yet it is a pedestrian work, on whose path Heidegger constitutes the major stumbling block. (See the Foreword to the second edition, p. vi.) The book ignores the essential coherence of *Sein* and *Nichts* in "What Is Metaphysics?" (see p. 309) and proclaims as its great discovery the "error" Heidegger commits when he capitalizes the "n" of *nichts,* thus "confusing" an indefinite pronoun for a substantive (pp. 311–12). The book does achieve a fleeting moment of truth, however, when Frau Kahl-Furthmann concedes, "A plethora of unanswered questions remains, making it impossible for us to derive from Heidegger's analysis of the nothing results which would advance our own investigation."

Steep'd amid honey'd morphine, my windpipe throttled in fakes of death,
At length let up again to feel the puzzle of puzzles,
And that we call Being.

William James, exalting the "hoary loafer" who composed "Crossing Brooklyn Ferry," refers to a similar sort of experience. "There is life," he writes, "and there, a step away is death. There is the only kind of beauty there ever was." James continues,

> To be rapt with satisfied attention, like Whitman, to the mere spectacle of the world's presence, is one way, and the most fundamental way, of confessing one's sense of its unfathomable significance and importance. But how can one attain to the feeling of the vital significance of an experience, if one have it not to begin with? There is no receipt which one can follow. Being a secret and a mystery, it often comes in mysteriously unexpected ways. It blossoms sometimes from out of the very grave wherein we imagined that our happiness was buried.[48]

Whether and to what extent other moods duplicate the characteristics of anxiety—its bewildering calm, speechlessness, and uncanniness in the face of the slipping away of beings as a whole—remains an intriguing existential-ontological problem.[49] The meta-ontological significance of attunement remains nonetheless clear: "Being held out into the nothing," Dasein is in some way "out beyond" beings. By grace of nihilation, Dasein is trans-ontical, is (finite) transcendence. By grace of nihilation, Dasein is *meta-physical.* "Metaphysics is the

---

[48] William James, "On a Certain Blindness in Human Beings," in Joseph L. Blau, ed. *Pragmatism and Other Essays,* (New York: Washington Square, 1963), pp. 263–64. I introduce these lyric and pragmatic American sources to suggest that "nihilation" need not merely be the result of Heidegger's failure to locate "fixed" semantic and syntactic "units" for "protocol sentences" and "empirical propositions" about "possible experience." See Rudolf Carnap, "Overcoming Metaphysics," pp. 60–81. Although Carnap's conjecture (p. 80) "that metaphysics is a substitute, albeit an inadequate one, for art" remains thought-provoking, especially because he cites Nietzsche as the one who "almost entirely" avoids confusing science with artistic expression, it does seem as though nihilation—celebrated in art and interrogated in thought—remains a "possible experience." Indeed, for Heidegger, nihilation is the possibility of experience as such.

[49] See August Seiffert, "Ernüchterung um das Nichts," in *Zeitschrift für philosophische Forschung,* 1951, *6,* 528–46, for an ascerbic treatment.

basic occurrence of Dasein. It is Dasein itself."[50] But such transcendence, selfhood, and freedom as are at the disposal of Dasein are not metaphysical in the traditional ontotheological sense; they manifest themselves in the interstices of beings as *negation,* and in sundry contexts of beleaguered human behavior as *nihilation.* Nihilation is both broader and deeper than negation:

> Unyielding antagonism and stinging rebuke have a more abysmal source than the measured negation of thought. Galling failure and merciless prohibition require some deeper answer. Bitter privation is more burdensome.[51]

It is therefore comprehensible that metaphysics, spawned in the opening of the nothing, should leave its own origins in obscurity and busy itself with beings. While the classical metaphysical proposition *ex nihilo nihil fit*—from nothing, nothing comes to be—is essential for the fundamental conception of Being in antiquity, the sense of the *nihil* itself "never really becomes a problem."[52] The Platonistic, Aristotelian, and Plotinian conceptions of becoming (*genesis*) and matter (*hyle*) as properly nothing (*to mē on*), become as it were the cracked looking-glass for Western conceptions of Being. In the Augustinian transformation of the ancient principle, which now reads *ex nihilo fit—ens creatum,* from nothing comes created being, a second crack intersects the first and forms what Schelling will call "the cross of the Intellect."[53] Hegel's *Logic* only appears to draw the consequences of the resulting distorted reflection: it equates pure Being and pure Nothing as "concepts" that are equally immediate and

---

[50] Martin Heidegger, "Was ist Metaphysik?" in *Wegmarken* (Frankfurt am Main: V. Klostermann, 1967), p. 18; in *Basic Writings,* p. 112.

[51] Heidegger, *Wegmarken,* p. 14; *Basic Writings,* p. 107.

[52] Heidegger, *Wegmarken,* p. 16; *Basic Writings,* p. 109.

[53] See F. W. J. Schelling, *Sämmtliche Werke* (1860), VII, 373, n. 2. For Schelling's God, that crack becomes a wound from which the Absolute will never recover. Schelling calls that wound "the will of ground," *der Wille des Grundes* (p. 375). From this gaping "ground," in spite of all that Schelling can do to anneal it, flows "a source of sadness," a "profound, indestructible melancholy in all life" (p. 399). Heidegger, who was teaching courses on Schelling immediately before and after the Nietzsche lectures, recognized the wound—the fatal split between *Grund* and *Existenz*—as the demise of Schelling's God *and* his system. See Martin Heidegger, *Schellings Abhandlung über das Wesen der menschlichen Freiheit* (*1809*), ed. Hildegard Feick (Tübingen: M. Niemeyer, 1971), esp. p. 194.

indeterminate, then proceeds to derive Becoming from their interpenetration, in strict conformity with the metaphysical tradition. For Heidegger too, Being and the nothing belong together, although not merely as concepts, "because Being itself is essentially finite and reveals itself only in the transcendence of Dasein which is held out into the nothing."[54] Being itself, *das Sein,* is finite, pervaded by the nothing. At this juncture, *Sein* and *Dasein* become wholly indistinguishable; indeed, Heidegger now speaks of "the nothing of *Dasein*" in which alone beings as a whole can come to themselves in their own way; that is to say, a finite way. *Sein, Dasein,* and *das Seiende im Ganzen* converge in nihilation. But if that is so, then the introduction of beings as a whole as a "new" horizon for fundamental ontology, the meta-ontological turn, seems to turn us back toward the same cluster of problems. As Heidegger himself puts it: in the question of Being, horizons form only to dissolve.[55] Not into new *grounds,* but into old *questions,* for example, that posed by Leibniz in his *Principles of Nature and of Grace, Founded on Reason* (1714): "Why are there beings at all, and why not rather nothing?"

Heidegger lets that same question resound in his 1944–46 treatise, "Nihilism as Determined by the History of Being" (p. 208, above). In fact it can be heard throughout the Nietzsche lectures in Heidegger's emphasis on Nietzsche's experience of nihilism—the futility of the "why?" question, and the "coming to nothing" of beings as a whole and Being itself. The Leibnizian question is furthermore a leitmotif in a number of lectures and essays immediately prior to, and directly subsequent to, the Nietzsche lectures.[56] All the same, I want to pursue the enigma of the nothing not in these but in several later texts where the Leibnizian question concerning beings fades before the question of Being.[57] Study of these later texts discloses the lasting quality of the

[54] Heidegger, *Wegmarken,* p. 17; *Basic Writings,* p. 110.

[55] See Heidegger, *Anfangsgründe,* p. 198.

[56] In addition to the sources just cited, see Heidegger's *Einführung in die Metaphysik* (lectures given in 1935), esp. pp. 18–24; English translation, pp. 19–25. See also the 1943 "Afterword" and 1949 "Introduction" to "What Is Metaphysics?" in *Wegmarken,* pp. 99–108, 195–211. Finally, see the 1946–47 "Letter on Humanism," *Wegmarken,* esp. pp. 176–78, 189–91; in *Basic Writings,* pp. 225–27, 237–38.

[57] Martin Heidegger, "Zur Seinsfrage," first published in 1955, now in *Wegmarken,*

issue of ground and nullity. Such study makes it impossible to assent to that interpretation of Heidegger's career which asserts that the problem of the nothing pertains to an "existentialist" phase that is soon tranquilized into "releasement" by "thankfulness to Being." If one interpretation deserves another—to counter it—then mine would be as follows: Heidegger's thought, early and late, inquiring into the finitude of human being (as being-toward-death and as mortal), the finitude of philosophy (including both fundamental ontology and "the other thinking"), the finitude of Being (as revealing-concealing) and of Time (as presencing-absencing), and the finitude of *Ereignis* itself, brings Nietzsche's accomplishment—ecstatic nihilism—to an apotheosis.

Heidegger grapples with the relation of ground to nullity once again in his 1955–56 lecture course on the "principle of sufficient reason," *Der Satz vom Grund.* That course offers us a matchless opportunity to trace the development of Heidegger's thoughts on ground from the period of *Being and Time* through his later thought.[58] Without being able to attempt such a tracing here, I at least want to indicate one of Heidegger's strategies in the later lecture course. He stresses the principle of sufficient reason, *Nihil est sine ratio,* "Nothing is without grounds," as it is normally asserted: "*Nothing* is *without* grounds." Curiously, when we stress the word "nothing" we tend to pass *through* it, to think it *away,* to proceed to beings *without* it—the nothing. Oddly, when we stress the nothing the principle sounds wholly positive, conclusive, self-evident. It lays a claim on all beings which is utterly transparent: *Nihil . . . sine* executes a perfectly choreographed dialectic, a negation of negation that guarantees universal rationality. But Heidegger now alters the emphasis, ironically downplaying the nothing and invoking the ostensibly fully positive identity of being and reason: "Nothing *is* without *grounds.*" Finally, he inserts a hiatus into the principle, which now proclaims something disconcerting:

pp. 213–53; "Bauen Wohnen Denken" (1951), "Das Ding" (1950), and "Dichterisch Wohnet der Mensch" (1951), now in *Vorträge und Aufsätze,* pp. 145–204; English translations in *Poetry, Language, Thought,* pp. 145–86 and 213–29; and Martin Heidegger, *Der Satz vom Grund* (Pfullingen: G. Neske, 1957), complete.

[58] From the period of *Being and Time,* see "Vom Wesen des Grundes," in *Wegmarken,* pp. 21–71, and the lecture course on which that essay was based, reprinted as *Anfangsgründe.*

"Nothing *is*—without *grounds,*" *Nichts* ist—*ohne* Grund. The identity between Being and the rationalist project of ground, the identity of *einai* and *noein,* precisely when it is stressed, is undercut by the scarcely heard "Nothing . . . without."

True, when all is said and done, Heidegger is here only playing with words, or worse, is letting words play with him. He knows that. For Heidegger such play is in earnest, and goes for the highest stakes—it is the child's play that rules the world:

> The question evoked by our leap into the altered emphasis of the principle of sufficient reason asks: Can the essence of play be defined appropriately in terms of Being as ground, or must we think Being and ground, Being as abyss [*Ab-Grund*], in terms of the essence of play, indeed, of that play to which we mortals are introduced, being mortal only because we dwell in proximity to death, which, as the uttermost possibility of Dasein, is capable of the supreme lighting of Being and of Being's truth? Death is the still unthought standard of the immeasurable, that is, of that supreme play to which man is introduced on earth, and in which he is at stake.[59]

So much for a Heidegger II who would rescue us from Heidegger I: the circle of themes in *Being and Time* (anxiety, the nothing, death, disclosure, and nullity-as-ground) is never broken. It never traces a line one might cross.

To the *Festschrift* for Heidegger's sixtieth birthday Ernst Jünger contributed an essay entitled *Über die Linie,* "Over the Line." The "line" in question was the boundary demarcating the historical region of nihilism from the still uncharted domain where a new relationship to Being might become possible. Five years later, Heidegger contributed to the *Festschrift* for Jünger's sixtieth birthday an open letter entitled *Über 'Die Linie,'* "About 'The Line.'"

Heidegger's title liberates the *Über* from the quotation marks and thus focuses on the question of "the line" as such. It transmutes Jünger's title and his intention: the *Über* is no longer a command to cross over the boundary but a question about the boundary itself. For Heidegger, nihilism is not a matter that can be left behind by a crossing; there is no promised land *trans linea,* no meta-level hovering over the

[59] Heidegger, *Satz vom Grund,* pp. 186–87.

terrain of the nothing. Heidegger's title is not *trans linea* but *de linea*: his essay does not cross the line but moves about (*peri*) the periphery of the zone or dimension where the *nihil* comes to the fore. Much about the two *Festschrift* essays is similar. For example, Nietzsche is the principal witness for both, invoking nihilism as the "uncanniest of guests" and defining it as the collapse of the uppermost values. But the major difference between the two essays emerges in Heidegger's droll comment on that "guest":

> He is called the *unheimlichste* ["uncanniest"] because, as the unconditioned will-to-will, he wills *Heimatlosigkeit* ["homelessness"] as such. It doesn't help to show him the door because for a long time, and quite unseen, he has been making himself at home.[60]

Whereas Jünger's essay on nihilism—like most of the others I have seen—adopts a "medical attitude," venturing a diagnosis, risking a prognosis, and prescribing a predictable therapy, Heidegger's letter promises considerably less: "With regard to the *essence* of nihilism there is no prospect of, and no meaningful claim to, a cure."[61] The *essence* of actual, destructive nihilism (which in the context of the present volume we would have to call the *nonessence* of the nothing) is a complex matter that cannot be reduced to definitions. Its zone is world-historical, its scope planetary. But Heidegger tries to shift attention from the multiple appearances of nihilism to its essential provenance. He abjures all reactive and restorative efforts, all attempts to vulcanize the blasted balloon tires of "value," in order to inquire into "the questionableness of man's metaphysical position."[62] Both his abjuration and his incipient inquiry derive from an insight into the peculiar quandary that language gets into when it speaks of the nothing. Jünger speaks the same language whether he is contemplating this or that "side" of the "line." Heidegger remarks,

> There is a kind of thinking that endeavors to cross over the line. What language does the basic plan of such thinking speak? Shall a rescue operation lead the language of the metaphysics of will to power, *Gestalt*, and

60 Heidegger, "Zur Seinsfrage," *Wegmarken*, p. 215.
61 Ibid.
62 Ibid., p. 220.

> values across the critical line? Why should we want to do that, if it is the language of metaphysics itself (whether of the living or the dead God) which *as* metaphysics has erected those barriers that obstruct passage across the line and so prevent the overcoming of nihilism? If that is how matters indeed stand, then would not a crossing of the line necessarily have to involve a transformation of saying; would it not demand a transformed relation to the essence of language?[63]

But the metamorphosis of saying and the transformed relation to the essence of language here assume a disconcerting form. Heidegger begins to write the word "Being," which according to a long tradition is the word that says the very opposite of "nothing" and so would be the key word for overcoming nihilism, as ~~Being~~. Whereas Jünger envisions a new "turn to Being" as the prerequisite for a successful crossing of the line, Heidegger "crosses out" Being. It appears that the thinker whose sole passion it was to raise anew the question of Being now surrenders his own question to nihilation. For what would it mean to ask about ~~Being~~?

The motivation for Heidegger's crossing of Being is not capitulation to nihilism. It springs from an active resistance to the customary way of posing the question of the "relationship" of Being and Man. That is the question in which both parts of the present volume culminate. Heidegger notes,

> We always say *too little* about "Being itself" when, uttering "Being," we leave out of account presencing *to* the human *presence* [*das An-wesen* zum *Menschen*wesen], thereby ignoring the fact that the latter presence itself participates in constituting "Being." We always say *too little* about man as well when, uttering "Being" (N.B.: not human being), we posit man for himself and only then bring what we have posited into relation to "Being." . . . The talk about "Being" drives representational thought from one quandary into another, without the source of such helplessness ever showing itself.[64]

The "individualizing" and "separating" words *Sein* and *Mensch* are hence to be dispatched. Between ~~Being~~ and ~~Man~~ there can be no

[63] Ibid., p. 233.
[64] Ibid., pp. 235–36.

relation, not even full identity. In ~~Being~~ and ~~Man~~ we confront a duplicitous convergence that is neither identity nor difference in the usual sense. But with the nihilation of Being and Man there seems to be *nothing* left. Or can we scratch the nothing as well, and so, as though there were ~~nothing~~ to it, slip unobtrusively over the line? What would grant us the power to scratch the nothing?

It is so little a question of dispatching the nothing that we must rather say the very opposite: a transformed relation to the essence of language, as the sole way "to the question of Being," must allow the nothing to advene and to take up residence among and within mortals.[65] But by mentioning the "mortals" we invade the dimension of *the fourfold* as discussed in the essays "Building Dwelling Thinking," "The Thing," and "Poetically Man Dwells." In fact, Heidegger explicitly directs the reader of *Zur Seinsfrage* to these essays, with the hint that the fourfold will tell him something essential about "the line."

If we try to sketch the fourfold as envisioned in these essays, to make of it a kind of pictogram and rebus, we establish a periphery about the dimension of Being:

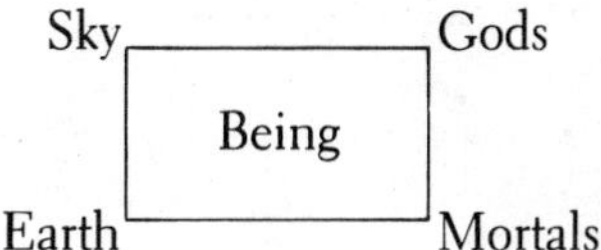

Accordingly, the crossing of Being would be, not mere *Durchstreichung,* but a *Durchkreuzen*—not a crossing *out,* but a crossing *through:*

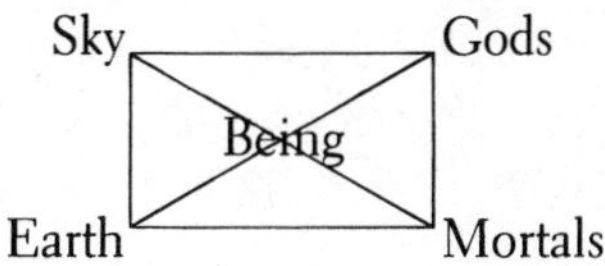

[65] Ibid., p. 238.

By virtue of the crossing, each member of the fourfold could proceed not only about the periphery of the dimension but toward its very center. The cohesion of the fourfold thus would depend on the nihilation of Being. ~~Being~~ would express the finite transcendence of Dasein; mortal Dasein would be the same as ~~Sein~~. But because it is the thinking by mortals that thinks the other three along with itself, mortal Dasein could be said to inhabit the heart of the fourfold dimension of ~~Being~~ in a special way. Does that mean that mortals can, perhaps like the original androgynes, roll up that inclined plane to the Sky, then across to the Gods, reducing divinity, nature, and history to elements of its self-contained autonoesis? If not, how is the unity of the fourfold sustained? What is this "crossing"?

While it is true that a sacrificial vessel ("The Thing") is not a broken hammer (*Being and Time*), such things remain the accoutrements of mortal man, on this earth. They, and the mortals, have their specific gravity. Mortality is joined by the nothing—so that the crossing cannot be a matter of clambering up divided-lines and ladders of love—joined by the nothing in both its *living* and its *naming.* With respect to naming, or rather, his reticence about naming the dimension,[66] Heidegger testifies to the lack of an irrefragable standard of measure for speech. A late poem of Hölderlin contains the lines:

> Is there a measure on earth? There is
> None.

With respect to the living, Heidegger writes,

> Mortals are men. Men are called mortals because they can die. To die means to make death possible as death. . . . Death is the shrine of the nothing, of that which is never in any respect a mere being, but which all the same comes to presence as the very mystery of Being itself. As the shrine of the nothing, death shelters the presencing of Being in itself. . . . The mortals are who they are, as mortal, presencing in the shelter of Being. They are the presencing relation to Being as Being.[67]

Perhaps Heidegger should have written, "the presencing relation to

[66] Heidegger, "Dichterisch Wohnet der Mensch," *Vorträge und Aufsätze,* p. 195.
[67] Heidegger, "Das Ding," *Vorträge und Aufsätze,* p. 177.

~~Being~~ as ~~Being~~." As for human beings, the preceding passage has already crossed them through, not by outfitting them with a cross of the Intellect, but by addressing them as mortals, the ones for whom death is, in the words of *Being and Time,* "ownmost, nonrelational, and insurmountable," at once "certain and indefinite."[68] There is no crossing over the line. There is no line. Only the zone or dimension whose very openness and anonymity require the shelter, the protective screen, of nihilation. To advance *de linea,* about the periphery, then to cross through, is to confront and accompany the nothing. Without dreaming of escape.

But when I read over the above lines, which try to compress the contents of several of Heidegger's essays into a few lines, complete with pictures, and to follow the trajectory of Heidegger's thought back to the one experience that spawned *Being and Time,* back to *the* fundamental experience of Heidegger's thought *as such,* I am struck by their resemblance to the ridiculous bathos of Pierre's scribblings. As though both naming and living were consumed in writing! As though writing itself were the crossing! Of ~~Being~~ Jacques Derrida writes,

> This erasure is the last inscription of an epoch. Under its traced lines the presence of a transcendental signified is effaced—while remaining legible. Effaces itself while remaining readable; destroys itself while making manifest the very idea of a sign. Inasmuch as it de-limits ontotheology, metaphysics of presence, and logocentrism, this last inscription is also the first.[69]

The first, that is to say, of a new epoch of writing.

Indeed, the question of the *nihil* has struck not only contemporary philosophy but also contemporary literature and literary criticism. I am thinking for example of a recent statement by three inquisitive critics who, peering into Dedalus' "cracked looking-glass of a servant" (a second looking-glass, or the same one?), descry the "shattered image" of contemporary criticism as a whole:

> What one sees . . . is *dispersal:* a broken, discontinuous, jagged series of fragments stripped of all illusory, mystifying *images* of unity, revealed in all its particularity and unevenness—not the One, the Word, Identity, but the

[68] Heidegger, *Sein und Zeit,* pp. 263–65.

[69] Jacques Derrida, *De la grammatologie* (Paris: Éditions de Minuit, 1967), p. 38.

> many, words, difference. The one who stares into the mirror is unmasked: there he finds the same figures of disruption, of failed recuperation, of the nostalgic desire to *create* or *project* a unified image of critical activity—where none is to be found. We can connect nothing with nothing, one might say.[70]

I am thinking too of a recent thought-provoking essay by J. Hillis Miller, "The Critic as Host."[71] In the second section of his paper Miller raises the question of nihilism with respect to deconstructive criticism, tracing the very path we have traveled here, from Nietzsche to Ernst Jünger to Heidegger. Miller too experiences the nothing, not as a disease he hopes to eradicate, but as a permanent though hardly comfortable symbiosis of "parasite and host" in the critical encounter. Whether it be in a self-subverting text of metaphysics, a poem, or a piece of criticism, "nihilism is the latent ghost encrypted within any expression of a logocentric system."[72] Yet, to repeat, it is not an apotropaic ritual that Miller is looking for, neither exorcism nor pacification. "Deconstruction does not provide an escape from nihilism, nor from metaphysics, nor from their uncanny inherence in one another. There is no escape."[73]

---

[70] William V. Spanos, Daniel T. O'Hara, and Paul A. Bové, Introduction to "The Problems of Reading in Contemporary American Criticism: A Symposium," *boundary 2,* 1979, *8*(1), 8.

[71] In Harold Bloom et al., eds., *Deconstruction and Criticism* (New York: Seabury Press, 1979), pp. 217–53.

[72] Miller, p. 228.

[73] However, deconstruction does, according to Miller, (p. 231),

> move back and forth within this inherence. It makes the inherence oscillate in such a way that one enters a strange borderland, a frontier region which seems to give the widest glimpse into the other land ("beyond metaphysics"), though this land may not by any means be entered and does not in fact exist for Western man. By this form of interpretation, however, the border zone itself may be made sensible, as quattrocento painting makes the Tuscan air visible in its invisibility. The zone may be appropriated in the torsion of the mind's expropriation, its experience of an inability to comprehend logically. This procedure is an attempt to reach clarity in a region where clarity is not possible. In the failure of that attempt, however, something moves, a limit is encountered. This encounter may be compared to the uncanny experience of reaching a frontier where there is no visible barrier, as when Wordsworth found he had crossed the Alps without knowing he was doing so. It is as if the "prisonhouse of language" were like that universe finite but unbounded which some modern cosmologies posit.

Toward the close of his letter to Ernst Jünger, Heidegger again invokes Nietzsche—"in whose light and shadow all of us today, with our 'pro-Nietzsche' or 'contra-Nietzsche,' are thinking and writing."[74] Nietzsche responded to the call to reflect on the fate and fatality of humanity's inheritance of the earth.

> He followed that call along the path of metaphysical thinking which was his lot, and he collapsed while under way. So it seems, at least, to the historian's eye. Perhaps he did not collapse, however, but went as far as his thinking could go.[75]

"As far as his thinking could go. . . ." The phrase still seems to betray a residual judgment or *evaluation* of Nietzsche, as though Heidegger had crossed the line to the meta-level of the historian's unrestricted vision, the level that would permit a final settling of accounts with Nietzsche. Yet that is not the case. A thinking that goes as far as it can—Heidegger never claimed such success for his own thought.

> The fact that Nietzsche's thought left to posterity such weighty and difficult matters should remind us in a different and more rigorous way than ever before of the long provenance of the question of nihilism which stirred in him. The question has not become any easier for us.[76]

My Analysis in the first volume of Heidegger's *Nietzsche* opened with an innocent though perhaps preposterous anecdote: because the

---

> One may move everywhere freely within this enclosure without ever encountering a wall, and yet it is limited. It is a prison, a milieu without origin or edge. Such a place is therefore all frontier zone without either peaceful homeland, in one direction, land of hosts and domesticity, nor, in the other direction, any alien land of hostile strangers, "beyond the line."

Cf. Maurice Blanchot, "The Limits of Experience: Nihilism," in David B. Allison's excellent collection, *The New Nietzsche: Contemporary Styles of Interpretation* (New York: Delta Books, 1977), pp. 121–27. Blanchot calls nihilism "an extreme that cannot be gotten beyond," but also "the only true path of going beyond": "Nihilism is the impossibility of coming to an end and finding an outcome in this end. . . . Nihilism would be identical with the will to overcome Nihilism *absolutely*." Finally, for a discussion of nihilism in the context of Heidegger's remarks on p. 48 of the present volume, see D. F. Krell, "Results," in *The Monist*, 1981, *64* (4), 467–80.

[74] Heidegger, "Zur Seinsfrage," *Wegmarken* p. 252.

[75] Ibid., pp. 252–53.

[76] Ibid., p. 253.

designer of the German volumes printed merely the two names *heidegger* and *nietzsche* on the spine of the books, and because Nietzsche was, as he himself had said, "born posthumously," no one could tell which was the author and which the title. By the time we have worked through the lecture and essay on nihilism we cannot but have noticed that these volumes are shaped as much by their subject as by their author. In one of his notes on nihilism Nietzsche pledges to relate "the history of the next two centuries." Heidegger is well within the scope of that "history," as are those now translating or reading the volumes. It will not surprise us therefore, since Heidegger has prepared us well for it, that our own questions to Heidegger's text revert to Nietzsche's texts—as though the matter for further thought were nietzsche's heidegger.

> Perhaps what we must do is, not remove Nietzsche from the Heideggerian reading, but on the contrary deliver him over to it totally, subscribe to that interpretation without reservation. In a *certain manner,* and precisely at the point where the content of the Nietzschean discourse is all but lost in the question of Being, the form of that discourse recovers its absolute strangeness. At that point Nietzsche's text finally calls for another kind of reading, one more faithful to his type of writing: since *what* Nietzsche wrote, he *wrote.*[77]

[77] Derrida, pp. 32–33.

Glossary

abandonment	*die Verlassenheit*
abode	*die Unterkunft*
absence	*die Abwesenheit*
absolute	*unbedingt, absolut*
abyss, abyssal	*der Abgrund, abgründig*
to accomplish	*vollbringen*
actual	*wirklich*
to address	*ansprechen*
advent	*die Ankunft*
affect	*der Affekt*
appearance	*der Schein, die Erscheinung*
articulation	*das Gefüge*
aspect, outward	*das Aussehen,* eidos
at hand	*vorhanden*
authentic	*eigentlich*
basic experience	*die Grunderfahrung*
basic occurrence	*das Grundgeschehen*
basically, at bottom	*im Grunde*
becoming	*das Werden*
Being	*das Sein*
being(s), the being	*das Seiende*
being(s) as a whole	*das Seiende im Ganzen*
beingness	*die Seiendheit*
belonging	*die Zugehörigkeit*
claim	*die Ansprechung, der Anspruch*

coherence, cohesion	*die Zusammengehörigkeit*
coinage	*die Prägung*
completion	*die Vollendung*
concealing	*die Verbergung*
concealment	*die Verborgenheit*
conception	*der Begriff, die Auffassung*
configuration	*die Gestalt*
confrontation	*die Auseinandersetzung*
continuance	*die Beständigkeit*
countermovement	*die Gegenbewegung*
default	*das Ausbleiben*
to define	*bestimmen*
definitive	*massgebend*
deliberative thought	*das Bedenken,* dubitare
de-limitation	*die Ent-schränkung*
destiny	*das Geschick*
to determine	*bestimmen*
difference	*die Differenz, der Unterschied*
differentiation	*die Unterscheidung*
discordance	*der Zwiespalt*
disjunction	*die Abkehr*
disposition	*die Verfügung*
distinction	*der Unterschied*
dominance, dominion	*die Herrschaft*
to doubt	*bezweifeln,* dubitare
drawing pull	*der Bezug*
drive	*der Trieb*
ecstative	*ekstatisch*
effectiveness	*die Wirksamkeit*
encounter in thought	*entgegendenken*
enframing	*das Ge-stell*
enhancement	*die Steigerung*
enigma	*das Rätsel*
to enjoin	*über etwas verfügen*

essence	*das Wesen*
essential determination	*die Wesensbestimmung*
essential unfolding	*wesen* (verbal)
to estimate	*schätzen (ab-, ein-)*
eternal recurrence of the same	*die ewige Wiederkehr des Gleichen*
eternal return	*die ewige Wiederkunft*
event	*das Ereignis*
exaction	*die Zumutung*
explicit(ly)	*ausdrücklich, eigens*
expression	*der Ausdruck*
expressly	*eigens*
feeling	*das Gefühl*
fixation	*die Festmachung*
force	*die Kraft*
fore, to come to the	*zum Vorschein kommen*
forgottenness	*die Vergessenheit*
form	*die Form, die Gestalt*
free region	*das Freie*
fulfillment	*die Vollendung*
fullness, plentitude	*die Fülle*
fundamental experience	*die Grunderfahrung*
fundamental metaphysical position	*die metaphysische Grundstellung*
genuine	*echt, eigentlich*
to grasp	*begreifen, fassen*
ground(s)	*der Grund*
grounding question	*die Grundfrage*
guiding question	*die Leitfrage*
hale	*das Heilsame*
to harbor, shelter	*bergen*
to heed	*achten, beachten*
hierarchy	*die Rangordnung*

historicity	*die Geschichtlichkeit*
history of Being	*die Seinsgeschichte*
to hold sway	*walten*
idea	*die Idee,* idea
illusion	*der Anschein*
impact	*das Erwirken, die Tragweite*
in-cipient	*an-fänglich*
inherence	*das Innestehen*
insistence	*die Inständigkeit*
jointure	*der Fug*
justification	*die Gerechtigkeit*
to keep to itself	*ansichhalten*
lawfulness	*die Gesetzlichkeit*
to lighten	*lichten*
lighting	*die Lichtung*
to linger, tarry	*verweilen*
locale	*die Ortschaft*
main, major work, magnum opus	*das Hauptwerk*
matter (of thought)	*die Sache (des Denkens)*
measure	*das Mass*
measuredness	*die Mässigung*
to mediate	*vermitteln*
to meditate	*besinnen*
mood	*die Stimmung*
mystery, secret	*das Geheimnis*
need	*das Brauchen, die Not*
the nothing	*das Nichts*
vacuous nothingness	*das leere Nichts*
nullity	*die Nichtigkeit*

oblivion	*die Vergessenheit*
occur essentially	*wesen* (verbal)
on hand	*zuhanden*
the open (region)	*das Offene*
openness	*die Offenheit*
origin	*der Ursprung, die Herkunft*
original	*ursprünglich*
outset, at the	*anfänglich*
outward appearance (or aspect)	*das Aussenhen,* eidos, idea
perfection	*die Vollendung*
permanence	*die Beständigkeit*
the permanent	*das Beständige*
phenomena	*die Erscheinungen*
to place alongside	*bei-stellen*
playspace	*der Spielraum*
to ponder	*bedenken*
presence	*die Anwesenheit*
presencing, becoming present	*das Anwesen*
what is present	*das Anwesende*
to present to	*zu-stellen*
presumption	*die Anmassung*
to prevail	*walten, herrschen*
pre-vious	*das Vor-herige,* a priori
primordial	*anfänglich, ursprünglich*
proper	*eigentlich*
to be proper to	*gehören*
pro-posing	*das Vor-setzen*
proposition	*der Satz*
provenance	*die Herkunft*
proximity	*die Nähe*
radiance	*das Scheinen*
to radiate	*scheinen*
real, actual	*wirklich*

reality	*die Realität, die Wirklichkeit*
realm	*der Bereich*
to recall thoughtfully	*an-denken*
refusal	*die Verweigerung*
to reign	*walten*
rejection	*die Ab-sage*
relation	*die Beziehung*
relation(s) with beings	*das Verhältnis zum Seienden*
relationship to Being	*der Bezug zum Sein*
representable	*vorstellbar*
representation	*die Vorstellung, das Vorstellen*
representing	*das Vorstellen*
repudiation	*die Abwehr*
restriction	*die Beschränkung*
revealing	*die Entbergung*
to rule	*walten*
secret, mystery	*das Geheimnis*
to secure	*sichern*
securement	*die Sicherstellung*
securing of permanence	*die Bestandsicherung*
to seem	*scheinen*
the selfsame	*das Selbe*
self-assertion	*die Selbstbehauptung*
semblance	*der Schein*
settlement	*der Austrag*
shelter	*die Bleibe*
stability	*der Bestand*
standard	*massgebend*
statement	*der Satz*
to stay away	*ausbleiben*
stockpile	*der Bestand*
strength	*die Kraft*
subjecticity	*die Subiectität*
subjectivity	*die Subjektivität*
subsistence	*der Bestand*

suitable	*tauglich,* agathon
supersensuous	*übersinnlich*
surety	*die Sicherung*
surpassment	*der Überstieg*
the transcendent, supersensible	*das Übersinnliche*
transformation	*der Wandel*
transition	*der Übergang, der Überstieg*
the true	*das Wahre*
truth	*die Wahrheit,* alētheia
ultimately	*im Grunde*
the unconcealed	*das Unverborgene*
unconcealment	*die Unverborgenheit*
unconditioned	*unbedingt*
the underlying	*das Zugrundeliegende, das Zum Grunde Liegende*
upsurgence	*das Aufgehen,* physis
usage	*das Brauchen, der Brauch*
valuation	*die Wertsetzung*
valuative thought	*der Wertgedanke*
value estimation	*die Wertschätzung*
value thinking	*das Wertdenken*
viewpoint	*der Gesichtspunkt, der Blickpunkt*
visuality	*die Sichtsamkeit,* idea
to will, want	*wollen*
will to power	*der Wille zur Macht*
will-to-will	*der Wille zum Willen*
withdrawal	*der Entzug*
withholding	*der Vorenthalt*